Local Area Networking
with
Novell® Software

Michael J. Palmer
University of Wyoming

Alvin L. Rains
Truckee Meadows Community College

bf

boyd & fraser publishing company

Credits:

Publisher: Tom Walker
Acquisitions Editor: James H. Edwards
Editor: Donna Villanucci
Director of Production: Becky Herrington
Manufacturing Director: Dean Sherman
Cover Design/Illustration: Michael Broussard
Production Coordination: Beckwith-Clark, Inc.

bf © 1991 by boyd & fraser publishing
A Division of South-Western Publishing Company
Boston, MA 02116

Manufactured in the United States of America.

Trademarks

AT&T	Novell
AutoCAD	Paradox (Borland)
Carbon Copy	Prime
Compaq	Printer Assist (Fresh Technologies)
CompuAdd	Remote2 (Crosstalk)
dBase	Saber Software
Digital Equipment	SiteLock
DOS (MicroSoft)	SMARTDrive
Hewlett-Packard	SPEEDSTORE
IBM	SUN
BICC ISOLAN Multiport Repeater	Tandem
LAN Assist Plus (Fresh Technologies)	Telenet
Macintosh (Apple)	Tymnet
MAP Assist (Fresh Technologies)	Wollongong Group
MicroSoft Windows	WordStar
NetWare (Novell)	WordPerfect
Northgate	Zenith

Library of Congress Cataloging-in-Publication Data

Palmer, Michael J., 1948–
    Local Area Networking with Novell® Software / Michael J. Palmer, Alvin L. Rains.
        p.   cm.
    Includes index.
    ISBN 0-87835-497-2
        1. Local area networks (Computer networks)   2. NetWare (Computer operating system)   I. Rains, Alvin L., 1948–   . II. Title.
TK105.7.P28   1991
004.6—dc20   90-39941
                                                                          CIP

    2 3 4 5 6 7 8 9 10 MT 4 3 2 1

Dedication

To Sally, Shawn, and Kristy — MJP

To Deborah, Jennifer, and Greta — ALR

Contents

Preface

Novell's NetWare is installed on more local area networks than any other networking operating system. There are installations in the United States, Europe, Canada, New Zealand, and throughout the world. NetWare's popularity has made it a standard in the local area networking community.

ABOUT THIS BOOK

This book is intended to help students and NetWare system managers acquire an understanding of Novell local area networks. The book is written to transform beginning NetWare users to advanced users. And users who are already advanced will find new information to help manage networks more effectively.

Organization

Chapter 1 describes the need for local area networks and how the decision is made to implement a network. Chapter 2 introduces basic networking concepts and terms. Chapter 3 discusses the common types of networks and how networks are cabled. Chapter 4 introduces how computers communicate on networks. Chapters 5 and 6 describe the most important components of a network—file servers and workstations. Chapter 7 provides detailed information on the features of NetWare 286 and how to install the operating system. Chapter 8 shows how to use NetWare commands and utilities. Chapter 9 provides details about Novell's newest operating system, NetWare 386. Chapters 10, 11, and 12 show how to install software onto the network and how to successfully manage all aspects of a network. Chapter 13 explains how to interconnect different types of networks and resources so computer users can communicate across town or around the world.

Because the book is written with the student in mind, each chapter ends with a set of chapter questions. These questions are written to encourage you, the reader, to increase your understanding of networks and NetWare. Many of the questions pose real life problem situations that you are encouraged to resolve.

There is a glossary at the end of the book to help you quickly find the meaning of many networking and NetWare terms. And each time a term is introduced in the book, it is highlighted in bold to indicate it can also be found in the glossary.

As you increase your knowledge of NetWare, we know you will find this networking operating system to be versatile and powerful.

ACKNOWLEDGEMENTS

The authors especially thank Arthur Weisbach for his patient and thorough help in editing this manuscript. He has played a very important role in making this a more readable book. We also thank Donna Villanucci, Rosanne Coit, and Pat Donegan for all of their help in the production of the book. Jackie Cowlishaw has also played an important role as copy editor and proof reader. And we thank James Edwards of boyd & fraser publishing company who made this project possible. We also thank the reviewers, Alan M. Cohen of DataSys Corporation and George Gary Olson of Jefferson College, for their help in making the book better. Finally, and very importantly, we thank our families for their profound support.

Michael J. Palmer
Alvin L. Rains

1

Local Area Networking: The Planning Phase

INTRODUCTION

The use of local area networking (LAN) technology has grown phenomenally in businesses, public schools, industry, and higher education. LAN technology has proven to be very effective in making microcomputer applications available to many users. Also, new LAN software applications are rapidly emerging. More and more people now depend on LANs for processing and sharing information. LANs have taken over what were once firm minicomputer strongholds, and they are now even challenging the mainframe computer.

At the forefront of this technological upheaval is the Novell Corporation and its NetWare operating system for LANs. Novell has been very successful with LANs, in both industry and education.

Novell LANs have become popular for a variety of reasons. First, they enable a range of microcomputers or workstations to be linked together for information sharing. IBM, IBM compatible, Apple Macintosh, and other computers can be networked together to share messaging capabilities, common software, documents, reports, data, and desktop publications. Networks of these computers can be as small as three or as large as 250. These networks can operate as independent units, or they can be linked to other networks or to many popular mini and mainframe computers.

Another attractive option of Novell networks is that they can host nearly all commercially available microcomputer software. The options include word processors, spreadsheets, databases, desktop-publishing software, computer-language compilers, office-automation software, electronic mail, and computer-aided design (CAD) software.

Novell file servers, the heart of Novell LANs, can be made by any of a number of manufacturers. File servers can contain a host of add-on equipment, such as disk drives, disk controllers, memory expansion, and tape-backup equipment. Novell tests equipment for compatibility and provides that information to prospective buyers. Novell is not unique in offering these advantages, but it brings together one of the most effective software and hardware environments available.

This text is designed to explore that environment, along with specific ways to establish and enhance the Novell networking system.

LAN ISSUES

Two issues pertain to any introductory discussion of local area networking. The first issue relates to the acquisition and impact of the technology. The second issue focuses on the managerial processes that need to occur prior to installing a LAN. (Refer to Figure 1.1.)

FIGURE 1.1
LAN Acquisition Issues

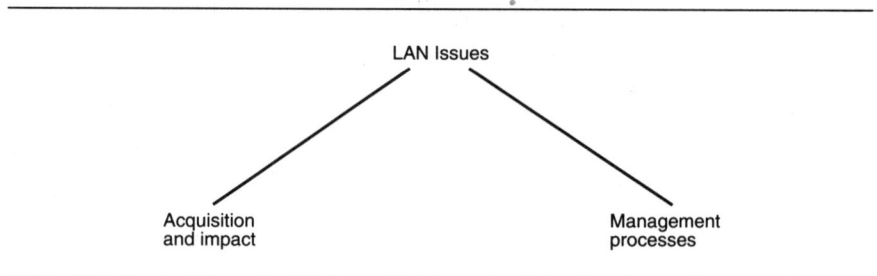

LAN ACQUISITION AND IMPACT

When buying a LAN, one must deal with three main concerns. The first concern is the impact the technology has on an organization. A second concern involves the costs incurred when purchasing LAN technology. The last issue addresses the pervasiveness and underlying complexity of the technology.

ORGANIZATIONAL IMPACT

Generally, a technology is introduced into an organization when that technology promises to increase profits or reduce costs. Adopting new technology should be attempted only when it harmonizes with management's strategic plans. This is an axiom of sound business management. However, pressures are often exerted on institutional personnel to upgrade technology for other than business reasons. Computer technology offers a prime example.

Changes occur rapidly in the computer industry. New models of computers are constantly offered to enable computer vendors to remain competitive and increase sales. As new computers are introduced, old models are phased out along with the accompanying maintenance options. Purchasers of the old equipment are often at the mercy of the vendors. As older computer models are phased out, their maintenance contracts become more expensive, and maintenance may be eliminated altogether. Consequently, new technology is forced on the computer owners, even if they are not ready for the change.

Newer machines have economic advantages over older machines. A favorite argument is to compare what $1000 will buy today to what the same amount could have bought five years ago. Newer computers are also usually more powerful, smaller in size, and easier to maintain.

The challenge for management is to determine which new technology will yield the highest benefits over cost. In evaluating technology, it's necessary to consider four kinds of costs:

- The cost of the new equipment
- The cost of maintenance
- The cost of support
- The cost as distributed over a range of years, based on the projected longevity of the equipment

The longevity of equipment is of particular interest when considering cost. But longevity itself is affected by at least three factors, all of which must be considered by management. These factors are listed and described below.

Amortized Value

Most computer analysts now say a single piece of equipment is viable for approximately five years. Once the equipment is purchased, the software and hardware technology are normally obsolete within this time span. This includes maintenance obsolescence.

Organizational Impact

Another important factor related to longevity is that technology causes institutions, such as businesses and schools, to change. If change is brought about too suddenly, employees will rebel. Employee resistance either causes the changes to fail, or delays full implementation of the changes. The result is added costs.

The perceived suddenness of changing technology is evident when management does not involve employees in the early stages of choosing the new equipment. When employees *are* involved and asked to participate, the problems and costs associated with implementing new technology are minimized.

Dependence

Once a new technology is fully embraced by an organization, the organization develops a level of dependence on that technology. This is certainly true with computer technology. An example can be seen in the reaction of management and employees when there is a power outage or equipment failure and suddenly computer systems are not available. In many offices the business of the day stops. Customer service orders can't be processed, reports can't be generated, data can't be accessed, and employees sit idle. Lost dollars mount with each passing minute.

When one is evaluating the impact that technology has on an organization, LAN implementations often become attractive. For example, LANs can be cost effective from the standpoint of computer obsolescence. If a LAN is capably installed, new equipment, maintenance, and support costs can be lower than those of mini and mainframe computer installations.

Employee resistance to LANs is likely to be low, since many employees will already be familiar with microcomputers. And LANs can be very reliable when designed and managed effectively.

COSTS

Two types of costs are associated with implementing any technology. The first cost is measured in dollars. Improvements required to upgrade building facilities, purchase of equipment, and consultant fees are examples. Cash expenses are frequently used to determine if the technology is affordable. Actual cash expenditures are also used to derive a cost/benefit ratio, which is used by management to justify investments in technology.

The second category of costs includes non-cash costs. Management may neglect to consider the significant negative contribution to institutional resources from non-cash expenditures. Lost productivity is the primary ingredient of non-cash expenditures. Every employee affected by a change in technology will go through a period of reduced productivity. Therefore, there will always be a period of training before the employee becomes productive.

It can be argued that non-cash expenditures impact an institution more than cash expenditures. The cash expenditures are relatively easy to project when evaluating new technology. The non-cash expenditures are difficult to project and measure, but must be evaluated in order to calculate a reliable cost estimate for any change in technology.

PERVASIVENESS AND COMPLEXITY

The pervasiveness and the underlying technology of a new system will determine the magnitude of impact on an institution. A pervasive system is one that impacts all or most of an institution. Of course, new telephone or computer systems are pervasive. Installing a new mail-sorting machine, however, does not impact people outside the mail room, and is not considered a pervasive system change. But what about the photocopy machine? Here, pervasiveness depends on access to the system. If all of the employees use the copier, then a new copier is pervasive technology. It's worth noting that a pervasive system requires more planning and resources than a system that impacts only one department in an institution.

Along with pervasiveness, one must consider the complexity of the technology. Different technologies pose different levels of complexity; telephones are relatively less complex than computer systems.

The complexity of a system's underlying technology can be the most important factor in determining its success or failure. The concept of underlying technology is well illustrated by comparing a phone system to a local area network.

Individuals

First, both phone and local area network technologies have a significant impact on the individuals of an institution.

From a human resource point of view, the phone system is low technology. The reasoning is not in the technology but in the time and costs associated with training users to use a new phone system. Even though a new phone system may have twice as many new features as older systems, the basic operation may not change. The telephone is also used frequently outside of work, thus reinforcing its acceptance.

Underlying Technology

The underlying technologies have an influence on the cost and success of a phone system and a local area network. On the other extreme of the technology spectrum from the telephone lies the LAN. Training employees to use a LAN requires significant time and expense. Users often require one-on-one training because the underlying technologies (programs, applications, and computer operations, as well as transport) may all affect the user. And users will seek outside help the minute something appears to be working incorrectly. Using a LAN causes changes in work patterns, whereas using a new phone system most often does not. Activities associated with using more-complex technological systems incur significant cash and non-cash costs.

MANAGERIAL PROCESSES AND LANS

Management needs to approach technology in the context of institutional objectives. Although it's tempting to examine technology feature by feature, it must be viewed in the *total* context. Features can be counted, tested, priced, and even used for gaining status, but these still remain secondary to the total impact of a technology.

Technology is frequently viewed differently by institutions and individuals. One worker may see the technology as threatening, while another sees it as a chance for advancement and a change for the better. Managers may see new technology as a way to increase their budgets and number of subordinates. (An old trick in mainframe environments is to rig the system clock to reflect more work being done than is actually accomplished. The false data recorded from the system clock might even be used to justify new computers.)

Computer systems have a life cycle, as all systems do, and the more sophisticated a system, the shorter the life cycle.

Both the phone system and the local area network can be explained and examined in a low-level scientific manner. But, when jargon begins to cloud the explanation of why a new system is needed, management should take a close look at the justifications. Factors, such as those discussed above, may be used to argue for newer technology, but the ultimate test lies in *institutional needs*.

In some institutions, having the latest system is a justifiable end. An educational institution may market itself as having the latest equipment on which the students can train. Older equipment would work, but purchasing the most up-to-date computers or lab equipment can be justified by higher enrollments. This is simply restating the adage of knowing what business you're in. Institutional success is determined not by technology alone, but by the technology meeting the objectives of the institution.

Let's take a final look at technology and institutional objectives. A critical objective of all institutions is to have a dependable information system. Some managers begin looking for computer technology to gather data and produce reports. These managers may conduct a study indicating that a local area network is the best option. Their decision is most likely based on sound technical evidence. Upper management, however, must take a wider view of the circumstances. For instance, where does the company's information originate? If the company transacts most of its business over the telephone, management may determine that a new telephone system is required before a computer system can be installed. Installing a local area network would not be the right technology at that time. The institution, after installing a new phone system, may then determine there is a requirement for a LAN. Installing the LAN before the phone system would not make the best use of currently available resources.

A timeline is a convenient tool to illustrate the management processes involved in acquiring a LAN. (Refer to Figure 1.2 on page 8.) The timeline begins with a perceived need to change technology within the institution. Planning is the second phase of the process to acquire technology. This begins at high levels of management and extends to the lowest level managers and supervisors. Technological changes frequently reach across institutional boundaries. All personnel, from department heads to physical plant supervisors, need to be involved in the planning. Each person will determine how the new technology will best impact his or her area. The department head may focus on productivity issues and the physical plant personnel may determine if the technology involves fire and safety codes.

After the planning or feasibility analysis, management looks at vendors of the technology, who are sent a Request for Proposal (RFP).

FIGURE 1.2
LAN Acquisition Timeline

LAN Management Timeline

Need for change	Phase 1
Planning/feasibility	Phase 2
RFP	Phase 3
Equipment purchase	Phase 4
Installation/testing	Phase 5
Training	Phase 6
Growth	Phase 7

The RFP is a detailed list of the features required, and the terms under which the institution expects the vendor to perform. RFPs require many weeks and months to finalize. The desired features must be researched to ensure the system will meet the needs of the institution.

Once the required features are determined, the RFP is written. The institution's lawyer will either write the RFP or review it. Finally, the RFP is mailed to the vendor. There may be some changes made but the final RFP specifies the features to be delivered and the timetable for installation, testing, and final acceptance.

For example, in one situation the RFP may indicate the need to have a LAN operate over four floors of a building. The vendors' responses to the RFP would indicate what specific hardware and equipment would be used to service the four floors. Since the proposed hardware would likely be new to management, there needs to be research into exactly how the hardware will perform within the context of the institution's operation. Will the hardware meet the demands of future growth? Researching hardware features is time consuming and costly. Companies will often hire consultants to determine what features of a new system best satisfy their requirements.

There are other institutional activities in progress during the RFP phase. The RFP may specify that the institution's physical plant make the necessary building, wiring, or air-conditioning modifications. These changes can be contracted and another RFP may need to be prepared for them. The financial officer will begin the process of funding the future system. Documents for a loan, bond, or stock sale may need to be prepared. At the completion of the RFP, which is when all parties have signed, the purchase of equipment begins.

Purchasing agents or other qualified personnel are responsible for determining that delivered equipment is properly received and stored until installation. Equipment will need to be safeguarded and stored under the manufacturers' specifications. Institutional personnel must also ensure that delivered equipment meets the requirements set forth in the RFP, or that the equipment exceeds the stated RFP requirements. In some situations, the vendor will substitute equipment to meet delivery deadlines.

Institutional personnel may be required to oversee the installation of equipment. This function can also be performed by a contractor with the necessary technical expertise. For instance, non-institutional personnel might be needed to oversee installation of equipment when the equipment connects to a public utility, such as the phone system.

Testing the new system requires institutional personnel to test all the features, ensuring each feature functions as specified in the RFP or as specified by the equipment manufacturer. (RFPs do not always state room temperatures for computer equipment, but there will be a manufacturer's specification for temperature ranges under which a computer is to operate.)

Another element involved in the installation/testing phase is *training*. System managers, as well as the users, may need to be trained. Internal documentation for the new system may also become part of the training phase.

At the end of the timeline is the *growth phase*, which begins as soon as the LAN is installed. (For instance, users will want more applications.) This requires hard disk upgrades. Next, more workstations are added to the LAN. At some point, management begins to feel the need to reevaluate the current state of technology. This reevaluation brings the timeline full circle and the process begins again.

SUMMARY

LAN implementations are becoming more of a reality in all kinds of institutions, from schools to the business community. New technology, as represented by LANs, forces change within any institution. To prepare for institutional change related to the introduction of new computer systems, management must consider several important factors:

1. The human resources required to make a new computer system successful
2. The impact of the new system in terms of total costs in both productivity and equipment acquisition
3. The pervasiveness and complexity of the new computer system
4. The management planning required to develop a timeline for equipment purchase, installation, and testing
5. A mechanism by which to plan for future growth

CHAPTER QUESTIONS

1. Explain the two primary issues related to local area networking.
2. What types of costs are associated with evaluating a new technology?
3. What types of costs are associated with implementing a new technology?
4. Prepare an example scenario showing how a business might profit from the installation of a local area network.
5. Develop a plan showing how employees might be brought into the planning and implementation of a new LAN system.
6. Explain the management timeline associated with the acquisition of a LAN.

2

Networking Basics

LOCAL AREA NETWORK

A local area network is a system that permits computing devices to communicate with one another over distances from a few feet to six miles. The computing devices include:

- Terminals
- Microcomputers
- Workstations
- Minicomputers
- Mainframe computers
- Printers
- Voice communication equipment

Devices on the LAN coexist in a **decentralized** relationship, which means that the network gives each device the same priority. No single device has more access to the network than any other device. By comparison, a mainframe computer exerts **centralized** control, where some devices have higher priority than others.

Communication distances on a LAN are defined as "moderate" by the Institute of Electrical and Electronics Engineers (IEEE). (This group consists of committees that work to establish standards for LANs.) LANs link computer devices within a single building, or among several adjacent buildings within a range of up to six miles.

Communication speeds on a LAN are also defined as moderate by the IEEE. Speeds are rated in terms of the number of data bits per second (bps), which are transmitted over a communications medium, such as a cable. Transmission speeds for LANs without fiber-optic cable range from 1 Mbps to 20 Mbps. LANs that use fiber-optic cable can attain data transmission rates of 100 Mbps. (See the Transmission Rate section in this chapter for more information about data transmission speeds.)

Several LANs can be connected to one another so a user on one LAN can access information on a different LAN. One or more LANs connected together form an **internetwork.**

WIDE AREA NETWORK

A **wide area network** (WAN) links computer users who are separated over a wide geographic area. WANs use public and private telecommunications facilities to access computers all over the world. For example, BITNET is a wide area network that connects educational computer users in the United States and in several foreign countries. NSFNET is a network started by the National Science Foundation to provide access to supercomputer sites throughout the United States.

LANs, or an internetwork of LANs, can be connected to a wide area network. Thus, a scientist in Colorado can use a microcomputer to log onto a LAN in his or her building and reach a supercomputer in Champaign, Illinois, by connecting to a WAN.

WHY A LAN?

Computing is an evolving technology. Twenty years ago most computing was done on mainframe computers. Ten years ago smaller minicomputers began to compete with mainframes for certain kinds of installations. Today LANs are competing in areas once dominated by mainframes and minicomputers.

Why is the LAN such a popular technology? There are several reasons. First, *the success of the LAN is linked to the success of the microcomputer*. The microcomputer has introduced large numbers of people to computing, such as business people, secretaries, teachers, students, and factory workers. The LAN offers a way for people in a small geographic area to communicate with one another and share microcomputer resources.

The LAN also provides a way for microcomputer users to communicate through electronic mail. Electronic mail enables users to send messages to one another and to establish bulletin boards of common information.

Resources such as programs and files can be made available for common use. It is no longer necessary to have twenty separate copies of a word processing application for twenty microcomputers. One LAN version with twenty licenses can be installed instead. And two users can share the same word processing file without walking from desk to desk with a diskette.

Devices are also shared on a LAN. For example, it's unnecessary for every microcomputer user to have his or her own printer. Twenty microcomputer users can share two or three printers; or they can share one modem.

Cost is a second reason LANs are popular. Because resources are shared, the cost of equipment goes down. Fewer printers are needed, as compared to stand-alone microcomputer installations. Also, the cost of software is reduced on a LAN.

Maintenance is a third advantage of the LAN. With stand-alone computers, there may be twenty users each with a copy of a word-processing application. When an upgrade to that application becomes available, it is necessary to install the upgrade twenty times. On a LAN with twenty word processing users, only one copy of the upgrade needs to be installed.

MAINFRAMES AND MINIS VS. LANS

Mainframe and minicomputers are based on a centralized CPU (central processing unit) design. They consist of terminals or workstations connected directly to the mainframe or mini. Access to these computers is controlled by the CPU. Each connection gets a "timeslice" of the CPU or is assigned a priority level. The timeslice is the amount of

CPU time the connection shares with all other connections. If the timeslice is small for a particular connection, that user has less access to the computer's resources than another user with a higher timeslice. Or, if the connection's priority is low, the user has less access than users with connections assigned a higher priority.

Programs and data files are also centralized on mainframe and minicomputers. They do not reside on individual terminals or workstations.

LANs are not based on centralized computing; they are *decentralized*. Each user has the same access to the LAN. Also, because the LAN is decentralized, programs and data files can be distributed over the LAN. Programs and files may be stored on individual workstations or on the LAN.

Programs stored on the LAN file server are not run from the file server. Instead, when a workstation requests the use of a program, the server loads that program into the workstation's memory. The program is then run from the workstation. Mainframe and minicomputer programs are not transferred to the workstation or terminal. They are run on the host computer.

Most mainframe and minicomputers must be installed in a machine room where the temperature and humidity are carefully controlled with expensive equipment. These machines also require purchasing a costly maintenance contract from the vendor.

LAN equipment will operate at normal room temperature, which equates to cost savings when compared to mainframe and minicomputers. LAN components are also less expensive than mainframe and minicomputer components. Because components are less expensive, the cost of maintenance is less, too. Many types of LAN maintenance can be performed by the local computer center staff.

Mainframe and minicomputer software is written for specific brands and models of computers. Thus, software that runs on one computer may not be available on another model, even when both computers are made by the same company. Data files, too, are often not compatible between different models.

Because LAN technology is based on the microcomputer, there is a large volume of applications software available. The software will work on most LAN equipment without compatibility problems. For example, the Lotus 1-2-3 spreadsheet program will run on IBM, Zenith, Compaq, Northgate, CompuAdd, and many other computers. A data file created on a Zenith computer can be ported to a Compaq computer.

Figure 2.1 lists the differences between mainframes and minicomputers versus LANs.

FIGURE 2.1
Mainframes and Minicomputers Compared to LANs

Mainframes and Minicomputers Compared to LANs	
Mainframes and Minicomputers	**LANs**
Centralized processing	Decentralized processing
Programs run on the host	Programs run on the workstation
Machine room required	No machine room required
Limited range of software	Wide range of software
Costly maintenance	Less costly maintenance

FILE SERVERS AND WORKSTATIONS

NetWare LANs consist of one or more file servers and workstations. The **file server** is a microcomputer that allows other microcomputers to share its resources. Novell's NetWare is installed on the file server, and this **operating system** makes the server's resources available to the microcomputers that log on to it. In one sense, the file server is a large hard disk that stores programs and files for other microcomputers. The file server also connects to printers, which are made available to logged-on microcomputers.

The NetWare operating system is an administrator of resources, similar to DOS (disk operating system). They both control input/output activities, access to the CPU, and the commands that are available to the computer user. However, NetWare permits more than one user to access programs and files. DOS is a single-user system.

Because DOS is a popular operating system, NetWare provides a way to use DOS commands. NetWare is loaded onto the file server, and DOS is loaded like any other software program onto the NetWare file server.

Microcomputers that log on to a file server are called **workstations**. Workstations may be as small as a microcomputer with an 8088 CPU, or as large as an 80486 microcomputer or Macintosh. They can also vary in brand and model. Some workstations have no disk drives, and rely entirely on the file server's network drive.

NETWORK SHELL

The network **shell** is software that is loaded onto the workstation. In the Novell operating system, the shell consists of two files, IPX.COM and NETx.COM. These files enable a DOS workstation to communicate with NetWare. The NETx.COM file is customized to the version of DOS on the workstation. For example, a workstation with DOS version 3.xx uses NET3.COM.

NODE

Any device that is connected to the network is called a **node**. Nodes consist of file servers, workstations, communications devices, and printer devices. Nodes have access to network and communication services. All nodes have a unique network address.

PROTOCOL

Workstations communicate with each other and the file server through a **protocol**. A protocol is a set of rules that determine the formatting, timing, sequencing, and error checking in communications. NetWare uses protocols called **Internetwork Packet Exchange** (IPX) and **Sequenced Packet Exchange** (SPX).

CABLING

Nodes are connected to the LAN through **cabling.** The cable provides a medium for transmission of electronic signals. The physical layout of cable connections is the LAN **topology**. Nodes can be connected in several different ways, such as in a star layout or a ring pattern.

PACKETS

Data travels from one node to another in **packets**. A packet is a discrete unit of data bits. Each packet contains the following information:

- The address of the node that sent the packet
- The address of the node that is to receive the packet
- The data to be transmitted
- Error-control information

TRANSMISSION RATE

The speed at which data packets travel on a LAN is called the **transmission rate.** The transmission rate is measured in **bits per second** (bps). Each LAN cabling method has a bps rating from 1 Mbps to 100 Mbps. The rating applies to ideal transmission conditions only.

In a typical LAN installation, there are many factors that reduce the time it takes for information to go from one node to another. For example, some LANs have a high number of *packet collisions.* When packets collide they have to be retransmitted, which slows the rate of communication. Another example of slower communications is the network where cabling runs exceed the maximum lengths as specified by the vendor. These networks will experience low transmission rates and a high number of lost packets.

Communication rates are also affected by the characteristics of file servers and workstations. A file server with a slow CPU clock speed, such as 8 MHz, will slow the exchange of information more than a server with a higher clock speed. And communications will be slow to a workstation having low memory access and low disk drive access ratings.

SUMMARY

This chapter has introduced networking basics defining LANs and WANs. LANs are a group of devices, separated by moderate distances, which share resources. WANs connect different computer devices over a wide geographic area.

A comparison of LANs is made to mainframe and minicomputers. The comparison shows that LANs are decentralized, whereas mainframes and minicomputers are centralized.

Finally, networking components, such as file servers and workstations, are discussed. Networking terms, such as protocol, are introduced in the context of their relevance to networking components.

CHAPTER QUESTIONS

1. How is a local area network defined? How is a wide area network defined?
2. What factors have made LANs popular?
3. How might a LAN and a mainframe or minicomputer be integrated to take advantage of both technologies?

4. You have a LAN that can transmit data at speeds up to 10 Mbps. However, the actual rate of transmission is 1 Mbps. What factors may be causing the slow-down?

5. What is a protocol? What protocol is used by NetWare? Name two protocols used by other networks.

6. How is a workstation able to communicate with a Novell network?

3

LAN Topologies
and Cabling

INTRODUCTION

A local area network connects rooms in a building, or it connects a series of buildings together, with cable. LANs typically are confined to a small geographic area, hence the term local. Two important local area networking considerations are the layout of the network *nodes*, or computers, and the *medium*, or cable connecting the nodes. Nodes are typically desktop computers. Connecting the nodes with cable or linking computers is like drawing lines from desk to desk. The lines take the shape of a geometric figure, which is referred to as the *topology*.

The choice of topology and cable has significant impact on the success or failure of a network. Each topology and cable has characteristics that determine cost, performance, and manageability. Designing a network topology requires examining the following considerations:

Segmentation   This refers to the network's capability to be divided into smaller sections, which improve network support and reliability.

Diagnostics and troubleshooting   The network must be accompanied by diagnostic software and hardware to facilitate the analysis of network

19

problems. An important consideration is whether the network diagnostics can be used without shutting down the network.

Bandwidth   This refers to the network-cable transmission qualities. It's important to consider whether the transmission design enables smooth and fast flow of data along the cabling, without bottlenecks.

Manageability   The network topology must support management control systems. Is there sufficient ability to control access, security, and user applications?

Bridging   Will the topology allow additional LANs or mini and mainframe computers to be connected for future growth?

Expansion   The network topology must provide for expansion. Relative considerations are whether new nodes can be added and moved easily.

This chapter explains network topologies and discusses LAN cabling. The topologies covered here include bus, ring, and star. Also, the characteristics and performance of twisted pair, coaxial, and fiber optic cable are described and compared. Finally, the installation of cabling is explained.

NETWORK TOPOLOGY

Network topology is the geometric or physical layout of the nodes on a network. The nodes are connected together with sections of cable, which are often called **links**. At its simplest, a network can be considered a series of nodes and links. The resulting layout of the network is then largely determined by the building containing the network.

When nodes are linked one after another down a hallway, the layout is a straight line or **bus** topology. Another possibility is to connect each node with a separate cable. In a roughly drawn layout, this arrangement resembles, and is named, a **star**. A third common topology is the **ring**, which is like a bus with the two end links coming together at the same node. Figure 3.1 lists the three topologies.

The three topologies are considered below in terms of comparative cost, support, and performance. All three of these factors are important and have an impact on the decision of which type of network to install.

FIGURE 3.1
Topologies

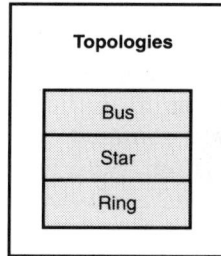

Topologies

Bus
Star
Ring

Bus Topology

The bus is the most common topology. As an observer might determine by examining the physical layout of offices and the links connecting the offices, this topology generally results in the shortest network links or amount of cable. Cable length is certainly a cost factor when evaluating topology alternatives. Figure 3.2 illustrates a bus topology in an office building. The cable is run from office to office, each node is connected to another node, and the file servers can be connected at any location on the cable, as can workstations. The bus

FIGURE 3.2
Bus Topology

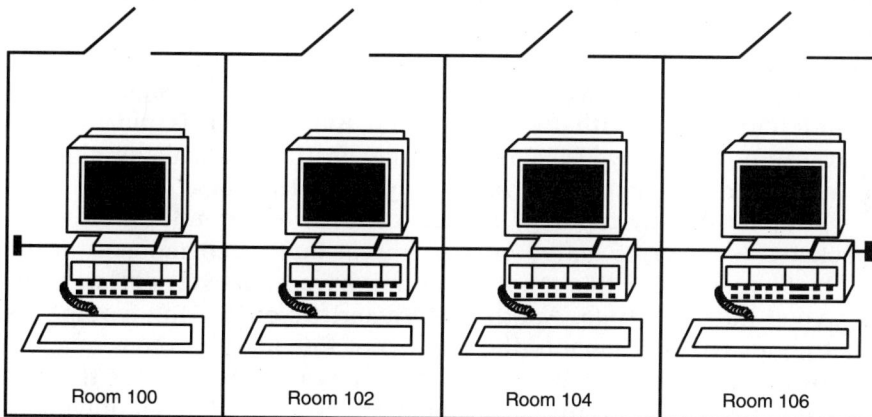

| Room 100 | Room 102 | Room 104 | Room 106 |

topology has two distinct ends, which are fitted with terminating devices so the signal is not lost.

The digital signal is sent from one node to all the other nodes on the cable, much in the same way as a city bus picks up passengers and goes to all stops on its route. Passengers then get off at their designated stops. Just as the city bus goes from one stop to the next, the network bus topology goes from one point to the next on the network in what is called **point-to-point** data communications. The obvious problem occurs when the city bus stops running. All the passengers on the route are affected. On the electronic route, if one link is broken, the entire network goes down.

The bus topology uses the least amount of cable to link the nodes, and also closely fits the physical layout of most offices. The cost advantage of using less cable is more than offset by the higher support costs of keeping the network operational. If one link is faulty, communication is broken to all of the nodes on the network. Further, adding nodes to the bus requires that the cable be broken and the network be shut down. Troubleshooting cable problems requires investigating the entire cable from one terminator node to the other.

Ring Topology

As the name "ring" implies, a ring topology is a network where the nodes are physically connected to two adjacent nodes to form a closed loop. In the standard design, the signal travels around the loop in a single direction, usually clockwise. The data is sent around the ring until the desired node is reached, at which time the next node takes its turn to send data around the ring. Figure 3.3 illustrates the standard ring design topology.

Variations on the ring topology can include two rings: one where the signal travels clockwise, and another where the signal moves counterclockwise. With two rings, each unit of data is put on both rings simultaneously. Data reaches the destination via the shortest route. Figure 3.4 shows this variation on ring topology.

The classic ring topology is characterized by permitting only one packet of data to be active on the ring at any given moment. More efficient versions of this topology permit several packets of data to be active at the same time. Another characteristic of the ring topology is that nodes will see some traffic that is not intended for them.

In most ring topologies, to add or remove nodes requires that the ring be broken. The result is that the network must be taken down and defective nodes must be switched out of the ring and bypassed.

FIGURE 3.3
Classic Ring Topology

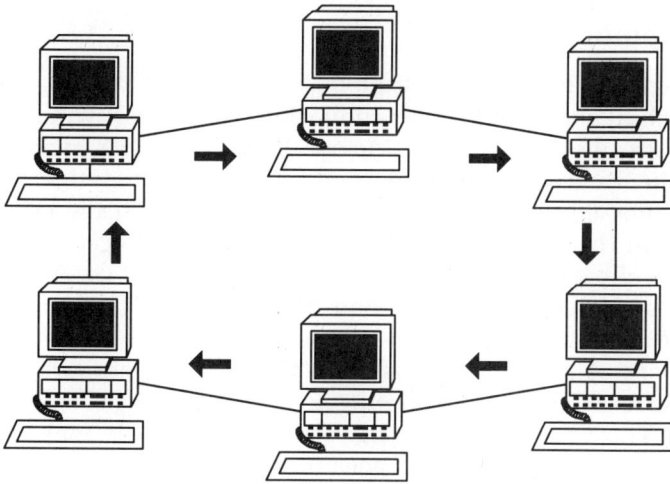

FIGURE 3.4
Ring Topology

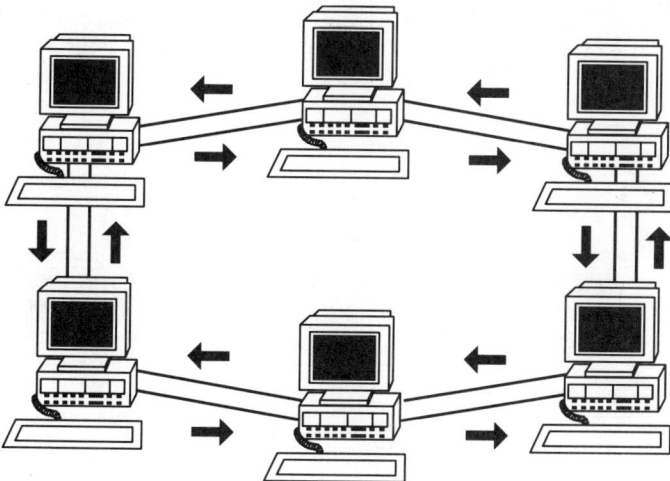

Therefore, the ring and bus topologies share many of the same benefits and weaknesses.

Star Topology

The typical star topology has each node sending data through a central hub, much like telephone lines connected to a central switching office. The hub can be an intelligent device like a data PBX switch, which takes data from one node and sends it to another designated node. Passive hubs do not switch signals, but simply split the signal to all branches in the star. Each node is responsible for receiving the data. Figure 3.5 shows the typical star topology.

Nodes are added at the hub and do not require the network to be disrupted. A node can also be removed from the hub without affecting the network. A star topology is therefore easier to support than other topologies because troubleshooting and wiring changes are isolated to the hub. The prime disadvantage of this topology is that if the hub goes down, the entire network goes down, too.

FIGURE 3.5
Typical Star Topology

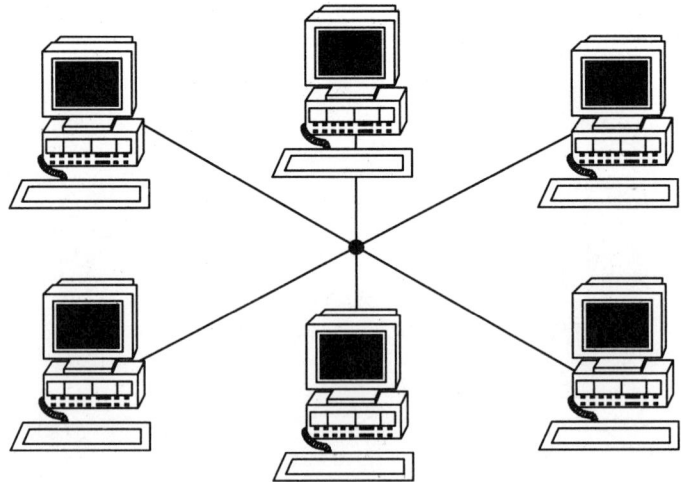

A variation on the typical star topology uses dedicated wiring to connect all nodes to one another. The single point of failure in the centralized hub design is eliminated, since data can be routed through an intermediary node. The disadvantage of this topology is that cabling expenses are high, because of the elaborate redundancy built into the design. See Figure 3.6 for an example of this topology.

FIGURE 3.6
Star Topology Without a Centralized Hub

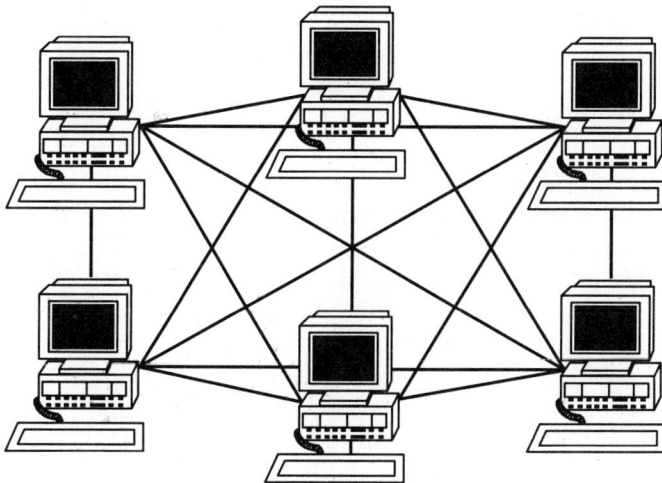

Table 3.1 provides a comparison among the common topologies.

TABLE 3.1
Comparative Analysis of Topologies

Bus	Ring	Star
Adding or removing nodes requires breaking the bus, causing down time	Ring is broken to add or remove nodes, causing down time	Nodes are added and removed without causing down time

PHYSICAL TOPOLOGY, ELECTRICAL TOPOLOGY, AND CABLING

Cable is the medium used to connect or link network nodes. There are two ways cabling affects a LAN. One is the **physical topology**, the other is the **electrical topology**. The chapter sections describing the bus, star, and ring topologies concern the physical layout of the cable. The physical layout is an important consideration because it affects cabling costs and maintenance.

The electrical topology concerns how the cable transmits signals or data packets across the cable, such as the bandwidth of the cable. It also involves concerns about electrical interference from nearby devices, which can degrade transmission of data packets.

ELECTRICAL TOPOLOGY

Cables carry an electronic signal with encoded data. There are many types of cable used in networks, and each cable has characteristics that determine the reliability and speed with which data is transmitted. Knowing the characteristics of cable types will help you design a LAN.

The first step to successful cabling is to contact a reputable supplier. He or she will know the electrical characteristics of different brands of cable and can recommend which cable is best for your installation.

Cabling is the one component of a LAN that, once it is installed, is costly and nearly impossible to replace. Therefore, it's critical to purchase the right cable and install it correctly the first time. Also, plan to purchase 15–20 percent more cable than you need. You will reduce the likelihood of running out of cable and having to purchase a different brand. Different brands and types of cable should not be mixed on the same network.

There are three types of cable: **coaxial, twisted pair**, and **fiber optic**. Any of these can be used in the three predominant network topologies. Important factors to consider when selecting network cable are the following:

Signal frequency/bandwidth   The frequency and bandwidth of cables can be dramatically different. Bandwidths can vary from 1–2 MHz to 3 GHz.

Data propagation levels   Cable data speeds can be as low as 300–9600 bps or as high as 1 Gbps (gigabit per second).

Signal loss and degradation   Signal loss and degradation affect how long the cable can extend without the need for signal amplification devices.

Noise subjectivity   The cable's susceptibility to electrical interference or noise will affect the overall performance of the network.

All of the above factors, along with other characteristics, will be considered for each of the three cable types.

Coaxial Cable

Coaxial cable is available in two general types, thick and thin. Thin coaxial is sometimes called *cheaper net*. More specific designations for coaxial cable are RG58, RG59, and RG62. RG58 cable is 50 ohm, RG59 is 75 ohm, and RG62 is 95 ohm cable. RG75 cable is used for television. (RG comes from a military designation for "Radio Government.") The RG designation is marked on the outer cover of the cable. Some cable will have a designation such as RG58/Type, which allows a cable manufacturer to substitute cable.

The impedance of the cable measured in ohms is important to consider, because the signaling devices on the network must be compatible. Figure 3.7 shows the cross section of a coaxial cable.

All types of coaxial cable have the same physical characteristics with a few exceptions. Thick coaxial has a yellow outer plastic cover. The plastic cover keeps moisture away from the center conductor, which carries electric current and the data signal. The outer cover may also be Teflon or plenum cable. Teflon coating allows the cable to

FIGURE 3.7
Coaxial Cable

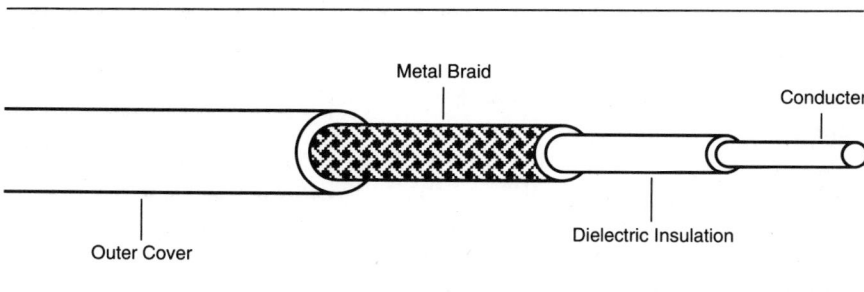

be used in plenum areas of a building. Plastic (PVC) covered cable, if installed in a plenum, must be installed in conduit to protect people from poisonous fumes in the event the cable is ignited in a fire.

Under the outer cover there is a metal braid or foil. The braid is either bare copper or tinned copper and serves as a ground or return current path. The braid does not serve as an insulator.

The layer just inside the braid is called the dielectric. This is either foam or solid insulation. Its function is to keep out electronic noise while sustaining the electric current at the same time.

At the center of the coaxial cable is the conductor, which can be solid, stranded, or tinned copper. The signaling capacity is largely determined by the type of conductor inside the cable. The larger the conductor, the farther the signal can be transmitted. The tradeoff, however, is that larger conductors make the cable less flexible, harder to work with, and more costly. Other types of coaxial cables that have not been described are *twinax*, *triax*, and *quadrax*. These cables are largely distinguished by their number of braids and conductors.

A network is not one continuous run of cable; at each node on the network, the cable has a connection that attaches the cable to the node. To make a connection, one must cut the cable and fit it with the appropriate connector.

Because coaxial cable has excellent shielding, it can be used in manufacturing environments where heavy machinery is operated. Coaxial is also used extensively around computers, particularly for computer-to-computer communication. Both of these environments generate high sources of electronic "noise." All cable that uses electronic current to transmit signals is susceptible to electromagnetic interference (EMI) and radio frequency interference (RFI). EMI is generated by computers, fluorescent lighting, broadcast stations, voltage lines, and electronic machines. Electronic emissions from these and other sources cause noise on the LAN cable. RFI is caused when the cable conductors act as receiving antennas or secondary windings of transformers. Both pick up noise from external sources.

Broadband and Baseband

The bandwidth of coaxial cable determines how many signals the cable can handle at once. Thick coax is a *broadband* medium, and thin coax is a *baseband* medium. Broadband cable allows several different signals to be transmitted at the same time, and has a number of frequencies or channels along which signals can run. Baseband cable can send only one signal over the cable at once and has a single channel for data transmission.

Twisted Pair

Twisted pair cable has been around longer than coaxial, but has only recently been used to carry data transmissions. Twisted pair cable is used to carry voice signals over the telephone network. The cable used for telephones has a plastic outer cover and insulated connectors inside. This cable is used in LANs.

Telephone cable is *unshielded twisted pair*. Shielded twisted pair cable is also available, but is not used with telephones. The distinctions between shielded and unshielded twisted pair are important when deciding whether to use existing telephone cable for a LAN.

Because unshielded twisted pair (UTP) does not have the noise immunity that coaxial has, UTP is more susceptible to electrical and radio frequency interference. This is why UTP has not been used in industrial plants or in computer rooms. Shielded twisted pair is more suited to environments where there is electrical interference.

Foil-shielded cable will shield some radio frequency interference. Braided shield cable will also shield against low-frequency interference. Double-shielded cable is designed to meet the most stringent electrical and radio frequency interference requirements.

Fiber Optic

Fiber-optic cable transmits light, rather than electronic signals. This single property accounts for fiber-optic cable's immunity to electrical and radio frequency interference. Figure 3.8 illustrates fiber-optic cable.

FIGURE 3.8
Fiber Optic Cable

The Lay of the LAN: Evaluating Topology & Cable
Fiber Optic Cable

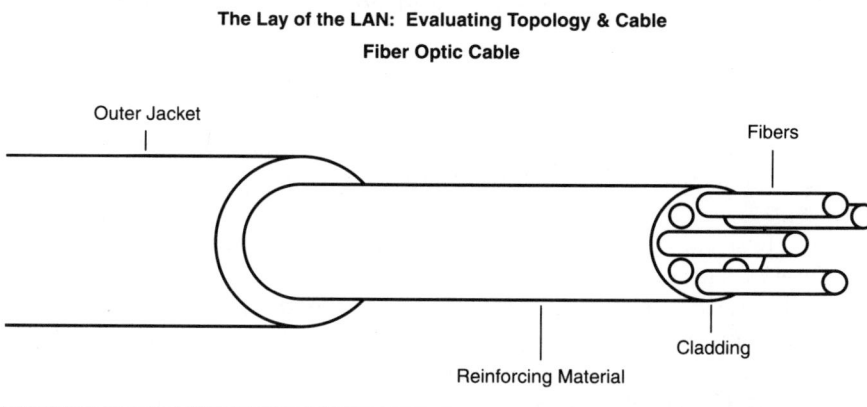

Outer Jacket

Fibers

Cladding

Reinforcing Material

The outer jacket of fiber-optic cable is plastic. The next layer is reinforcing material. This material serves to maintain the integrity of the cable during installation. Next, there is a buffer material called "cladding," which surrounds the optical fiber and aids in signal carrying. The optical fibers are glass or plastic strands that use light to transmit signals. Multiple strands are required, because light only moves in one direction. Fiber-optic cable comes in multistrands for sending and receiving signals, with some of the strands reserved for backup and growth.

Fiber cables are sized or graded by diameter. A common size is 100/140 cable. The fiber is 100 microns (millionths of a meter) in diameter and, with the cladding, is 140 microns. Currently, 100/140 is the de facto standard for LANs. This is likely to change to 62.5/125 cable. This is the standard proposed by the IEEE 802 Committee, which sets these standards. The 62.5/125 has a bandwidth of 150 MB, compared to 90 MB, for 50/125 cable.

A signal can be transmitted farther over fiber-optic cable than over either coax or twisted pair. The carrying capacity is about ten times that of twisted pair or coax. Currently, fiber-optic cable is mostly used to connect LANs between buildings. Connecting each node requires significantly more preparation of the cable. Thus, fiber optic installations are more expensive than coax or twisted pair installations.

CABLE INSTALLATION

All cable installation must be performed according to local building and wiring codes. Because of the importance and technical nature of cabling, only qualified personnel should install cable. What follows is a description of the kinds of cable and how to install them.

Types of Cable

Various types of cable are designed for different uses and applications. One LAN can use different combinations of cable, such as coaxial and fiber optic.

The first step in cabling is to obtain the local codes to determine the type of cable that can be used throughout a building. Local electrical codes will comply with the *National Electrical Code* (NEC). The NEC is a technical handbook published by the National Fire Protection Association. Generally, this requires that NEC compliant cable be used in the installation of a network. Compliant cable has met flame testing conducted by Underwriters Laboratories, which approves all data and telephone cable and classifies it into nine categories. All cable should be clearly marked with the UL codes. Some example cable markings to look for on the outer jacket are RG58/U Type CMP. This is coaxial cable with a Teflon sheath.

Class 2 cable (CL2) is power-limited, and is used for low-voltage digital transmission. CL2 can be used for RS-232 digital links and for speeds up to 16 Mbps. Communication cable (CM) is designed for optimal transmission of analog telephone signals and is referred to as "twisted pair." Used mostly to connect telephones, it can also be used to link LANs for speeds up to 10 Mbps.

General use cable (CL2, CM) is the least expensive. It has PVC insulation and a cable jacket, which is not fire retardant; it must be enclosed in conduit or non-combustible wireway for runs through vertical shafts or air plenums. (Plenums are used to recirculate air. They are found above drop ceilings and raised floors.)

Limited use cables (CL2X, CMX) are restricted to open work spaces with a maximum length of ten feet.

Riser cable (CL2R, CMR) is used where PVC cable cannot be used. Riser cable has a fire-retardant sheath, which prevents the cable from spreading flames up vertical shafts between floors. Riser cable does emit noxious fumes when burning, therefore requiring enclosure in conduit or non-combustible wireway for plenum areas.

Plenum cable (CL2P, CMP) has a low-flame- and low-fume-producing sheath. Plenum cable is frequently referred to as "Teflon cable" because Teflon is the predominant sheath material. Plenum cable can be run in both vertical shafts and plenum areas without protective enclosures.

Nonconductive optical fiber cable (OFN) must meet the same UL testing and restrictions as conductive cable.

Cable Connectors

It's one thing to have a length of cable available, but a network uses links, or cable segments, which have connectors at each end of the link. The connectors are attached (connectorized) to the nodes to make a network topology.

An easy solution to connectorizing cable is to purchase it cut to length and with connectors attached. This is costly but for small LANs and installations without trained installers this is the most viable option.

Each of these types of cable requires unique tools and techniques for attaching the connectors to the cable.

Connectors for coaxial cable require a special tool called a *crimper*. The outer layers down to the braid are stripped off with a *wire-stripping tool*. The crimping and stripping tools must match the diameter of the cable. (An RG58, or thin wire coax cable, requires different crimping and stripping tools than an RG59/62 cable.) The tool comes with die sets for the different sizes of cable, so two tools don't have to be purchased. Figure 3.9 illustrates a coaxial cable crimping tool.

FIGURE 3.9
Coaxial Crimp Tool

Stripping coaxial cable requires three strips, and each must be stripped to a specific length to guarantee a good connection. The first strip removes the insulation, the second removes the braid, and the dielectric material is cut away last, exposing the proper length of conductor. Although automatic stripping tools are available, stripping cable is the most tedious part of connectorizing cable.

For thin wire coaxial, or coax, a BNC connector is attached to the cable after it is stripped. The first step is to crimp a small connector pin to the coax conductor. Next, the hood and ferrule are placed onto the cable. Finally, the ferrule is crimped over the hood and the exposed braid to hold the BNC connector onto the cable. These crimps maintain the continuity of the connector and ground respectively. Failing to maintain the continuous ground and conductor through these connections results in the most frequent source of network failures. Something as simple as moving a desk with a computer connected to the network can cause the connection to fail and shut down the network. Users can unknowingly disconnect the cable with the same results.

FIGURE 3.10
BNC T Connector with Coaxial Cable Connecters

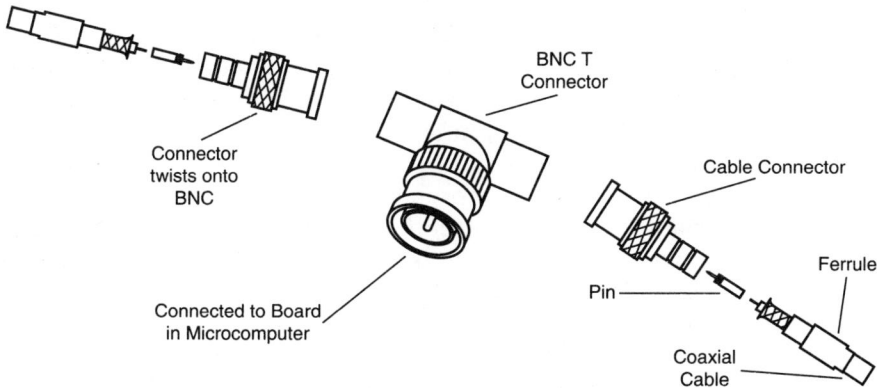

Figure 3.10 shows coaxial cable with a BNC connector. The BNC connector is the most commonly used type of connection on a LAN.

Rooms are now being wired for thin wire coaxial cable, which allows a node to be linked to the network by connecting the node to the wall plate, which has a thin-coax outlet.

Twisted pair connections on LANs are designated RJ-11 and RJ-45. RJ-11 connectors can take up to six wires, or three pairs, and are used for telephones with modular jacks. RJ-45 will connect eight wires or four pairs. There are crimping tools to crimp the connectors to the twisted pair cable, so stripping the cable is not required. With the proper crimping tools, twisted-pair cable is the easiest cable to connectorize.

Fiber-optic cable is the newest type of cable, and the most difficult to connectorize. It is used to connect building-to-building installations. The easiest way to buy a predetermined length of this cable is with the connectors already installed. Terminating connectors for fiber-optic cable do not go directly to a node on someone's desk. The cable is normally terminated in a wiring closet.

Fiber cable is significantly different from both coaxial and twisted pair when it comes to installation. All LAN cable is pulled from one point on the network to another. Great care must be exercised when pulling fiber-optic cable as it does not have the tensile strength of copper-conductor cable. Copper-conductor cable can be pulled by tying a pull cord to one end and pulling the cable through conduit. Fiber-optic cable requires the cord be taped to it at intervals of less than one foot. Taping at intervals reduces the chance of damaging the fiber core of the cable.

Installing cable requires a knowledge of the *bending radius* of the cable. Twisted pair can be bent at right angles without damaging the cable. Thin-wire coax is almost as flexible, and for installation purposes has no bending-radius limitations. Thick coax and fiber-optic cable both have a minimum bending radius. The rule here is to check the manufacturer's specification on bending radii.

The two main types of fiber-optic connectors are designated ST and SMA. ST connectors usually have a ceramic ferrule, and SMA have a metal ferrule. The ferrule holds the fiber to make the connection with a device or other connector.

ST and SMA connectors differ in cost and capability. ST connectors are more costly but result in less loss of signal. For long cable runs or networks with many fiber-optic segments, the ST connector is recommended.

TABLE 3.2
Comparison of Cable Alternatives

The Lay of the LAN: Evaluating Topology and Cable

Cable Media	Advantages	Disadvantages
Twisted pair	Easy to install and well understood technology and least expensive cable to buy and install. Can be used for all topologies.	Subject to electric interference, least security.
Thin coax	Greater resistance to interference than twisted pair.	More costly to install and less flexible than twisted pair.
Thick coax	Can be used over greater distances, and has more bandwidth than thin coax. Good immunity to outside interference.	More difficult to install and costly to install.
Fiber optics	Highest bandwidth and least problems with interference. Small size and light weight.	Most difficult and expensive to purchase and install.

The process of connectorizing fiber-optic cable is both difficult and time-consuming. There are six phases to connectorizing fiber-optic cable:

- Preparing fibers
- Terminating fibers
- Crimping
- Completing assembly
- Polishing
- Testing the completed connector

Table 3.2 compares twisted pair, coaxial, and fiber-optic cable showing the advantages and disadvantages of each.

LAN Cabling

A building's existing wiring conduit, wire runs, and wire closets are used, when possible, for cabling a LAN. Figure 3.11 depicts a LAN cabled with both thin and thick coaxial cable, and fiber-optic cable. A

FIGURE 3.11

Ethernet Network Using Thin and Thick Coax and Fiber-Optic Cable

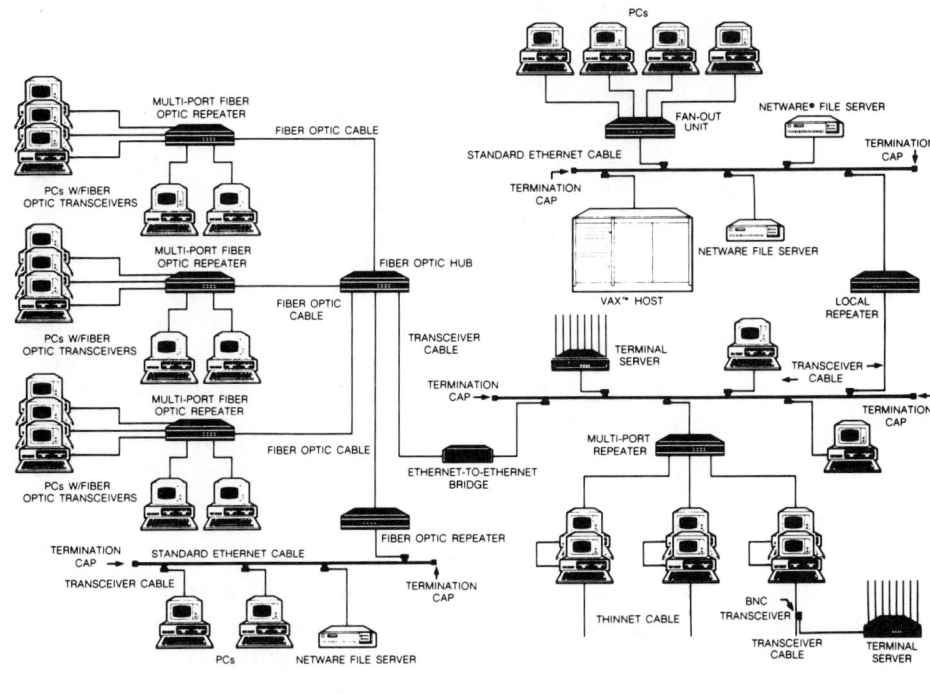

LAN residing in one room would not use thick coaxial or fiber-optic cable. The choices would be thin coax or twisted-pair cable. Thick coax and fiber-optic cable are not linked directly to nodes. Both these cable types require either thin wire coax or twisted pair to be connected from the cable to the node using a transceiver and transceiver cable.

Cable Costs

Table 3.3 offers a cost comparison of the different types of cable, including preassembled connectors or links. Preassembled links cost more, because each link has the connector attached to the cable. Unassembled links require the use of appropriate tools. To make a comparison between the preassembled and unassembled links, the cost of tools must be added to the unassembled costs.

TABLE 3.3
Comparative Cable Costs with Preassembled Links

Coaxial Cable	
Cable Type	Cost
Thin Coax PVC	$11.75 + 0.35/ft
Thin Coax Teflon	11.75 + 0.75/ft
Thick Coax	40.00 + 1.25/ft
Transceiver Cable	28.00 + 1.20/ft

Twisted-Pair Cable	
Cable Length	Cost
7 feet	$1.44
14 feet	1.98
25 feet	2.70

Fiber-Optic Cable	
Cable Type	Cost
62.5 Micron Core	$153.50 + 0.50/ft

SUMMARY

Installing a LAN is a complicated undertaking. It requires making decisions about which topology to use: bus, ring, or star. Several considerations that affect the selection of topology include whether the network can be divided into smaller segments; how easy it is to diagnose network problems; bridging and growth capabilities; security and access needs; and cable transmission capabilities.

Another issue related to topology is the type of cable that can be used. Whether to use twisted pair, coaxial, or fiber cable depends on such factors as cost, building characteristics, and presence of electrical interference. Two important goals in selecting topology and cabling are to achieve a reliable computing environment with low maintenance.

CHAPTER QUESTIONS

1. Explain the term "topology."
2. What factors should be taken into account when designing a network topology?
3. What are the three major LAN topologies? Discuss each topology in terms of its advantages and disadvantages.
4. What considerations should be made when you purchase cable?
5. What kinds of cable are available for LANs?
6. What is the function of the dielectric in cable?
7. Explain the difference between broadband and baseband cable.
8. You have been asked to design a LAN installation. The installation consists of two buildings. One building is used for offices, the other is a manufacturing facility that houses heavy equipment. What kind of cable would you use in the office building? Why? What kind of cable would you use in the manufacturing facility? Why? What kind of cable would you use to connect the two buildings? Why?
9. Describe the four factors that influence cable installation.

4

LAN Protocols

INTRODUCTION TO NETWORK PROTOCOLS

Protocols are standards for LAN communication. Ethernet, token ring, and ARCNET are protocols for connecting nodes to LANs and communicating on the LANs. Each of these protocols is explained in the following sections.

Ethernet Protocol

Currently the most popular protocol for LANs is ethernet. Ethernet, as defined by the IEEE 802.3 committee, uses Carrier Sense Multiple Access with Collision Detection (CSMA/CD) for media access control. In effect, the node, by means of the network interface card, "listens" for traffic on the medium. If no traffic is sensed, the node sends a packet of data on to the network. When the medium is busy, the node waits a period of time before retransmitting. If two stations try to access the medium at the same time, each node backs off and waits a random amount of time.

CSMA/CD is effective for networks transmitting for short durations, such as networks with a small number of nodes. When several nodes begin to transmit for long durations (five seconds or more), collisions occur. Collisions result in reduced throughput on the network. As more and more nodes try to access the medium and find it busy, nodes begin to experience delays. Determining whether CSMA/CD will have the desired response time requires some experimentation. The uncertainty of calculating how long it will take to send data between nodes is a major disadvantage.

The IEEE 802.3 CSMA/CD protocol works with five types of cable as shown in Figure 4.1.

FIGURE 4.1
IEEE 802.3 Cable Types

10 BASE 5	10 Mbps	50 ohm coax
10 BASE 2	10 Mbps	50 ohm coax
10 BROAD 36	10 Mbps	75 ohm coax
1 BASE 5	1 Mbps	twisted pair
10 BASE-T	10 Mbps	twisted pair

The 50 ohm is thin wire coaxial cable, and the 75 ohm is thick wire coaxial cable. Differences other than speed and cable type exist in how the data packets are constructed, in error handling, and in other protocol functions.

The 10 Mbps transmission rate shown in Figure 4.1 for coaxial and 10Base-T twisted pair cable needs to be explained. 10 Mbps is not an accurate description of the data throughput. Ethernet has enough overhead in the frames that the effective data transfer rate is, at best, 1 Mbps. Overhead includes the source and destination addresses, length of the frame, and the preamble, which synchronizes the sending and receiving nodes. The maximum packet size for ethernet is 1,500 bytes. Under normal network traffic conditions the transfer rate can be lower than 100 Kbps or 1/100 the raw transfer rate. Novell has a software utility called PERFORM.EXE, which can be run on the network to determine data throughput. PERFORM.EXE should be run under varying network loads to project the effective data throughput for nodes.

Ethernet networks are established in a bus topology. The ethernet cable begins at one node and is connected to additional nodes until all the nodes are connected. Connections are made according to ethernet specifications for distance and number of workstations per seg-

FIGURE 4.2
Ethernet Cable Specifications

Limitations	Thin Coax	Thick Coax
Maximum number of trunk segments	5	5
Maximum trunk segment length	185 m*	500 m
Maximum network trunk cable length	925 m	2,500 m
Maximum number of stations connected to one cable segment	30	100
Minimum distance between T-connectors	.5 m	.5 m

*m = meters

ment. The specifications are determined by the cable type. Figure 4.2 shows the ethernet specifications for thin and thick coaxial cable.

A **trunk segment** consists of the nodes and the cable. The trunk cable is a series of cable lengths connecting each node. One cable terminator to another terminator constitutes a trunk segment.

Using the specifications in Figure 4.2, a thin-wire ethernet LAN can be 185 meters long, or 607 feet, and have thirty nodes. To extend the distance and the number of nodes requires a *repeater*. A repeater is a box that amplifies the signal and has connections for adding cable segments. A popular and functional repeater is manufactured by BICC Data Networks. Their ISOLAN Multiport Repeater provides a means for connecting up to eight cable segments in a local area network; and it is designed to conform to IEEE 802.3 specifications. Six of the eight available ports (network connections) on the Multiport Repeater are dedicated to thin ethernet (IEEE 802.3 10 BASE 2) segments. The remaining two ports are of type AUI (Attachment Unit Interface). AUI ports can attach to thin, thick, or fiber-optic ethernet segments.

With the addition of repeaters, a LAN can be extended for thousands of feet.

Multiport repeaters have automatic partitioning and reconnection. These functions isolate a faulty segment from the rest of the network and reconnect the segment when the fault is cleared. The repeater also overcomes one of the limitations of the ethernet bus topology. On a bus topology, if the cable is disconnected to add a node, or is disconnected for any reason, the network cannot function. The repeater allows each segment to be isolated. Individual segments can be downed to add or repair nodes. When a segment is reconnected, the repeater brings it back onto the network. Figure 4.3 demonstrates the extent to which an ethernet LAN can be configured.

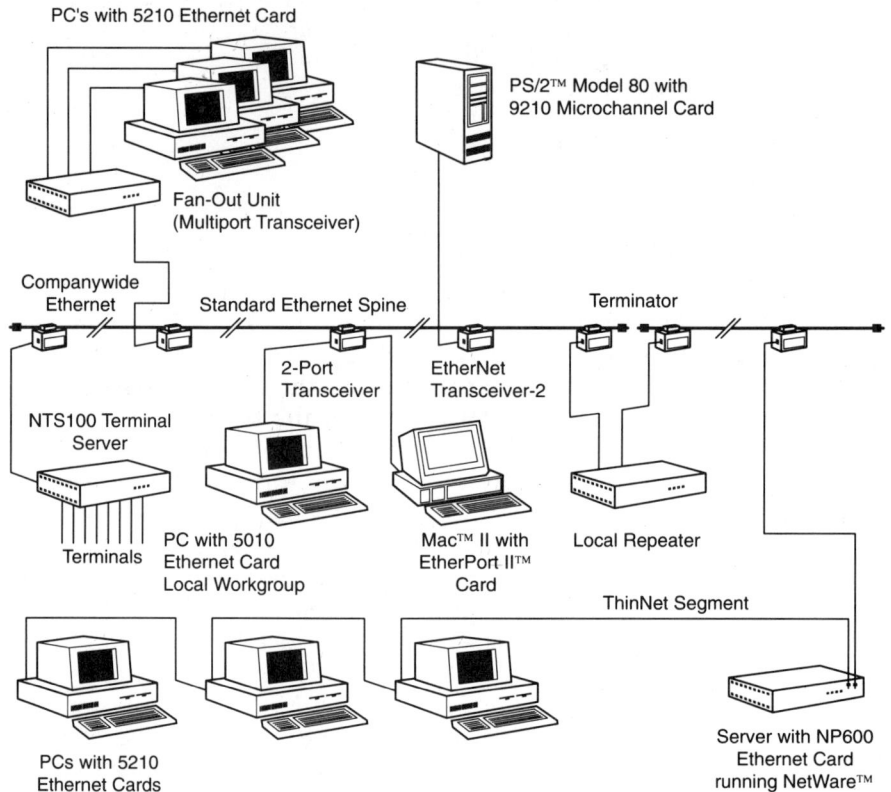

PC's with 5210 Ethernet Card

PS/2™ Model 80 with
9210 Microchannel Card

Fan-Out Unit
(Multiport Transceiver)

Companywide
Ethernet

Standard Ethernet Spine

Terminator

2-Port
Transceiver

EtherNet
Transceiver-2

NTS100 Terminal
Server

Terminals

PC with 5010
Ethernet Card
Local Workgroup

Mac™ II with
EtherPort II™
Card

Local Repeater

ThinNet Segment

PCs with 5210
Ethernet Cards

Server with NP600
Ethernet Card
running NetWare™

Ethernet on twisted pair cable is limited to a maximum segment length of 109 meters. Ethernet on fiber-optic cable has a maximum segment length of 1,200 meters.

Thick coaxial cable is not used to connect each node. It is used for connecting different LANs together or for connecting nodes that extend beyond the limitations of thin-wire coax. Thick-wire coax is used as a network **backbone**, which is a long cable connecting two or more LANs across a college or business campus.

Ethernet backbones can also use fiber-optic cable, which is now the preferred choice for backbones. Costs are similar for thick coax, but the signal capacity of fiber optic is ten times greater than thick coax.

Ethernet is the oldest network protocol and the most widely used. Because it has been used since the mid-1970s and is an established IEEE standard, ethernet enjoys the highest level of connectivity among all types and sizes of computers.

Token Ring Protocol

The IEEE 802.5 standard defines the token ring protocol for ring topology. This topology uses a data packet called a **token**.

The token circulates around the cable. Nodes wanting to transmit wait for the token to pass. When the token is taken by a node, the node changes the token to a start-of-frame sequence by changing one bit in the token. The node then appends and transmits the remaining fields of the data frame.

Once the node has removed the token by changing the bit pattern, no other nodes can transmit. This ensures that only one node can transmit at a time. The node which changed the token has control of the LAN until a new token is generated. The node generates a new token when both of the following conditions are met:

- The station has completed transmission of its frame.
- The leading edge of its transmitted frame has returned (after a complete circulation of the ring) to the station.

Once a new token is on the ring, the next node can take it and transmit data. The token ring protocol gives each node equal access to the network. Networks with heavy traffic benefit from a token ring protocol because there are no collisions, as with the CSMA/CD protocol.

A token ring protocol does have the ability to set priorities. There are situations where a node is shut down because it interrupts the priority sequence for the token, or because the token is corrupt.

When a node sends a packet to another node, the sending node detects one of three outcomes:

- The receiving node is nonexistent or not active.
- The receiving node exists, but the contents of the packet are not copied.
- The contents of the packet are copied.

A packet contains such information as the data to be transmitted and information that helps test for transmission errors. The maximum packet size for a 4 Mbps token ring is 4 KB, and for 16 Mbps is 16 KB.

Each token ring node has a network interface card. There is a Multistation Access Unit (MAU), which is a device that connects up to eight nodes in a network. The token ring eight-foot adaptor cable has a NIC adaptor on one end and an IBM Cabling System connector that connects to either a patch cable or to an MAU. Patch cables are IBM type 6 cable with an IBM Cabling System connector on each end. Patch cables are available in 8, 30, 75, and 150-foot lengths. Patch cables can be connected to each other, to adapter cables, or to an MAU. Token-ring network specifications are listed in Figure 4.4.

The limitations on speed are determined by either the IEEE or IBM standard. For IEEE, token ring can transmit at 1–4 Mbps. The IBM standard allows for 16 Mbps on shielded twisted-pair or on fiber-optic cable.

ARCNET Protocol

ARCNET protocol is not an officially recognized standard, even though it has been used since 1977. ARCNET, developed by Datapoint Corporation, is a combination of two acronyms—ARC, attached resource computer, and NET, network. Even though ARCNET does not fall under IEEE standards, there are over 600,000 users, as reported in the *ARCNET Factory LAN Primer*, written by Contemporary Control Systems, Inc. In fact, this publication is an excellent resource for the ARCNET protocol.

ARCNET is a token-passing protocol, which with the use of active hubs has a star topology. An active hub is a signal regenerator, and will split the signal onto other segments connected to the active hub.

FIGURE 4.4
Token Ring Specifications

- Maximum number of stations is 96.
- Maximum number of MAU units is 12.
- Maximum patch cable distance between an MAU and a station is 150 feet.
- Maximum patch cable distance between two MAUs is 150 feet.
- Maximum patch cable distance connecting all MAUs is 400 feet.
- The total length of the main ring must not exceed 1200 feet.
- One eight-station hub counts as 16 feet of cable.
- One non-bridged main ring will support up to 33 eight-station hubs.
- The maximum number of nodes one main ring can support is 255.

The cabling medium is RG62 A/U coaxial cable. Twisted pair and fiber-optic cable are also used.

The ARCNET network interface card has a set of eight switches that can be used to set a node address from 1 to 255. An ARCNET network is therefore limited to 255 nodes. The address 0 is used by ARCNET to send broadcast messages on the network. Each node must have a unique address. (See Figure 4.5.)

Since ARCNET is a token-passing system, each node has equal access to the network. The token is passed to the node that has the next higher address. After the token reaches the highest active node, that node sends the token to the lowest active node address. The token circulates in a logical ring, which may not resemble the physical ring. Figure 4.6 demonstrates the logical and physical relationship between nodes on an ARCNET LAN.

ARCNET data packets hold from 1 to 508 characters. The maximum ARCNET packet size is 512 bytes. The token is passed to the next node after one packet is sent. When the data exceeds 512 bytes, additional packets must be sent.

FIGURE 4.5
ARCNET NIC
Courtesy of Interface Corporation

FIGURE 4.6
FIGURE 4.6
ARCNET Logical Versus Physical Network Configuration

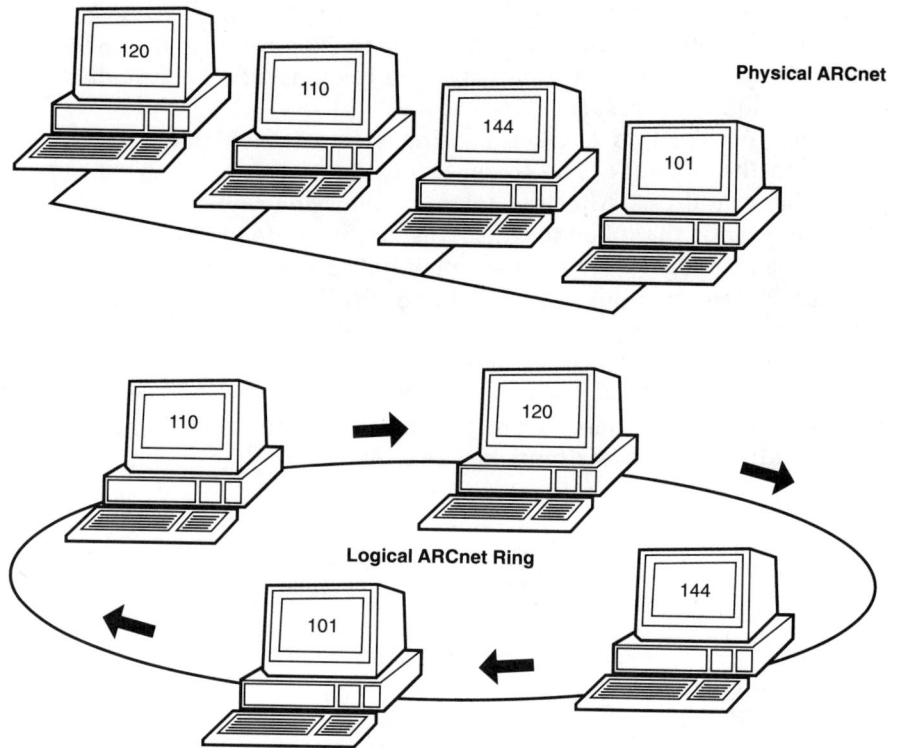

For the token to pass successfully around the network, each node only needs to know the active node with the next highest address.

The specifications shown in Figure 4.7 apply to ARCNET using RG62 A/U cable.

FIGURE 4.7
ARCNET Specifications

- Maximum cable distance from one end of the network to another is 20,000 feet.

- Maximum distance between active hubs is 2,000 feet.

- Maximum distance between an active hub and a network node is 2,000 feet.

- Maximum distance between an active hub and a passive hub is 100 feet.

- Maximum distance between a passive hub and a station is 100 feet.

SUMMARY

Three data transmission protocols were discussed in this chapter: ethernet, token ring, and ARCNET. Of these, ethernet is the most popular. The ethernet protocol uses CSMA/CD as the access method to the network. The token-ring protocol uses token-passing as a way for data to access the network. Finally, ARCNET also uses token-passing for network access.

CHAPTER QUESTIONS

1. What body defines protocol standards for networks?
2. Explain the CSMA/CD access method.
3. Explain the token-passing access methods used by token-ring protocol and by ARCNET.
4. What type of cabling works best for a backbone? Why?
5. What is the purpose of a repeater?
6. What is the purpose of a hub?
7. Compare the advantages of ethernet, token ring, and ARCNET.
8. You are designing a network that will have seventy users on one server in the same building. What topology, protocol, and cable would you use? Why?

5

The Novell File Server
A Look at the Hardware

INTRODUCTION TO NOVELL FILE SERVERS

Novell's NetWare operating system is available on 80286, 80386, minicomputers, and VAX mainframe platforms. The 80286 platform is used in the largest number of NetWare installations. This chapter discusses the many options available when selecting the hardware components of a file server. The file server hardware plays a major role in the performance and reliability of the network.

When selecting a file server, one must first select an 80286 or 80386 computer that has been *certified* by Novell. Hardware vendors can "hire" Novell to certify that their hardware works with Novell's operating systems. Novell publishes overall results of the tests, specific configuration results, and any qualifications regarding certification. (For example, the CPU functions at a clock speed of 12 Mhz, but not at 16 Mhz.)

Before deciding on a hardware platform, one must determine if the computer is certified by Novell. The same applies to file server components such as disk drives.

49

File servers can be purchased fully configured with hardware, or the 80286/80386 computer can be purchased and configured by the network installer.

Once the file server is on site, the vendor's hardware diagnostics should be run before the NetWare operating system is loaded. These diagnostics test the memory, disk drives, monitor, and keyboard. Normally, the diagnostics are run for a 24-hour "burn in" period, which allows sufficient time to detect any problems.

If additional disk drives, serial ports, or other components are to be added to the server, it's a good idea to ensure the original server hardware is working first (by running the diagnostics). Then the installer can add the new components one at a time. The equipment manufacturer's diagnostics should be run with each new component before adding another component. (Most disk drive, serial port, and network interface card vendors provide diagnostics with their equipment.) By following this method, hardware problems can be identified and resolved before loading the operating system.

HOW TO CONFIGURE A FILE SERVER

A bare bones 80286 or 80386 computer has 1 MB of memory (RAM) and one floppy disk drive. To allow for expansion, only computers with six or more expansion slots should be purchased. The computer needs to have the capability for memory expansion either directly on the mother board or through expansion slots. These expansion capabilities make it possible to increase memory, install one or more NICs, add disk drives, and add other hardware that may be needed later.

SELECTING DISK DRIVES

Selecting disk drives should be the first decision for configuring the file server. As the name "file server" implies, the primary function of a LAN is to provide shared disk access for applications and data. The disk drive may not be a large initial dollar investment, but the disk will soon contain thousands of dollars' worth of application software and perhaps tens of thousands of dollars' worth of data files. Therefore, it is advisable to select only Novell-certified disk drives, or drives that are shown to be reliable in network environments. Figure 5.1 contains a list of recommendations for selecting disk drives.

FIGURE 5.1
Recommendations for Disk Drive Systems

- Select only Novell-certified disk drives and controllers.
- Select ESDI or SCSI type disk drives and controllers.
- Select 40 MB or larger disk drives.
- Record disk drive information.
- Have only qualified personnel install disk drives and controllers.
- Coordinate disk size with memory.

One important requirement of a disk drive is that track 0, or the boot track, must be defect-free. Novell's NetWare 286 will not function if track 0 does not meet this condition.

NetWare allows expansion to thirty-two disk volumes, with a single volume limit of 255 megabytes. The file server maximum is 2 GB (2 billion bytes) of disk storage.

The amount of disk storage required for a given installation depends on three factors:

- The anticipated number of users
- The types of applications
- Whether users will store data files on the server

Disk storage requirements increase as the number of users increases. Storage requirements also increase with the complexity of applications. For instance, computer-aided design applications, such as AutoCAD, need more disk storage than word processing applications. And disk storage needs are particularly great if users store their data files on the network disk. For example, consider the following environment:

1. There is an anticipated maximum of 15 users.
2. The network software consists of a word processor, a spreadsheet, electronic mail, and several small database applications.
3. Only the database files are stored on the server (other files are stored on individual floppy diskettes).

This environment does not require a large amount of disk storage, particularly since word processing and spreadsheet files are not stored on the network disk. The number of users is comparatively small, and the applications require a relatively small amount of disk storage. A 40–70 MB hard disk will adequately service this environment.

A more demanding environment would be the following:

1. There is a maximum of thirty users.

2. There is software consisting of desktop publishing applications, a word processor, desktop publishing fonts, a computer-aided design (CAD) package, graphics art packages, downloading fonts, and a spreadsheet.

3. The users store data files on the file server.

The above environment will require 150–300 MB or more of disk storage. Storage demands will be very high with thirty users creating desktop publishing documents and CAD drawings. Desktop publishing or CAD files can easily be 2 MB or more in size. Many of these files are too large to store on floppy diskette and must be stored on the network.

Beyond storage requirements, it's necessary to consider disk drive performance. There are four areas related to disk performance: the disk controller, the speed of the disk, disk integrity, and disk reliability. All of these areas should be considered before purchasing a file server disk drive.

Disk Controllers

The **disk controller** is a circuit board that controls how data is written onto or read from a disk drive. The controller may be a separate board that fits in a slot in the computer, or it can be built into the disk drive. There are three disk controller technologies available: ST506, ESDI, and SCSI.

The most common controller technology is *ST506*, which was developed before microcomputer hard disks. It is the least sophisticated and slowest of the three controllers. The raw-data transfer rate is 5 megabits per second. The ST506 knows how to spin the drive and move the heads, but it knows nothing about the information on the disk.

The data-coding patterns commonly used by the ST506 are *modified frequency modulation* (MFM), *run length limited* (RLL), and *advanced run length limited* (ARLL). Both the data coding system supplied by the controller and the capabilities of the hard drive must be compatible. An MFM disk cannot be used with an RLL controller.

Enhanced small device interface (ESDI) controllers are more recent technology. ESDI is a standard developed by disk controller manufacturers. Transfer rates of 5 to 15 megabits per second are possible with this type of controller. ESDI incorporates defect-mapping information on the disk drive. Defect or bad disk track information is stored on the disk like other data.

Instead of sending raw data like the MFM controller, the ESDI controller communicates in NRZ (not-return-zero) code. The result is faster and more reliable transfer of data. An ESDI controller must be used with an ESDI disk drive. It will not work with an ST506 drive, even though the two can be physically connected together.

Whereas the ST506 and ESDI controllers are separate boards, the *SCSI* controller is built into the disk drive. SCSI, or *small computer system interface,* is the most recent disk technology. ST506 and ESDI are designed as device-level disk connections, but the SCSI can interface with hard disks, tape drives, and other hardware that works with the SCSI standard.

The SCSI board inserted into the computer is not truly a controller but a host adapter, which allows disk drives and tape drives to act independently of the computer. The advantage of using a SCSI interface is that there is the flexibility to connect hardware, such as a tape drive. The disadvantage is that the SCSI interface is the least standardized interface.

Disk Speed

The previous discussion about transfer rates applies to the speed with which data is transferred between the disk drive and the computer's memory. A manufacturer's drive information includes the *average access time* and the *data transfer rate.* Access time is the time required to move the read/write heads to the data. Transfer rate is how fast the data moves to memory once the heads have been positioned over the data. For fast data retrieval, it's best to have a low access time and a high transfer rate.

ESDI drives have a high transfer rate (5–15 Mbps). They also have a low access time (under 20 milliseconds). This makes ESDI drives faster than ST506 drives, which have lower transfer rates (5 Mbps) and higher access times (80–40 milliseconds). SCSI drives are comparable to ESDI transfer rates and access times.

Disk Integrity and Throughput

The manufacturer's drive information is stated in optimal terms. It does not accurately reflect the true data throughput of a disk drive. The actual data throughput is determined by:

- The low-level format of the disk
- The coding method (MFM, RLL, etc.) that stores the data
- The DMA, or direct memory access

- The performance of the computer
- Bad-sector data as supplied by the manufacturer

The disk drive manufacturer performs a low-level format before the disk is sold. Results of the format (bad disk sectors) are printed on a label and pasted on the disk drive. This information should be recorded if Novell's COMPSURF is used, because the COMPSURF utility asks for bad-sector information. COMPSURF (for comprehensive surface analysis) is a NetWare utility that tests the disk drive. The installation can be completed without the bad sector information, because COMPSURF is not required. COMPSURF is not required because NetWare has a "hot-fix" feature, which determines when a bad spot on the disk has been accessed and redirects the data to another location.

Disk Reliability

The reliability of the disk system is critical. It does little good to install a disk system if it lasts only three months. Many low-end 40 MB disk drives are not designed to the specifications required for a file server. File server disks frequently run for weeks or months without being powered down. The mean time between failure (MTBF) must be sufficient to ensure a long-lasting disk. For example, some ESDI drives have a seven year MTBF.

INSTALLING DISK DRIVES

A file server may be purchased with the hard disk pre-installed. However, many organizations prefer to install their own hard disks. The physical installation of a hard disk is not a difficult procedure, as long as the manufacturer's instructions are followed.

Every disk drive will have a drive type indicated somewhere on the drive or in the drive installation guide. The drive type tells the computer what kind of drive is installed. For example, on an IBM computer, a type 1 disk drive has 306 cylinders, four heads, write precomp 128, landing zone cylinder 305, and a capacity of 10 MB.

The drive type is entered into the computer's setup program, which provides the computer with information about what hardware has been installed. This includes the type of disk drives, the amount of memory, and the number of serial communication ports. Figure 5.2 illustrates how this information is entered.

Once the setup information is entered, it is helpful to record the drive type for later reference. A file server may lose its setup informa-

FIGURE 5.2
Setup Program Screen

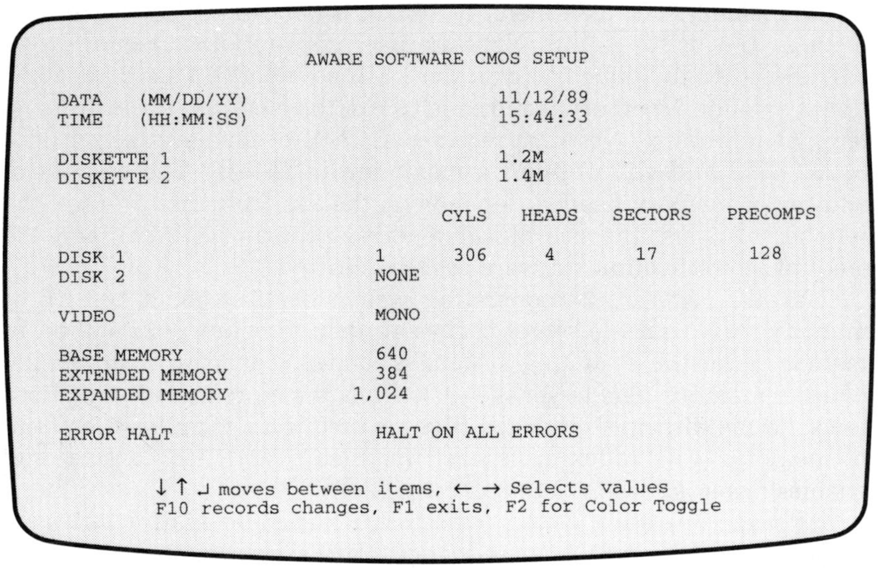

```
                    AWARE SOFTWARE CMOS SETUP

   DATA   (MM/DD/YY)               11/12/89
   TIME   (HH:MM:SS)               15:44:33

   DISKETTE 1                      1.2M
   DISKETTE 2                      1.4M

                        CYLS    HEADS    SECTORS    PRECOMPS

   DISK 1           1   306      4         17         128
   DISK 2           NONE

   VIDEO            MONO

   BASE MEMORY      640
   EXTENDED MEMORY  384
   EXPANDED MEMORY  1,024

   ERROR HALT       HALT ON ALL ERRORS

         ↓ ↑ ↵ moves between items, ← → Selects values
         F10 records changes, F1 exits, F2 for Color Toggle
```

tion, requiring the setup to be reinstalled. This can happen if the computer's battery stops functioning. Without the correct setup information, the file server will not function. Someone who is not familiar with the hardware may have difficulty supplying the setup information. If a reference sheet is available, the information can be restored quickly.

Once the hard disk is installed and the computer put back together, the disk must be formatted. It is possible to purchase formatted disks. Some Novell certified disk drives are formatted and ready to install and use.

The format utility is supplied by the computer vendor or by the disk drive manufacturer. There is also third-party hard disk setup software. Two popular hard disk programs are DISK MANAGER from Ontrack Computer Systems and SPEEDSTOR from Storage Dimensions. These programs format hard drives and expand the options available for installing a drive.

Novell's COMPSURF utility can also be used to format and test the disk drive. When using COMPSURF, it is wise to consult the *NetWare 286 Maintenance* manual.

MEMORY

A standard 80286/80386 computer will come with a maximum of 1 MB of memory. The base memory, which is 640 KB, is the only usable memory out of the 1 MB. NetWare uses conventional memory (640 KB) and extended memory (over the 1 MB boundary). Therefore, additional extended memory is required to run the NetWare operating system. At minimum, NetWare requires 1.5 MB of memory to run on a 80286 CPU and will support a maximum of 15 MB. The amount of additional memory needed depends on the available disk storage, the number of users, the use of value-added programs (VAPs), and the amount of application software caching desired.

Novell's NetWare 286 operating system requires about 400 KB of memory. A Novell file server caches all disk directory information in memory after the operating system is loaded. Each file requires 100 bytes of memory. The larger the disk drive, the more memory required to cache the directory. **Indexed files** also require a significant amount of memory. (File indexing is used for files over 1 MB in size, and enables faster access to data in a large file.)

After the operating system, directories, and indexed directories are loaded into memory, VAPs are loaded. (VAPs are programs that work with the operating system to manage the file server or to provide added services to the users.)

NetWare supports up to 100 concurrent users and each user requires 4 KB of file server memory. Further, at least one **communication buffer** is created for each user. This is in addition to a base of forty buffers. (Communication buffers are used to store data until the server can process it. For twenty users, at least sixty communication buffers would be created.) Each communication buffer occupies half a KB of memory.

Any remaining memory is used to cache applications and data. Caching enables frequently requested applications or data to be stored in memory. For example, when several workstations request WordPerfect, it is loaded into cache after the first request. Each workstation receives WordPerfect more quickly because it is accessed from the server's cache instead of from disk. (Accessing data from cache can be up to 100 times faster than accessing it from disk.) The greater the amount of cached memory, the greater the number of applications that can be stored in memory. The benefits of caching include reduced disk operations and faster access to applications.

A direct way to establish the memory requirements for a server involves assessing the disk size, number of users, and need for services, such as indexed files. For instance, if there is an 80 MB disk on the server, at least 2 MB of memory should be used. If there will be over twenty-five users and a need for file indexing, then over 4 MB should be used. Smooth operation of a file server depends on having sufficient memory. For this reason, many experienced NetWare installers recommend the purchase of as much memory as you can afford.

Memory Installation

During the setup process, the installer specifies the type and amount of memory in the computer. The setup information must match the actual memory installed. Additional memory is installed on the motherboard or by inserting a separate memory board into the computer. These simple rules should be followed when adding memory:

1. Determine the type and speed of the existing memory chips.
2. Purchase memory that runs at the same speed as the existing memory in the computer (such as 80 or 120 nanoseconds).
3. Take steps to prevent static discharges.
4. Add memory to the motherboard first.
5. Add more memory using a separate memory board.
6. Set any hardware settings on the memory boards by following the manufacturer's instructions.
7. Use the computer's setup routine to reflect the added memory.

If the file server does not have enough memory, or if the setup information is not correct, the file server will not boot. The resulting error message does not indicate a shortage of memory. Instead, it is a *general protection interrupt* (GPI) error, which is interpreted to mean the computer has run out of memory.

NETWORK INTERFACE CARD

A **network interface card** (NIC) is available for each type of network protocol (ethernet, token ring, ARCNET, etc.) used on a LAN. A minimum of one NIC is required, and up to four can be installed on a file server. There are many NIC manufacturers for each network protocol. On the surface, choosing a NIC is easy because many NICs are marketed. Determining which NIC has the best performance, however, is not easy. The NIC must be evaluated in conjunction with the performance of the network. The bottom line in the evaluation is the throughput of the NIC. The performance also varies, depending on the amount of memory on the NIC.

A NIC has several hardware settings that must be correct before the NIC can be installed in the file server. These settings are established by moving dip switches or by pulling jumpers on the circuit board. NIC manufacturers supply documentation explaining how to set the switches and jumpers. The particular settings used are influenced by software drivers provided by Novell or by the NIC manufacturer. A driver is used to enable the NIC to communicate with the network software. Figure 5.3 shows a NIC.

FIGURE 5.3
File Server Network Interface Card

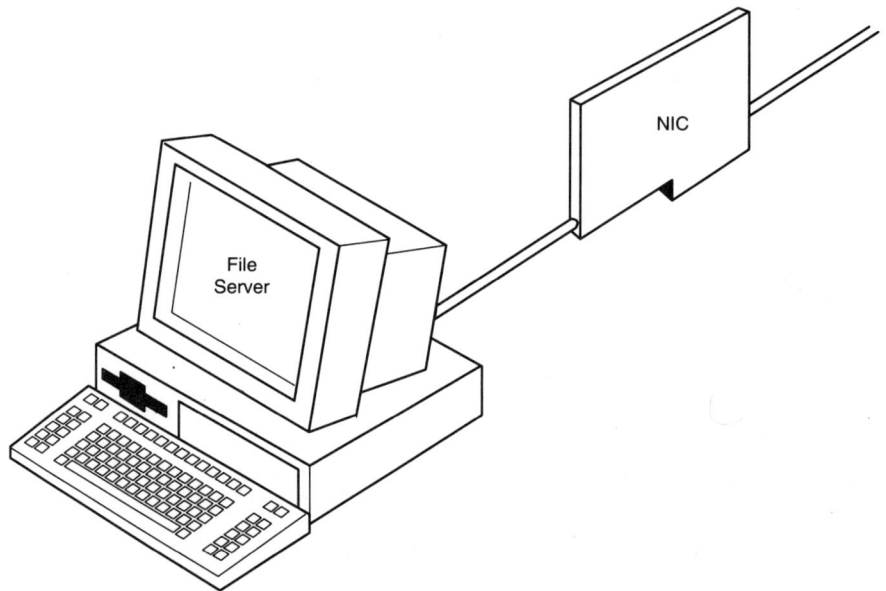

Chapter 7 discusses the procedure for selecting the LAN driver software. Briefly, the generation of the operating system includes selection of the NIC(s). The NIC driver configuration is selected as an option. Each configuration option represents hardware settings on the NIC. For example, option 0 might require the I/O base address to be 300h, the IRQ number to be 3, and the base memory address to be C800:0. An I/O base is an input/output storage area in the server's memory, which is used by the NIC. The IRQ is a hardware interrupt line used to process signals from a device, such as a hard disk drive or a NIC. And the base memory address is a location in the server's memory used by the NIC to process information.

The appropriate dip switches or jumpers must be set on the NIC to match option 0. There are situations where the settings for the NIC conflict with other hardware in the file server. For example, the IRQ is used to signal the microprocessor that a hardware device needs attention. The IRQ used for the NIC cannot be used for another hardware device. For instance, IRQ 3 is used on many computers for the second communication port (COM2). If the NIC is set to IRQ3, the second communications port will not work.

Selecting the correct NIC setting is vital if the file server is to function. Fortunately, when the file server goes through its boot-up procedures, the devices in the server and the NIC must be compatible. Otherwise, the message "UNABLE TO INITIALIZE LAN A" is displayed on the file server console, and the file server stops its boot-up procedure.

If the file server does not boot-up, the NIC settings should be checked—they may be in conflict with other hardware settings on the file server, such as a serial port. Another problem area may be the LAN cable, which is connected to the NIC. It may not be properly connected or terminated. Installing the NIC without connecting it to the cable will result in the file server's not booting.

FILE SERVER MONITOR

Any monitor that will work with 80286 or 80386 computers will also work with the file server. The file server operates primarily without user intervention. Thus, an inexpensive monochrome monitor is the best option.

FLOPPY DISK DRIVE

An important component of the file server is a floppy disk drive. Either a 5¼" or a 3½" floppy disk drive will work. The floppy drive is used to load and reconfigure the operating system.

PRINTER PORTS

The number and type of printers connected to the file server are determined by the number of serial and parallel printer ports. Usually an

80286 or 80386 computer will have one serial and one parallel printer port. Additional printer ports can be installed in one of the expansion slots.

ADDITIONAL CONFIGURATION ISSUES

Once the disk drives, memory, NICs, and printer ports are in place, it is important to consider the amount of heat generated inside the server chassis. A circulation fan may need to be installed to reduce the heat. Environmental considerations, such as temperature and power, play a major role in the up-time of a file server.

Although it is not a component of a file server, an **uninterruptible power source** (UPS) should be considered. A UPS is connected between the wall outlet and the server. There are two types of UPS: on-line and off-line. The off-line UPS does not supply power to the file server until AC power is lost. There is a brief switching time when no power is supplied to the server while the UPS switches to backup battery power. The server may go down during the switching time, causing file errors.

An on-line UPS is the best alternative. The on-line UPS supplies power to the file server through a battery. The battery is charged when the AC power is working. When the AC power is lost, the battery continues to supply power without a switch-over delay or power fluctuations. Depending on the load the file server is drawing and the size of the UPS, the file server will continue to function ten to thirty minutes without AC power. This is enough time to shut down the file server.

Since the file server's disk directory is cached in memory, sudden loss of power can result in directory structure errors. This occurs because the cache directory has not updated the disk directory. These errors can be repaired by using NetWare's VREPAIR utility (see Chapter 11). But a safer alternative is to reduce the effects of power loss with a UPS.

Power sags and surges are other power problems addressed by a UPS. (Sags occur when power on the line drops well below 120 volts. Surges occur when power exceeds the normal 120 volt level.) A good UPS will condition the line to eliminate dramatic sags or surges.

The need for a UPS is sometimes difficult to evaluate. The first step is to use a power monitor, plugged into the AC power outlet, to measure power fluctuations. Frequent fluctuations indicate a need for a UPS. Unfortunately, power problems are among the most difficult to troubleshoot. Any time the file server experiences frequent unexplained memory errors or disk problems, a UPS is recommended.

The file server will draw 200 to 240 watts. With the monitor and any other devices needed on a UPS, the total will be less than 500 watts. Depending on the amount of battery time required, a 500 or 750 watt UPS will prevent power-related problems.

SECURITY AND OPERATIONAL CONSIDERATIONS

Once the file server has been configured, where should it be located? It should be in a secure location so it is not tampered with or stolen. If printers are attached, it must be within about twenty-five feet of the printers. Otherwise, the file server can be located anywhere on the LAN cable. Under ideal conditions, the file server is powered-up, the operating system boots, and the file server is not touched until there is a problem or it is powered off. If a solid hardware platform is selected, a file server will run non-stop for months.

SUMMARY

The file server is the heart of the LAN and should be selected with care. The file server must be at least an 80286 or 80386 computer with enough expansion slots to add network interface cards, additional memory, more disk drives, and additional printer ports.

Configuring a file server involves providing adequate disk storage. The amount of disk storage required is related to the anticipated number of users, the types of applications to be used, and the number of user files to be stored on the server. Only Novell-certified disk drives should be used. The best disk drives are those with an ESDI or SCSI controller. The transfer rate and the access time of a drive also should be considered.

Installing sufficient memory in the server is critical to successful operation. There must be enough memory to provide for communication buffers, disk and directory caching, and file indexing.

Finally, configuring a server involves selecting an interface card. The card must have sufficient throughput to keep the server responsive to workstation requests. And installation of the card requires avoiding conflicts with other hardware in the server, such as serial ports.

Besides configuring the server, the electrical power conditions must be assessed. A UPS is a good investment against erratic power.

CHAPTER QUESTIONS

1. Describe what is likely to happen to a server if it loses its setup.
2. Why is an on-line UPS better protection than an off-line UPS?
3. What is an interrupt? Which interrupts are most commonly used by hardware (such as the disk drive, parallel port, etc.) on a micro-computer?
4. If data throughput begins to slow down on a file server, which components would you troubleshoot?
5. What is stored in a file server's memory?
6. How much memory would likely be needed for a server with forty users and a 150 MB disk drive?
7. What are the differences between SCSI, ESDI, and ST506 disk drives?
8. What information is required in the setup routine of a computer?

6

The LAN Workstation

THE WORKSTATION

From a user's perspective, the workstation is the most important component of the LAN. A workstation is a microcomputer residing on the user's desk. Previous chapters have used the term "node," which usually refers to a workstation on a network. For whatever reason, some users decide that when a microcomputer becomes a workstation on a network, it must function differently. In particular, they feel that the workstation is more difficult to use than a microcomputer and that the file server runs the application. In fact, the file server does just what it should: It provides application and data files to the workstation.

The workstation does all the processing once the application is downloaded to the workstation. The workstation on a LAN should be as easy to use as is a stand-alone microcomputer. Ideally, a user should not know where his or her application or data comes from. Well-functioning LANs are an extension of a workstation, not the reverse.

THE WORKSTATION PROCESSOR

Any IBM compatible or Macintosh microcomputer can be used as a LAN workstation. The minimum recommended memory is 640 KB. For workstations using ethernet, about 70 KB is used to access NetWare. The remaining memory is available for applications. For users also using additional memory-resident utilities, the 640 KB is required.

If you are networking existing 8088 microcomputers, be sure each one has 640 KB memory. For new workstations, select 80286 or 80386 platforms. Both will increase network performance because of the faster data transfer from the LAN cable to the workstation memory. Faster platforms will increase data throughput on the network.

WORKSTATION DISK DRIVES

The selection of workstation disks relates to the selection of disk space on the file server. If the decision is to have each user store data on his or her workstation, then the workstation will require at least one floppy disk drive. Any other disks are optional. In fact, there are diskless workstations.

Diskless workstations can be microcomputers in a keyboard. The memory and NIC are built into the keyboard. Diskless workstations are less expensive than others, and they ensure that applications and data are not copied. Earth Computer Technologies makes diskless workstations for ethernet and ARCNET. The Earthstation-IIe uses an 80286 CPU. It comes with thin and thick coaxial interfaces. Memory is expandable to 4 MB. Also, within the keyboard is a multimode adaptor for VGA, EGA, CGA, and Hercules video, as well as parallel and serial ports.

WORKSTATION INTERFACE CARD

Every workstation must have a network interface card. This NIC plugs into an expansion slot inside the microcomputer.

Installing the NIC is simple. Remove the cover of the microcomputer. At the back of the computer and the end of an unused slot, remove the metal cover which is attached with one screw. Insert the NIC in the slot and use the screw to secure the NIC. NICs come in 8-bit, 16-bit, and 32-bit varieties. Therefore, there must be a corresponding available open slot. Figure 6.1 shows an example of a NIC.

Selecting the NIC requires knowing the type of medium or cable, along with the network protocol. The NIC provides the physical port connecting the workstation to the cable. For example, if the cable type is thin-wire coaxial, the NIC needs a **BNC**-type connection (Bayonet-

FIGURE 6.1
NIC and Workstation

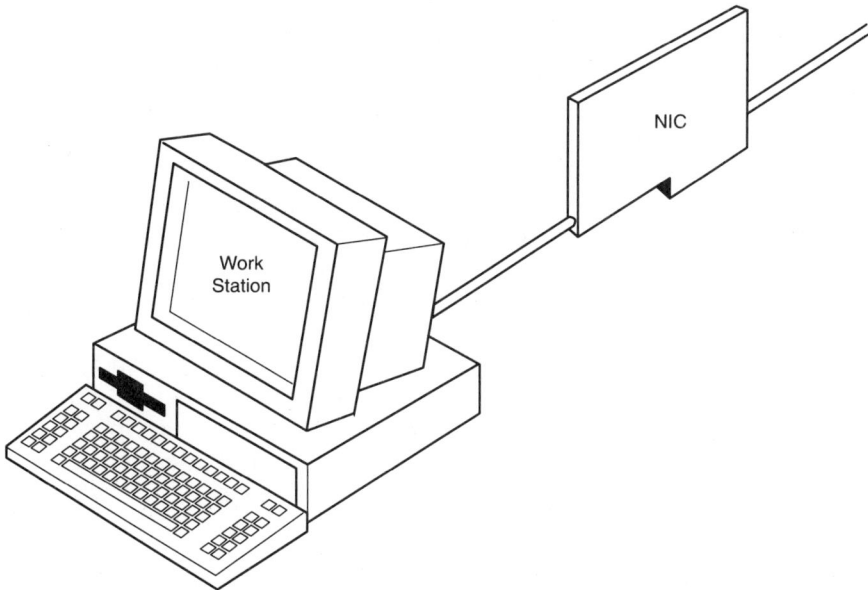

Neill-Concelman). A BNC connector is shaped like the letter *T*. One end connects to the NIC and two ends connect to the LAN cable.

Note that having a properly installed cable is vital to a successful network. This includes the cable connectors and the connections to the NICs. (You may want to refer to Chapter 3 to review cabling issues.)

NICs have characteristics other than those of the physical interface that also determine their performance. These are: *access method, on-board processors,* and *NIC-to-Host transfer.*

Access Method The access method determines use of the shared cable. For instance, two popular access methods are token-passing and contention (see Chapter 4).

Onboard Processors Some NICs have a coprocessor that augments the computer's CPU. A poorly designed coprocessor will likely hinder the data transfer rate by adding processing overhead. Unless it has been demonstrated that the coprocessor improves performance, do not use a NIC with a coprocessor.

NIC-to-Host Transfer LAN performance is greatly affected by the speed at which data can be transferred between the microcomputer (called the host) and the NIC. The NIC-to-host data transfer can be implemented with: *shared memory, direct memory access* (DMA), and a *shared I/O port* (I/O mapped). A given NIC may use any or a combination of these. The fastest method is shared memory, then I/O ports, then DMA.

The final hardware consideration for NICs is that they may conflict with other hardware components in the workstation. Just as a NIC will use memory, so will the workstation's video. If there is any memory overlap, the NIC and the video will not work. It is also possible to install a NIC that conflicts with the host's hard drive, printer ports, and communication ports.

Depending on the type of NIC, the NIC board will need to have switches set to avoid hardware conflicts and to correspond to the NIC software. Workstation configurations may differ requiring more than one hardware setting for the NICs. You should configure the software before installing the NIC. Detailed information is supplied with the NIC to assist with switch settings. Usually the only tools required are a small screwdriver and small-nosed pliers.

WORKSTATION SOFTWARE

Once the hardware is installed, software is installed to control the interaction between the workstation and the NIC. Before the specifics of installing the NIC software are discussed, a general overview of the operations between a workstation and file server is presented.

NetWare resides on the file server, and DOS resides on the workstation. By themselves they do not communicate with each other, even if they are physically cabled together on a network. An interpreter, or **shell**, is loaded into the workstation's memory, which allows the two operating systems to communicate. (The operation of shells is described in detail below.) Figure 6.2 shows the interaction among an application, such as a word processor, DOS, the shell, and NetWare.

The workstation shell passes communications and requests between DOS and the NetWare operating system. Commands determined by the shell to be DOS commands are turned over to the workstation. Commands determined to require the file server are routed to the file server by way of the shell. DIR and NDIR are examples of commands

FIGURE 6.2
Interaction Between Application Software,
DOS, IPX, COM and NetWare

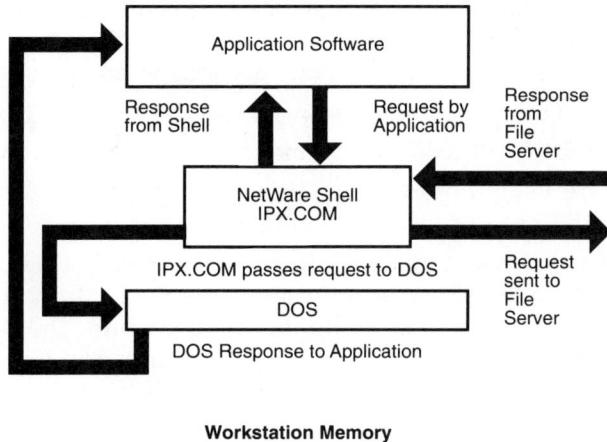

Application Software

Response from Shell   Request by Application   Response from File Server

NetWare Shell
IPX.COM

IPX.COM passes request to DOS   Request sent to File Server

DOS

DOS Response to Application

Workstation Memory

that show how the shell performs its function. When a user enters DIR, a DOS directory is displayed. When NDIR (a NetWare command) is entered, a request is sent to the file server to download NDIR.EXE to the workstation and execute it. The network directory information is much more comprehensive and specific to the file server's directory. A user will access an application, such as WordPerfect, in the same manner, whether the application is located on the file server or on the workstation. Application access and installation are explained more in Chapter 10.

The shell is generated with NetWare. The shell that is generated depends on the type of NIC and the software driver supplied by the NIC manufacturer. In situations where all the workstations have the same hardware configuration and protocols, only one shell version is created. Otherwise, several shell versions may need to be created for each protocol and hardware configuration. Ethernet and ARCNET protocols each use different shells. Likewise, AT and XT computers have different hardware and may require different shells.

CREATING A WORKSTATION SHELL

Creation of the Shell

The shell is a program file created on any IBM-compatible computer. The recommended approach is to load the required NetWare files onto a hard disk system or another network. The shell can also be generated by using floppy disks.

The procedures used to generate a workstation shell are:

1. Make working copies of the NetWare disks SHGEN-1 and SHGEN-2 with the DOS DISKCOPY command.

2. If you are using floppy disks, insert SHGEN-1 and enter SHGEN. Follow the prompt for inserting the required disks.

3. For a hard drive or network installation, use NetWare's installation procedure. The appropriate directory structure will be created, and the files will be loaded into the directories. SHGEN.EXE should be in the NetWare directory. Begin the hard disk or network generation by entering SHGEN from the NetWare directory. The screen is shown in Figure 6.3.

FIGURE 6.3
Shell Configuration Level Menu

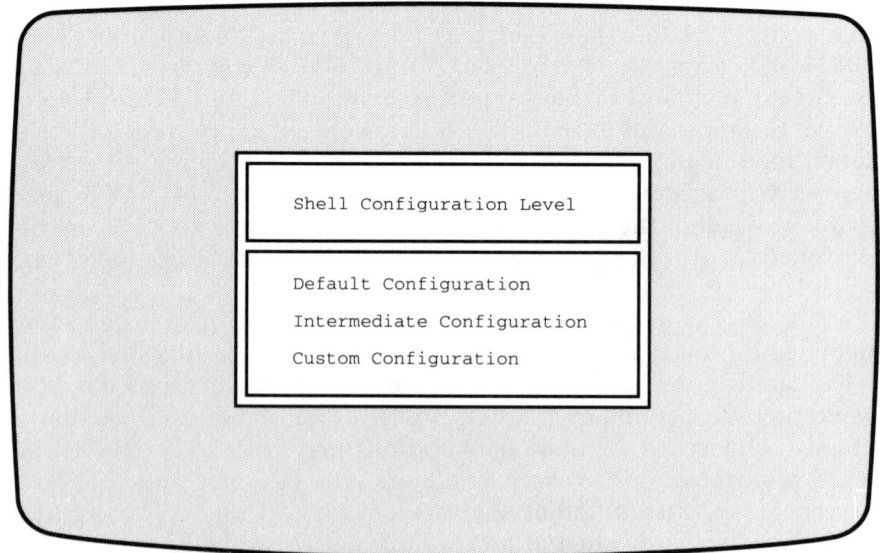

```
        Shell Configuration Level

        Default Configuration
        Intermediate Configuration
        Custom Configuration
```

4. It is possible to configure a shell using any of the displayed options. The *Custom Configuration* option is recommended, because it provides the most control over selection of options. However, the default and intermediate options will work in many circumstances.

5. The next two screens prompt for where SHGEN.EXE is located.

   Enter the letter of the drive that contains the SHGEN.EXE program. The "Shell Configuration Option" menu is displayed. See Figure 6.4.

FIGURE 6.4
Shell Configuration Option Menu

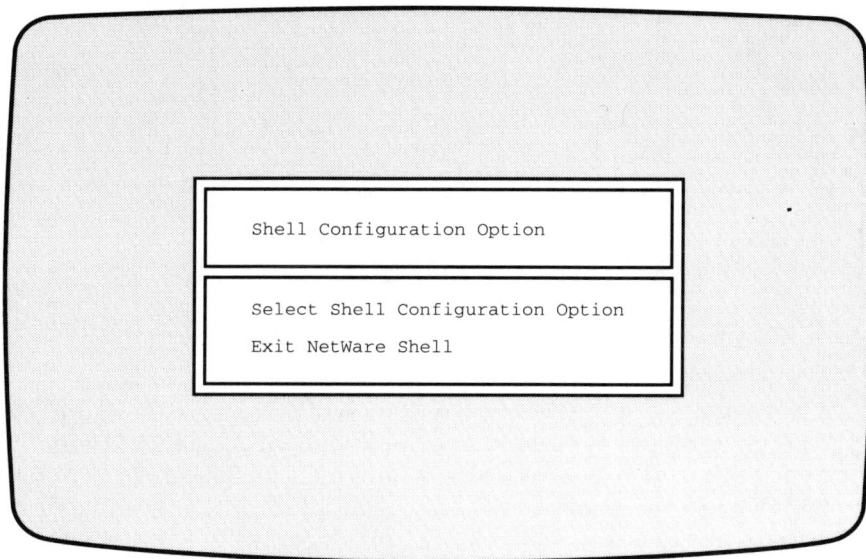

```
    Shell Configuration Option

    Select Shell Configuration Option
    Exit NetWare Shell
```

6. Choose the *Select Shell Configuration* option. The next screen is shown in Figure 6.5.

FIGURE 6.5
Available Options Menu

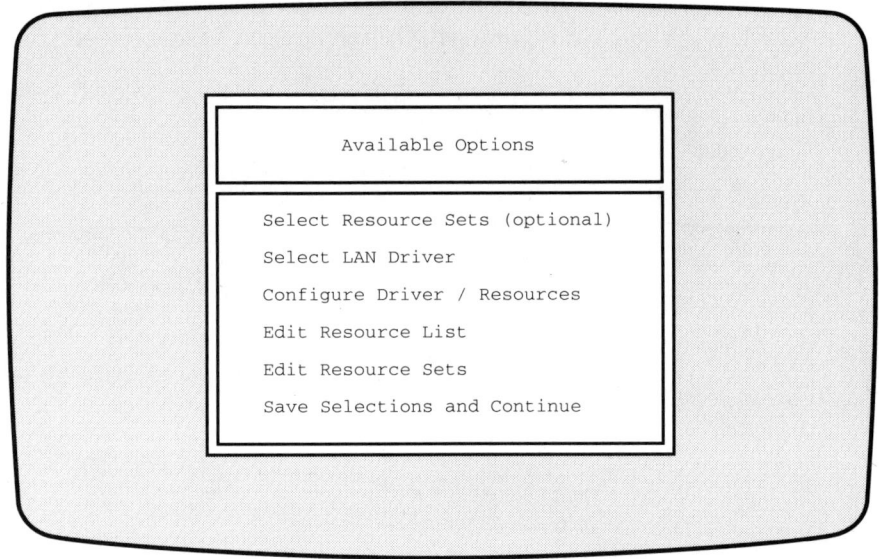

```
                    Available Options


      Select Resource Sets (optional)

      Select LAN Driver

      Configure Driver / Resources

      Edit Resource List

      Edit Resource Sets

      Save Selections and Continue
```

7. Choose the *Select LAN Driver* option, which appears in Figure 6.5. Another window appears where you highlight the *Select Available Item* option to use LAN Drivers provided by Novell (see Figure 6.6). Or use the *Load and Select Item* option if you are installing non-Novell drivers. Use the NIC manufacturer's instructions for this type of installation. A window showing the drivers appears as in Figure 6.7.

FIGURE 6.6
LAN Driver Options Menu

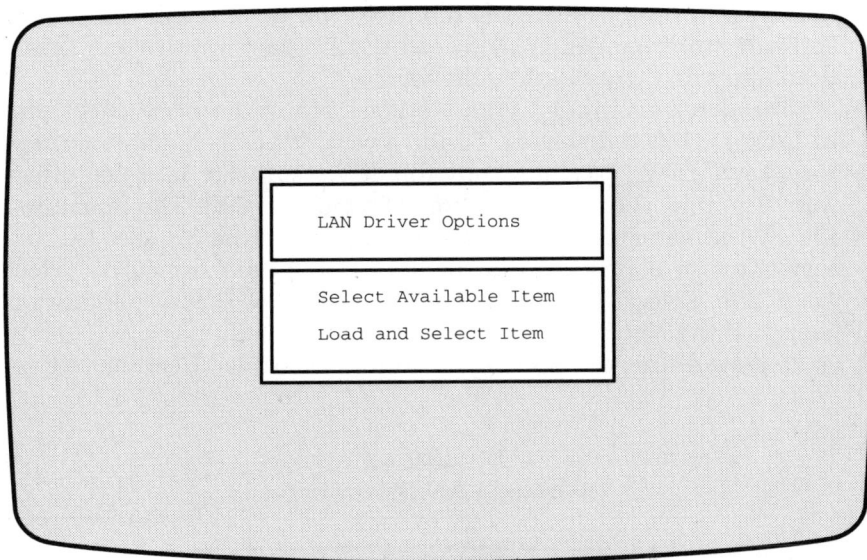

```
          ┌─────────────────────────────┐
          │                             │
          │    LAN Driver Options       │
          │                             │
          ├─────────────────────────────┤
          │                             │
          │    Select Available Item    │
          │    Load and Select Item     │
          │                             │
          └─────────────────────────────┘
```

FIGURE 6.7
Available LAN Drivers Menu

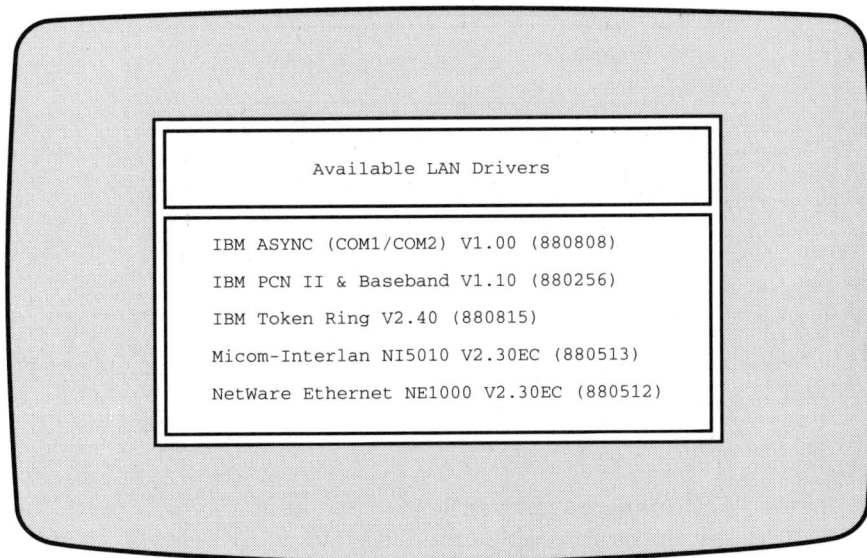

```
     ┌────────────────────────────────────────┐
     │                                        │
     │          Available LAN Drivers         │
     │                                        │
     ├────────────────────────────────────────┤
     │                                        │
     │  IBM ASYNC (COM1/COM2) V1.00 (880808)  │
     │                                        │
     │  IBM PCN II & Baseband V1.10 (880256)  │
     │                                        │
     │  IBM Token Ring V2.40 (880815)         │
     │                                        │
     │  Micom-Interlan NI5010 V2.30EC (880513)│
     │                                        │
     │  NetWare Ethernet NE1000 V2.30EC (880512)│
     │                                        │
     └────────────────────────────────────────┘
```

8. Highlight a driver from the list and select it by using the arrow keys and the ENTER key. Press the ESC key to exit if the selection is correct. Note that the driver for the NIC you have may not be listed as an option. If this is the case, you must obtain the driver software from the vendor and load it onto the hard drive or insert the floppy disk provided by the vendor.

   The drivers supplied with NetWare are in the LAN_DRV_.001 or LAN_DRV.002 diskettes. To add a vendor's driver, create a directory, LAN_DRV_.003, and copy the driver software into that directory. The files should have a file extension of .OBJ. The remaining files, with the extension .LAN, are copied into the SHGEN-1 directory. To use a driver from the LAN_DRV_.003 directory, select *Load and Select Item* from the Selected LAN Driver window in Step 7. If the NetWare Ethernet driver is selected, the next window is displayed. Use the ESC key to select this driver. See Figure 6.8.

FIGURE 6.8
Selected LAN Driver Screen

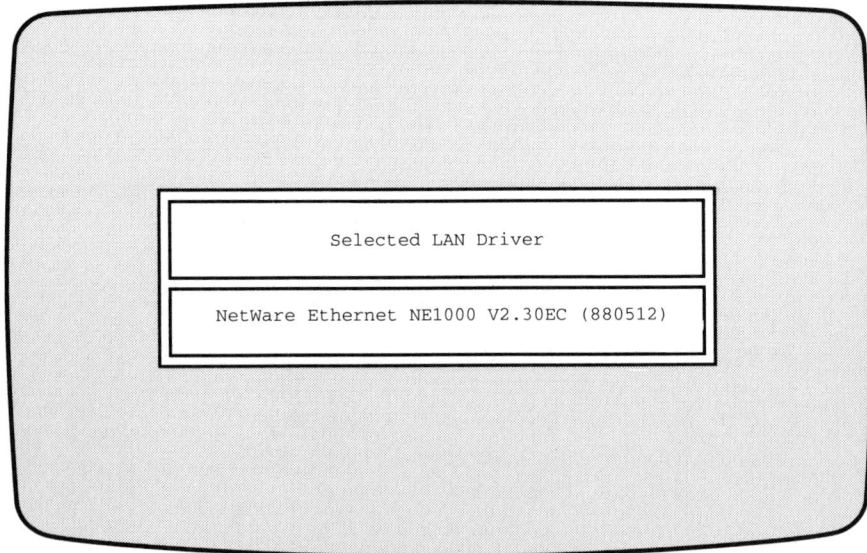

```
        Selected LAN Driver

  NetWare Ethernet NE1000 V2.30EC (880512)
```

9. Select the *Configure Driver/Resources* option. Then press the ENTER key in the Available Options window. A new window dis-

plays the driver selected in Step 8. Press the ENTER key again to select the driver for configuration. Three windows similar to those in Figure 6.9 are displayed.

FIGURE 6.9
Driver Configuration Menu

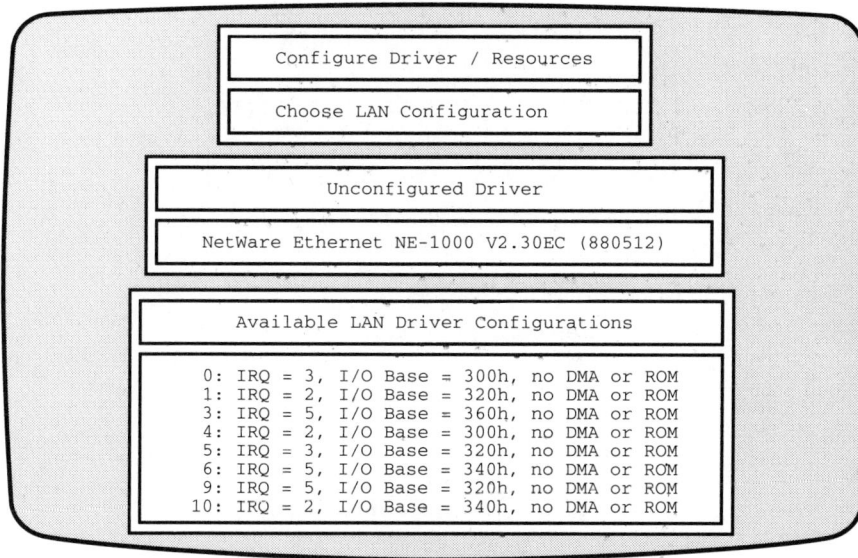

```
┌─────────────────────────────────────────────────────────────┐
│     ┌──────────────────────────────────────────────┐         │
│     │      Configure Driver / Resources             │        │
│     ├──────────────────────────────────────────────┤         │
│     │      Choose LAN Configuration                 │        │
│     └──────────────────────────────────────────────┘         │
│   ┌──────────────────────────────────────────────────┐       │
│   │            Unconfigured Driver                    │      │
│   ├──────────────────────────────────────────────────┤       │
│   │  NetWare Ethernet NE-1000 V2.30EC (880512)        │      │
│   └──────────────────────────────────────────────────┘       │
│   ┌──────────────────────────────────────────────────┐       │
│   │      Available LAN Driver Configurations          │      │
│   ├──────────────────────────────────────────────────┤       │
│   │   0: IRQ = 3, I/O Base = 300h, no DMA or ROM       │     │
│   │   1: IRQ = 2, I/O Base = 320h, no DMA or ROM       │     │
│   │   3: IRQ = 5, I/O Base = 360h, no DMA or ROM       │     │
│   │   4: IRQ = 2, I/O Base = 300h, no DMA or ROM       │     │
│   │   5: IRQ = 3, I/O Base = 320h, no DMA or ROM       │     │
│   │   6: IRQ = 5, I/O Base = 340h, no DMA or ROM       │     │
│   │   9: IRQ = 5, I/O Base = 320h, no DMA or ROM       │     │
│   │  10: IRQ = 2, I/O Base = 340h, no DMA or ROM       │     │
│   └──────────────────────────────────────────────────┘       │
└─────────────────────────────────────────────────────────────┘
```

10. Select a configuration option (0:–10:) that does not conflict with other hardware in the workstation. To do this, highlight the configuration option and press ENTER. (See Chapters 5 and 7 for additional information on hardware conflicts.) After selecting a configuration, select the first option from the window shown in Figure 6.10. Selecting the first option results in the window shown in Figure 6.11.

FIGURE 6.10
Configure Driver/Resources Menu

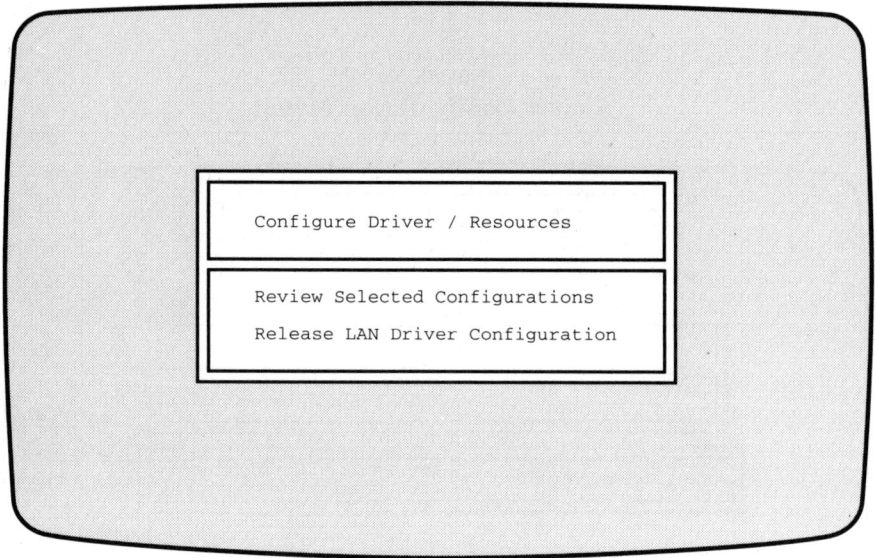

```
          Configure Driver / Resources

          Review Selected Configurations
          Release LAN Driver Configuration
```

FIGURE 6.11
Selected Configurations Screen

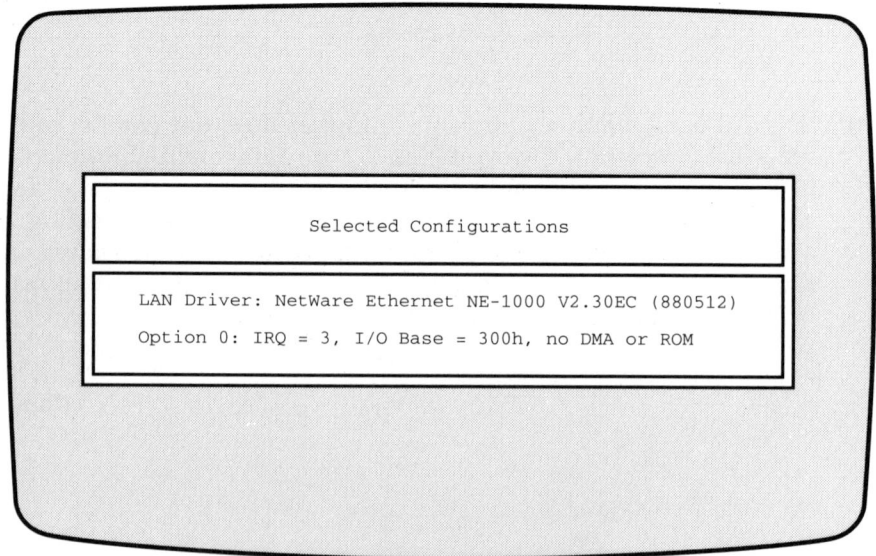

```
                Selected Configurations

   LAN Driver: NetWare Ethernet NE-1000 V2.30EC (880512)
   Option 0: IRQ = 3, I/O Base = 300h, no DMA or ROM
```

11. Use the ESC key to continue with the shell generation. A confirmation window appears. See Figure 6.12. Select "Yes" from the window. The Available Options menu is displayed.

FIGURE 6.12
Continue Shell Generation Using Selected
Configurations Menu

```
Continue Shell Generation Using Selected Configurations?

No

Yes
```

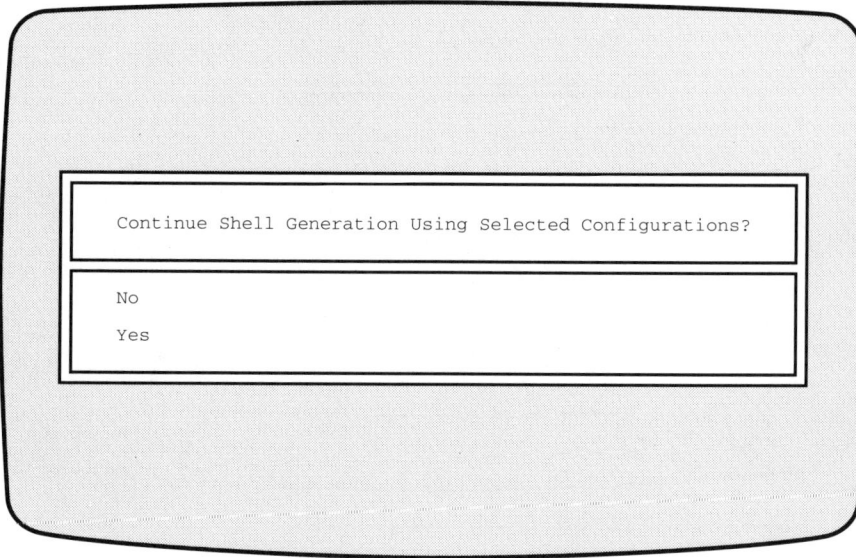

12. From the next window select the *Save Selections and Continue* option. Choose "Yes" from the next window to confirm the selection.

13. Select the *Link NetWare Shell* option from the Shell Generation Options menu in Figure 6.13. When you select *Link NetWare Shell*, SHGEN clears the screen and tells the user it is linking the shell. When the linking is finished, the screen in Figure 6.13 is displayed. At this point, select the *Exit SHGEN* option. It is possible to have a message that reads "error 9" displayed during the linking operation. This message means the drivers are not in the correct directory or disk; they are missing; or they are the wrong drivers. Selecting a driver also informs the linker program of files that must link the shell driver. For example, the linker may look in the LAN_DRV_.002 disk or directory when the required files are in LAN_DRV_.003. The problem is resolved by copying the

files into LAN_DRV_.002. It is also possible that the NIC vendor did not send the correct driver files.

FIGURE 6.13
Shell Generation Options Menu

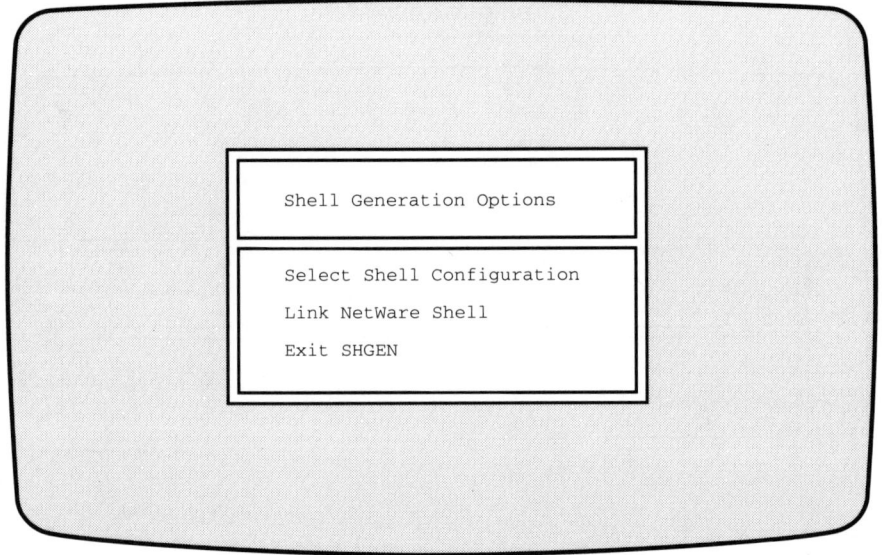

```
          Shell Generation Options

          Select Shell Configuration

          Link NetWare Shell

          Exit SHGEN
```

14. The shell generation is now complete. If SHGEN is run on a hard drive or network drive, copy the following files from the SHGEN-2 directory to a workstation boot disk:

   • IPX.COM

   • NET2.COM, NET3.COM, or NET4.COM

   NET2.COM is copied if the workstation is using DOS 2.x. Likewise, NET3.COM and NET4.COM are for workstations with DOS 3.x or DOS 4.x. The IPX.COM and NETx.COM files are explained in the following section.

BOOT DISK CONFIGURATION

Workstations use IPX.COM and either NET2.COM, NET3.COM, or NET4.COM to access the communication medium (such as ARCNET) and NetWare. IPX.COM and NETx.COM compose the NetWare shell. Both files are used by the workstation to link with NetWare. The

IPX.COM file communicates with the workstation NIC. It uses the IPX protocol to enable communication with other devices on the network, such as workstations and the file server. The SHGEN process customizes IPX.COM to match hardware characteristics of the NIC and the workstation.

NETx.COM interfaces with DOS on the workstation. It "surrounds" DOS, intercepting DOS and NetWare commands sent from the workstation. DOS commands are routed to DOS, and Novell commands are routed to NetWare.

The IPX.COM and NETx.COM files are stored on the workstation's boot disk. The boot disk can be a floppy or hard disk. This disk also needs other files that complement the functions of IPX.COM and NETx.COM. These files are listed in the following sections.

DOS System Files

The boot disk must contain the DOS system files. These files (MSDOS.SYS and IO.SYS) are not visible on the disk. When the workstation is booted, they load the DOS operating system.

COMMAND.COM File

The boot disk needs a COMMAND.COM file with a version level the same as that of the DOS system files. The system files and COMMAND.COM are available on the original DOS diskettes that accompany a workstation. They are copied onto the boot disk by using the DOS FORMAT command with the /S option. The COMMAND.COM file is a DOS interpreter, which interprets DOS functions, such as the directory command (DIR).

NETBIOS

Some applications are written to use the IBM communications protocol, **NETBIOS**. NETBIOS is a protocol developed by IBM for its PC LAN system. Novell provides a NETBIOS **emulator** in the file NETBIOS.COM, which simulates the NETBIOS protocol for applications that require it. If it is needed by an application, copy NETBIOS.COM to the workstation boot disk. It is used with another program called INT2.COM. Also copy INT2.COM to the boot disk.

CONFIG.SYS File

The boot disk needs a CONFIG.SYS file, which is loaded when the workstation boots. CONFIG.SYS is a text file that loads device drivers and DOS environment characteristics. The CONFIG.SYS file will usually contain four statements:

DEVICE = ANSI.SYS ANSI.SYS is a screen driver used by many software applications. (Note: When this statement is used, copy the ANSI.SYS file from the original DOS disk to the boot disk.)

SHELL = COMMAND.COM /P /E:1024 This command increases the DOS environment size, and prevents problems caused by the need to set **environment variables** for a program. (Environment variables are used to enable DOS to find files needed by it or by programs. Note: The SHELL command is only available in DOS versions 3.2 and above.)

BUFFERS = 20 Most software applications require a minimum number of 512 byte buffers for storing data on the workstation. Twenty buffers are enough for the normal range of software applications.

FILES = 20 This command determines the number of files that can be open (on the workstation) at the same time. Most software applications require twenty or fewer open files.

SHELL.CFG File

This file is placed on the boot disk. SHELL.CFG establishes shell parameters that affect NetWare. These parameters are:

File Handles This is the number of files the user can have open at the same time (on the network). If no number is set, the default is 40.

Local Printers This command tells the network how many printers are connected to the workstation. (Workstation printers are called **local printers**.) A LOCAL PRINTERS = 0 statement is used when there is no workstation printer (otherwise, the workstation will "hang" when jobs are sent to the local printer.)

Cache Buffers This is the number of data storage buffers available to the shell. Five buffers are automatically set when the statement is not used.

Long Machine Name This command tells the network the workstation's brand. The command is used when several manufacturers' versions of DOS are on the network, such as IBM, Zenith, and Northgate.

Create a separate network directory for each DOS version and use the command in the SHELL.CFG file (such as LONG MACHINE NAME = ZENITH). The default name is IBM_PC. See Chapter 12 for details about creating DOS directories.

Short Machine Type   This information enables NetWare to use appropriate screen formatting for some workstations, such as laptop computers. (Consult the Novell *Supervisor Reference* manual for a detailed explanation of this and other SHELL.CFG parameters.)

If no SHELL.CFG file is used on the boot disk, the default parameters automatically take effect.

AUTOEXEC.BAT File

The boot disk should have an AUTOEXEC.BAT file. This is optional and enables you to set up an automatic log-in procedure. The AUTOEXEC.BAT file is a text file with a stream of commands. The commands are executed after the workstation loads DOS. A typical AUTOEXEC.BAT will have the following command stream:

```
IPX
NET3
NETBIOS
INT2
F:
LOGIN FS1/USER1<A:PASS
^Z
```

In this command stream, IPX and NET3 are used to load the network shell. NETBIOS and INT2 are optional. They can be removed from the command stream if there are no applications that require them. The F: statement changes to the first network drive. The LOGIN command is used to log USER1 onto a file server named FS1. And <A:PASS is a DOS command that pipes the user's password to the network. In this example, the password is in a file called "PASS" on drive A.

The last command is a control Z character (CTRL-Z), which designates the end-of-file marker. It tells DOS there will be no more commands in the stream. This character prevents the network from trying to return to the AUTOEXEC.BAT file after log in. It eliminates conflicts when attempting to run a program.

BOOT DISK PROTECTION

Floppy boot disks should be write-protected to prevent users from deleting or adding files. Additional file protection can be obtained by hiding the files with a utility such as PCTools. Hidden files cannot be displayed with the DIR or TYPE command.

DISKLESS BOOTING

There are hardware configurations where boot disks are not used. In these configurations, the NIC has a remote reset boot PROM chip. In remote configurations, the boot files are on the file server. When a diskless workstation using a NIC with a remote boot-PROM boots, it looks to the file server for the boot files COMMAND.COM, CONFIG.SYS, IPX.COM, NETx.COM, and AUTOEXEC.BAT.

The remote boot-PROM can be an expensive and time-consuming alternative. Each boot PROM is specific to a DOS version level, such as DOS 3.2. When DOS is upgraded to a higher version, such as DOS 4.0, the PROM must be replaced. Also, when users first log into the network, all workstations must wait for the network to download the shells to each workstation logging in.

TESTING THE WORKSTATION CONNECTIVITY

A NetWare utility, COMCHECK, can be used to verify that the shell configuration and the NIC hardware settings are correct. The cabling must be in place and the workstations connected. Each workstation is first booted with DOS. Next, IPX.COM is run. All workstations and the file server can be tested. COMCHECK evaluates the communication path between the NIC and the cabling between the workstations. If the test fails, check that the SHGEN configuration option matches the hardware settings on the NIC. Also, check that the cable is correctly installed. COMCHECK is on NetWare's diagnostic disk.

SUMMARY

The user accesses a network through a workstation. He or she loads programs from the file server onto a workstation. Each program runs on the workstation, not on the file server. Any limits to running a program are those of the workstation and not of the server. Consequently, the configuration of the workstation depends on the applications it will run.

Every workstation should have at least 640 KB of memory. Workstations can be configured with or without disk drives, depending on the application program needs. However, all workstations must be equipped with a NIC. A network shell must also be generated for the workstation through the SHGEN process.

Once the shell is created, a boot disk is made for the workstation (or a boot directory is made for diskless workstations). Boot routines and workstation connections are tested with the COMCHECK program provided by Novell.

CHAPTER QUESTIONS

1. How are diskless workstations different from those with disk drives? Under what circumstances would diskless workstations be appropriate on a LAN?

2. What files are placed on a boot disk? Describe the purpose of each file.

3. What does an "error 9" mean in the SHGEN process?

4. Write an example AUTOEXEC.BAT for a workstation in a student lab on a college campus.

5. You have just created a network shell using SHGEN. When you run the shell on the workstation, it interacts properly with the NIC. However, it will not connect you to the network. What are the possible causes of the problem?

6. When you install a NIC in an XT (8088) type of workstation, you set the IRQ at 5. You then successfully generate the shell. When you boot the workstation, however, it hangs. What has happened?

7. What is the function of NETBIOS.COM. When would you use it?

8. What extra costs are associated with using boot PROMS?

9. You have just installed a network with ten workstations and one file server. One of your users complains that a desktop publishing application runs too slowly when it writes a data file to disk. What is the source of the problem, the workstation, or the server? Why?

7

The NetWare 286 Operating System: Features and Configuration

INTRODUCTION

The Novell operating system is available for several kinds of environments. These range from a network of two or three microcomputers to a DEC VAX-based network with NetWare on the VMS operating system. VMS NetWare makes the DEC VAX a file server.

The smallest option available from Novell is an ELS system meant for up to eight workstations. In the middle range, NetWare 286 is capable of handling 100 workstations. The largest Novell operating system is NetWare 386, which enables up to 250 workstation connections.

This chapter describes NetWare 286, which has thousands of installations worldwide. Novell's newer operating system, NetWare 386, is described in Chapter 9. NetWare 386 goes beyond NetWare 286 in three ways: It is easier to install; it provides more user connections; and it takes full advantage of the 80386 CPU capabilities.

NetWare 286 comes in two versions, Advanced and SFT. Advanced NetWare enables you to select between dedicated and nondedicated systems. Dedicated systems reserve the entire file server strictly for use by NetWare. Nondedicated systems permit you to have both the Novell operating system on the file server and another operating system, such as DOS.

SFT NetWare operates only in the dedicated mode. It offers **transaction tracking** (TTS), which protects updates to data files during power or system failures. TTS is one element in **system fault tolerance** (SFT). System fault tolerance consists of operating system features that maintain the integrity of the system after power or hardware failures. Fault tolerance keeps data from being altered or destroyed. (These and other features are listed in the next section of this chapter, "Operating System Overview.")

The latest edition of NetWare 286 is version 2.15. It offers the capability of connecting Apple Macintosh computers to the LAN.

Of the operating-system options described here, this chapter focuses mainly on SFT NetWare. This system is popular because it offers system fault tolerance.

OPERATING SYSTEM OVERVIEW

NetWare 286 is a robust environment that provides a variety of options to keep data secure, and to provide effective **multi-user** LAN operations.

Important operating system features include:

- Protection against directory and file-allocation table corruption
- Protection against disk-surface corruption
- Disk mirroring and duplexing
- Transaction tracking for data and file integrity
- Indexing for large files
- Uninterruptible power-source protection
- Dedicated and nondedicated file server options (in Advanced NetWare 286 only)
- Configuration flexibility for a variety of hardware options
- Directory and disk caching

Many of the features listed above are part of Novell's system-fault-tolerance operations. For example, *directory and file-allocation table protection* guards against power and computer failures. *Uninterruptible power source options* and *transaction tracking* also give protection against power and system failures.

Disk surface corruption is minimized in NetWare 286 through two features. The first is *hot fix redirection*, which prevents data from being written to a damaged portion of a hard disk. The second feature is *elevator seeking*, which reduces wear on a hard disk by minimizing the amount of mechanical movement needed to access data.

Disk mirroring and *disk duplexing* are other forms of fault tolerance. They guard against loss of data should a disk drive fail.

Indexing large files and *caching* are not fault tolerance features, but they do improve multi-user operations. Both features enable users to access data on a file server quickly.

NetWare's *configuration flexibility* is also intended for multi-user operations. The operating system can be customized to the number of users on a LAN. Later, it can be adjusted to accommodate new users and equipment.

If it's necessary for a file server to operate as a workstation, Advanced NetWare 286 fills the need. It permits a file server to operate in the nondedicated mode.

Each of these topics is discussed further in the sections that follow. (Figure 7.1 lists NetWare 286 operating system features.)

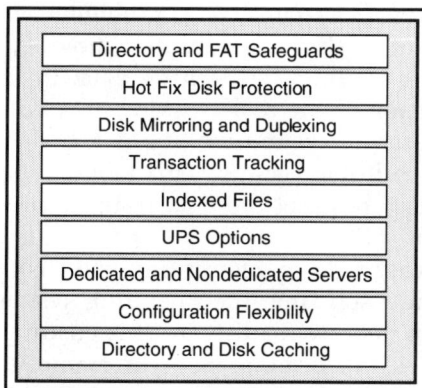

FIGURE 7.1
NetWare Operating System Features

| Directory and FAT Safeguards |
| Hot Fix Disk Protection |
| Disk Mirroring and Duplexing |
| Transaction Tracking |
| Indexed Files |
| UPS Options |
| Dedicated and Nondedicated Servers |
| Configuration Flexibility |
| Directory and Disk Caching |

DIRECTORY AND FILE ALLOCATION TABLE SAFEGUARDS

Many mainframe and minicomputers have built-in safeguards to protect sensitive data storage areas, such as important tables, operating system files, and data files. Similarly, Novell has the built-in ability to secure the data directory table and the file allocation table on the hard disk. Both of these structures contain information that provides the key to tracking and locating files on the file server. They hold pointers and addressing information to all of the production data on the disk. If either the directory or the file allocation tables become corrupt, some or all of the data stored on disk is rendered impossible to access.

The Novell operating system keeps two separate copies of the directory and file allocation tables. If a sector of data in one of these areas is corrupt, there is always a backup. Each time the file server is powered on, the operating system performs a check of the two tables. Whenever it finds a bad block, the server issues an error message to inform the LAN manager. It then marks the sector as bad, so no activity can be directed to that sector. And the information that was originally there is written to another portion of the disk. Normally, the LAN manager does not need to take any action to correct the disk corruption, with the possible exception of rebooting the server.

HOT-FIX DISK SURFACE PROTECTION

One of the most susceptible parts of a computer system is the hard disk. This is true for microcomputers, minicomputers, and mainframes. The hard disk is susceptible to problems because the mechanical portion of the disk is constantly moving, performing data searches, as well as reading and writing data. In the process, oxides may wear off a portion of the disk, making data vulnerable.

The Novell operating system maintains a hot-fix table to perform instant repairs on bad disk sectors. This table is used to identify bad spots on the disk and redirect the data in those bad sectors to a good portion of the disk.

A Novell tool that aids in identifying bad disk areas is the *read-after-write* function. Each time the operating system performs a disk write, it verifies the data by reading it. This ensures that what is written to disk matches the original data in memory. If there is not a match, several more data comparisons are performed. If the data is corrupt, the hot-fix function is invoked, and the data is directed to an area on the disk reserved for hot-fix redirection.

The hot fix table retains the address of each bad location it finds on the disk. Therefore, disk writes are not attempted to those locations. The hot-fix function is performed automatically, without user intervention. However, the hot-fix function must first be installed when the operating system is installed. The system installer has the option of determining the actual size of the hot-fix redirection area. This is a portion of the disk reserved for redirection of corrupt data as detected by the hot-fix function.

DISK ELEVATOR SEEKING

To improve the file server's disk access, Novell uses an elevator-seeking routine. Elevator seeking is used as an improvement over the disk-seeking method used by DOS. Under DOS, a disk drive will get a request to access a location on the disk. Once the data is accessed, the information is transferred to memory. This procedure is followed for each access request. If a file server with multiple users followed this disk-accessing method, the users would experience long delays in accessing the disk. Disk wear would also be high.

NetWare's elevator-seeking method works like an elevator in a building. The disk heads are the elevator. As the disk heads move across the disk, requests to read or write are serviced. Requests are not serviced on a first-come, first-served basis. Instead, requests are serviced based on the location of the heads on the disk.

Wear on the hard disk is reduced through elevator seeking. Users also experience fast access to data.

DISK MIRRORING AND DISK DUPLEXING

Hot-fix redirection can protect against bad disk sectors, but not against total disk failure. NetWare protection against disk failure is available through disk mirroring or disk duplexing.

Disk mirroring involves connecting two hard drives to the same channel or disk controller. One drive is designated as the *primary* drive, while the other is the *secondary* drive. Whenever data is written to the primary drive, the same data is also written to the secondary drive. However, the cold boot loader and selected system files are not stored on the secondary drive. If the primary drive fails, the system can be regenerated to copy the cold boot loader and other files to the secondary drive. The server then becomes a single-drive system, with all important data files fully intact.

Disk mirroring is limited in one important respect: If the disk controller fails, file server operations cannot be restored until the disk controller is replaced. Operation of the primary and secondary disks is dependent on the reliability of the disk controller.

Disk duplexing provides an alternative to disk mirroring. Disk duplexing involves establishing the primary and secondary drives on separate controllers. As with disk mirroring, both disks will contain the same data. If the primary disk fails, the secondary disk can take over operations, after the server is reconfigured as a one-disk system. If the disk controller fails on the primary disk, operations can still continue via the controller attached to the secondary disk.

When planning to use disk mirroring or disk duplexing, it's important to remember that the secondary disk must be equivalent in size to the primary disk. The primary disk cannot be larger, or full data replication will not be physically possible.

TRANSACTION TRACKING

Important applications programs, such as accounting programs or order-entry systems, require integrity of the database. That integrity may depend on files being in full synchronization. In an order-entry system, for instance, the ORDERS file may record information about an order for a product. At the same time the ORDERS file is updated, there may also be updates to accounts receivable files and to an inventory file. Consequently, one order will affect updates to several files. If the updating process is halted in the middle, then the files will be out of synch, because one will be updated and the other will not. This might happen if the updating process is interrupted by either a power or system failure.

Through its *transaction tracking system* (TTS), NetWare offers a way to prevent files from getting out of synch. With TTS, a group of database updates can be treated as a single transaction. If the transaction is not fully completed, it is backed out. In this way, either the affected range of files is fully updated, or no files are updated. In the example of order entry, if the ORDERS file is updated, and a power failure occurs before the accounts receivable and inventory files are updated, then the entry in the ORDERS file is backed out.

To use TTS, it must be turned on at the time the operating system is generated on the file server. Once TTS is installed, files that are to be designated for transaction tracking must be flagged. The transactional file attribute (a "T" flag) is used to mark files for transaction tracking.

INDEXED FILES

The speed of access to data in large files can be greatly increased if the file is flagged to take advantage of indexing. When a file is indexed,

NetWare creates an index table in memory for that file. The indexing makes random-access writes and reads much faster.

To take advantage of file indexing, the number of indexed files must be specified when the operating system is generated on the file server. Before generating the operating system, determine how many files will likely contain more than 1 MB. Next, increase the total number of the indexed files by two or three. Keep a record of the proposed number of indexed files handy, so it's available when the operating system is generated.

The maximum number of indexed files that can be specified is 1,000. However, the total number of indexed files should be kept to a minimum, because the operating system reserves a portion of memory for each indexed file. Disk caching, file indexing, open files, and communication buffers all vie for memory, so restraint is advisable when indexing files.

If speed of access is important, index a large file. If it's not important, do not index the file. Flagging files over 1 MB can speed up access to data two to four times. Once large files, such as database files, are identified for indexing, they must be flagged with an "I" for indexed files.

UNINTERRUPTIBLE POWER SOURCE

Power failures and power fluctuations are the greatest enemy of computers. Obviously, when the power goes out, no work can be performed on the computer; and work that was in process may be lost. However, it's even more damaging once power is restored, because the data may now be corrupt or hardware components may not work.

The best protection against power-related computer problems is a UPS (see Chapter 5). This is a box filled with rechargeable batteries. The UPS is connected to a power outlet, and the file server is connected to the UPS. With some UPS systems, there can also be a link between an interface board in the file server and a similar kind of board in the UPS. This link is used by the UPS to warn the file server when there is a power outage. The file server in turn warns the system users, who can take action to prevent loss of data. This gives users time to properly exit software, save files, and log off the network. If commercial power is not restored before the UPS batteries are exhausted, the server will then automatically down itself.

As long as commercial power is intact, the UPS batteries are constantly recharged. As soon as there is a commercial power interruption, the UPS takes over delivering power to the server. The length of time the UPS will deliver power to the file server depends on the capacity of the UPS and the power draw of the file server. Some UPS systems will maintain a server for just a few minutes, while others can deliver power for twenty to thirty minutes.

The file server and UPS system cannot communicate unless the system manager creates a CONFIG.UPS file. This file is stored in the SYSTEM directory on the file server. The file is read each time the server is booted. Consult the NetWare manual, *286 Maintenance* for information about the CONFIG.UPS file.

DEDICATED AND NONDEDICATED FILE SERVERS

A *dedicated* file server has only the NetWare operating system. A *nondedicated* server has operating systems that run at the same time as NetWare. Most nondedicated servers run DOS and NetWare. Advanced NetWare 286 permits a file server to operate in the nondedicated mode.

In many situations, the reason for installing a nondedicated server is to make the file server double as a workstation. The advantage is that it saves on the cost of a workstation. The disadvantage is that when the file server is used as a workstation, any software that hangs the workstation will hang the file server, too.

Because the file server is likely to be the life blood of many users, it's a good precaution not to plan on using the nondedicated option. There is likely to be a large investment in the file server, both in software applications and user productivity. Plan to configure the system for optimum performance to protect your investment. In the long term, it is most cost effective to have a reliable dedicated file server.

If you must use the nondedicated mode, up to four **partitions** can be created for different operating systems. (A partition is a section of disk reserved for an operating system, which can include DOS, OS/2, or UNIX.)

Any established partition can be designated as the boot partition. Using NetWare and DOS as examples, a file server partitioned with these operating systems can boot up from the DOS partition or from the NetWare partition.

CONFIGURATION FLEXIBILITY

Users require flexibility in generating a local-area network. The needed flexibility includes:

- Customizing the network to the number of users
- Adding disk drives
- Installing different brands of NICs
- Installing different hardware resources

The following sections describe each of these areas of flexibility.

Customizing for the Number of Users

NetWare can be "tuned" to match the number of users who will be connected. For example, users access the file server through communication buffers. These buffers store information in memory until it is processed by the CPU. There must be enough buffers to rapidly service each user, but if there are too many buffers, memory is wasted. You can vary the number of buffers to match what is needed by the number of users on the network.

The same need for customization applies to open files. The maximum number of files that can be open at one time is limited. This limit is established to make the file server use memory efficiently, since a portion of memory is reserved for each open file. The number of open files is related to the number of users on a network. A large number of users will require a large number of open files. Instructions showing how to establish the number of open files and communication buffers are provided later in this chapter.

Disk Drive Configurations

A file server can be configured for one disk drive or for many. Up to five hard disk channels can be configured, with up to eight hard disk controllers per channel. Hard disks attached to the server can vary in size, with some as large as 300 MB or more. And a full range of microcomputer disk controllers can be used. Some disk drives will also require specialized disk drivers for NetWare. These disk drivers are implemented during the installation process.

Network Interface Cards

Different brands of network interface cards can be installed in the file server and in each workstation. To install the interface card, you have choices regarding which hardware interrupt (IRQ) can be used and which memory locations are used to install the card in the workstations and the server. These choices depend on what other hardware is installed in the computer and what memory locations are used by specialized software applications. Each type of interface board will have its own drivers for generating the network shell for workstations, and the configuration used on the file server.

Resource Sets

Another area of flexibility lies in associating resource sets with the configured file server. These sets may include clock/calendar chips, display adapters, parallel and serial ports, tape-drive interfaces, and other specialized equipment. A resource set may be any combination of equipment that is given a resource set name. More than one resource set can be established, each with a unique name. A specific resource set is then associated with the file server at the time it's generated.

DIRECTORY CACHING AND DISK CACHING

When a directory is cached, a copy of the volume directory is stored in memory. Because data can be read faster from memory than from disk, caching provides fast access to information.

As a rule, the directory for the primary server volume, SYS, should be cached. Directories of any other volumes should also be cached if there is enough memory in the file server. Two MB of memory or more is normally enough to provide for caching of directory volumes.

In addition to directory caching, NetWare provides for disk caching to speed data access. At the time the system is generated, cache buffers are set up. Each cache buffer is partitioned into blocks consisting of 4,096 bytes. Every time a read request is issued to the file server, the data is read in blocks and cached into memory. This is done on the assumption that there are likely to be a number of requests for the same data. Later requests for data in the same block can be fulfilled quickly, because the data will already be in memory.

NETWARE INSTALLATION PREPARATION

The NetWare operating system is delivered on a series of 5¼″ or 3½″ diskettes, depending on what has been ordered. The first step in the installation process is to decide how the operating system will be loaded from these diskettes. The four methods are:

- Loading directly from floppy diskette
- Loading from a RAM disk
- Loading from a hard drive
- Loading from a pre-established network drive

Floppy and RAM Disk Methods

Loading directly from a floppy or from RAM disk is best suited for those who plan to generate one Novell file server. The first step when using either the floppy or RAM disk method is to make copies of each diskette, except the GENDATA disk. The GENDATA disk contains the operating system serial number, and is copy-protected. It should not be copied. Instead, the original diskette should be used in the installation process. If the RAM disk method is to be used, then a portion of the computer's memory must be reserved as a virtual disk prior to beginning NetWare installation.

Hard and Network Disk Methods

Generating the operating system from a hard disk or from a network disk is best suited for those who will be generating more than one network. If the hard disk method is used, all of the NetWare files must be copied to the hard disk. If the network method is used, files are copied to an appropriate network drive. The files are normally copied to a master directory called GENERATE. The volume names on each original diskette should be preserved as *subdirectory* names. For example, files on the NETGEN disk would be copied into a NETGEN subdirectory under the GENERATE directory on the hard or network disk drive.

Disk and LAN Drivers

If any special disk drivers are to be used, they must be loaded onto a diskette with the volume name DSK_DRV_.002 or DSK_DRV_.003, or whatever extension number is one higher than the extension used by the last DSK_DRV_.XXX disk that comes with the NetWare set of diskettes. For instance, if DSK_DRV.001 is the highest number diskette (there is only one disk driver diskette), then the diskette created for the special drivers must be formatted with the volume name DSK_DRV_.002.

The same process must be completed for any other special hardware drivers, such as network interface board drivers. Interface board drivers go into a LAN_DRV_.XXX diskette. The XXX stands for a number that is one more than the last-numbered system diskette. For example, if the diskettes LAN_DRV_.001 and LAN_DRV_.002 come with the NetWare disk set, the specialized drivers you wish to use will be copied onto a disk with the volume label LAN_DRV_.003.

Follow the same numbering process for any other special hardware drivers that are not for disk drives or network interface boards. These other hardware drivers should be copied onto a diskette with the volume name OTH_DRV_.001.

The remainder of this chapter concentrates on the NetWare 286 installation menus, which are used to generate the operating system. The following sections show how to generate the operating system, and provide techniques to avoid common pitfalls. For example, the custom generation method is suggested over other methods. It gives you more options to tune a network to your operating conditions.

The installation techniques explained here focus on the menus that are displayed, rather than on which diskette method is used. However, note that if the hard disk method is used, the system diskettes are first created on a stand-alone microcomputer. Then the NETGEN process is run from the system diskettes on the file server to load the operating system.

PREPARE THE HARD DRIVES

Prepare the hard drives in the file server before you begin NETGEN. This involves performing a low-level format on each hard disk. Use MS-DOS or PC-DOS for the format. To do this, boot the file server using DOS, then insert the DOS diskette that contains the PREP command. Run PREP on each hard drive. The DOS manuals accompanying your computer will have instructions on how to use PREP.

NETWARE INSTALLATION

To begin the NetWare installation process, boot the prospective file server under DOS. The DOS diskette you use to boot the system must contain a CONFIG.SYS file with the following lines:

FILES = 20
BUFFERS = 15

Once the computer is at the A> prompt, insert the NETGEN system diskette into Drive A (this diskette is the copy you created using the floppy or hard disk method). Or, if you plan to use the network method, log onto the file server that contains the Novell system files. Use a boot diskette in Drive A, as explained in Chapter 6. The boot diskette must contain the IPX.COM and NETx.COM files. (Consult the Novell manual, *NetWare 286 Installation,* for instructions on how to copy the system files to the network drive.)

From the A> prompt, type NETGEN to access the first NetWare menu. There are three "switches" that can be used when entering the NETGEN command:

- "N" for beginning a new NETGEN session
- "C" to designate the custom system option
- "D" to designate the default system option

The "N" switch is used to start a new NETGEN session. This option disregards any data that may have been entered during a previous session. The "C" switch permits you to customize the network to your operational needs. It enables you to select special network interface board drivers, to limit disk space for users, and to decide how to manage memory.

When you generate a new file server, use the "N" and "C" switches. The "N" switch ensures starting a new generation session from the beginning. The "C" switch gives the option to set any operational parameter without relying on defaults set by the NETGEN process.

The "D" switch uses the defaults established by NETGEN. Although the default settings are convenient, they do not ensure optimum performance. With the "D" switch, you give up decisions on how to allocate server memory and server disk space.

The format for entering a NETGEN session is:

NETGEN -NC

In this example, the "N" and "C" switches are used. The hyphen before the switches indicates a switch option is to be used. The NETGEN command also can be typed alone without specifying switches. When this is done, the first NetWare menu option asks whether the default or the custom configuration is to be used. A representation of this menu appears in Figure 7.2. Note that once this menu appears, you can exit the NETGEN process with the ESC key. This is true for most menus in NETGEN. Likewise, the ESC key can be

FIGURE 7.2
System Configuration Level Menu

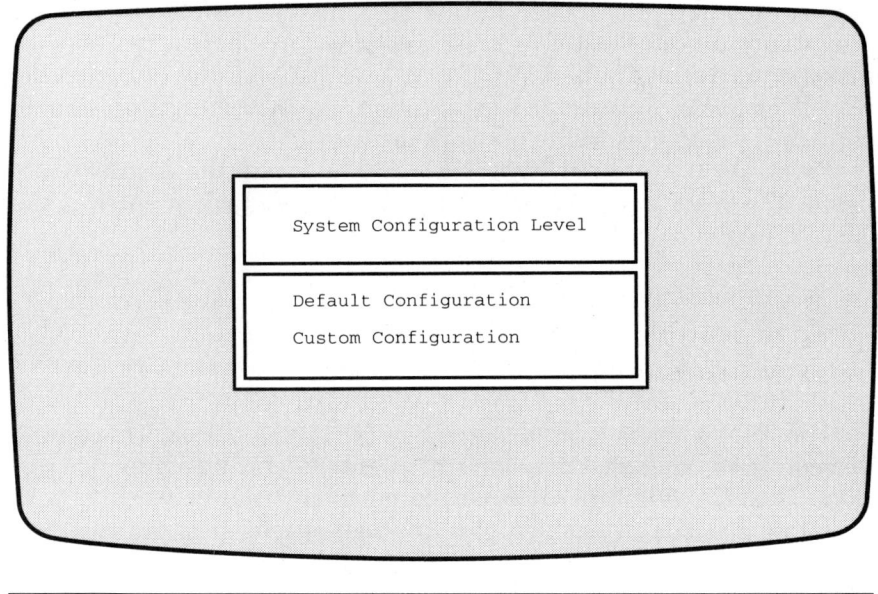

```
System Configuration Level

Default Configuration
Custom Configuration
```

used to return to a previous menu from most menus in the NETGEN process.

Following the initial System Configuration menu, NetWare asks which disk method you intend to use. The options include:

- Standard floppy diskette method
- RAM disk method
- Hard disk method
- Network drive method

These methods were described earlier. The selection depends on what hardware resources are available, as well as how many licensed operating systems will be generated (see Table 7.1). For example, if an existing network is available and several file servers are to be generated, the network drive is the easiest and fastest alternative. Figure 7.3 provides an illustration of this menu.

TABLE 7.1
Network Generation Method

Available Equipment	Number of Servers to Generate	Method
Server with floppy drive	1	Floppy disk
Server with floppy drive and 640 KB	1	RAM disk
Hard disk drive (stand-alone micro-computer)	1 to several	Hard disk
Existing Novell network	1 to several	Network drive

FIGURE 7.3
Netgen Run Options Menu

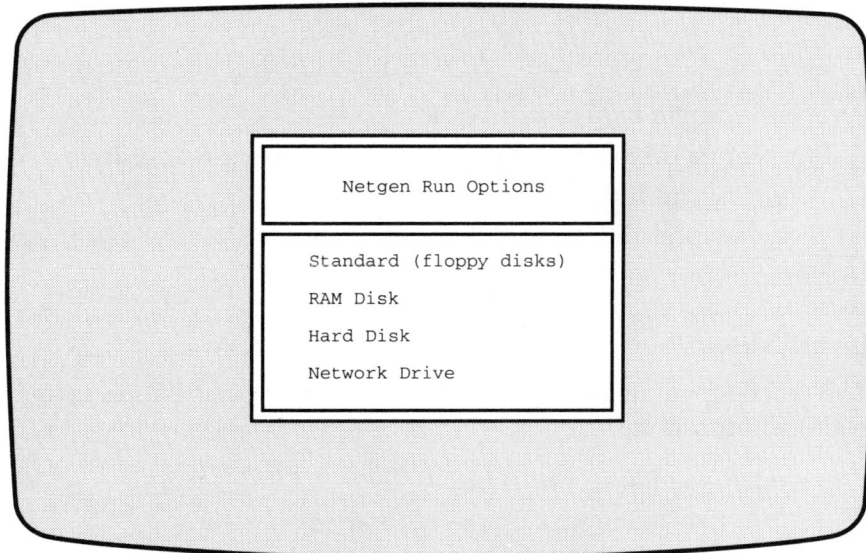

```
          Netgen Run Options

     Standard (floppy disks)

     RAM Disk

     Hard Disk

     Network Drive
```

NETWORK GENERATION LEVELS

Once the disk method is selected, NetWare provides the option to begin the first level of the network generation procedures. At this point, it is helpful to think of generation occurring on two levels. The first level deals with configuration and definition of the hardware. The second level specifies a variety of NetWare installation options, such as naming the file server.

Level One

The first level enables you to configure hardware including the disk drive types and the network interface board type. At this level, you can do the following:

- Select specific hardware resource sets
- Establish transaction tracking
- Select specific LAN drivers for interface boards
- Select specific hard disk drivers
- Incorporate drivers for unique hardware, such as a tape drive
- Configure and link the operating system
- Configure and link file server utilities, like VREPAIR (a utility to repair hard disk problems)

Level Two

The second level deals with the operating system installation options which allow you to:

- Establish the file server name
- Specify how many files can be open at any one time
- Establish the number of indexed files
- Establish the option to limit user disk space
- Specify the number of bindery objects
- Modify volume information, such as the number of permitted directory entries
- Specify whether to cache the directory
- Establish printer ports and spooler sequence
- Specify hot-fix table information
- Modify the partition table

HARDWARE CONFIGURATION

The network generation menu, which appears after the selection of the disk installation method, offers a variety of options designed to build information about the file server hardware into the operating system. The full Network Generation Options menu, which appears when the custom installation method is selected, is represented in Figure 7.4.

FIGURE 7.4
Network Generation Options Menu

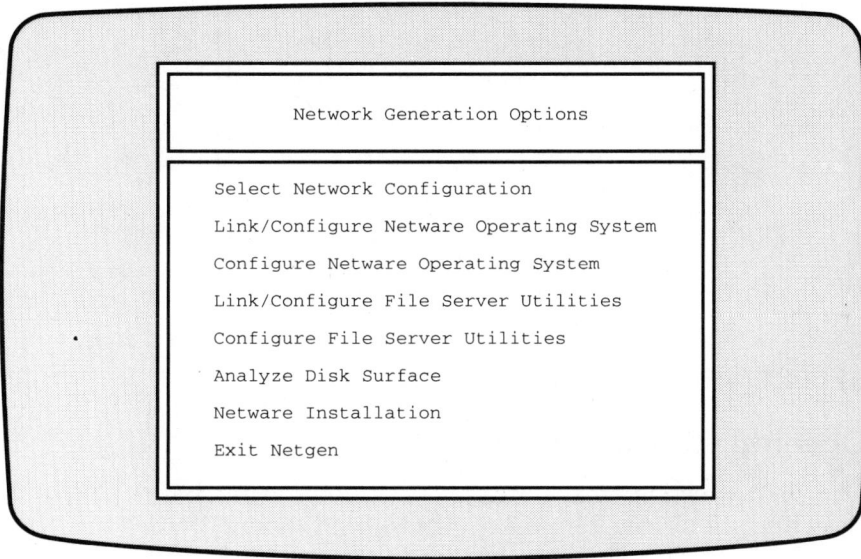

```
          Network Generation Options

    Select Network Configuration

    Link/Configure Netware Operating System

    Configure Netware Operating System

    Link/Configure File Server Utilities

    Configure File Server Utilities

    Analyze Disk Surface

    Netware Installation

    Exit Netgen
```

When this menu appears, take the first option, *Select Network Configuration*. This option provides choices to establish transaction tracking, select specialized LAN and disk drivers, and select resource sets. It branches to another menu, which appears in Figure 7.5.

FIGURE 7.5
Available Options Menu

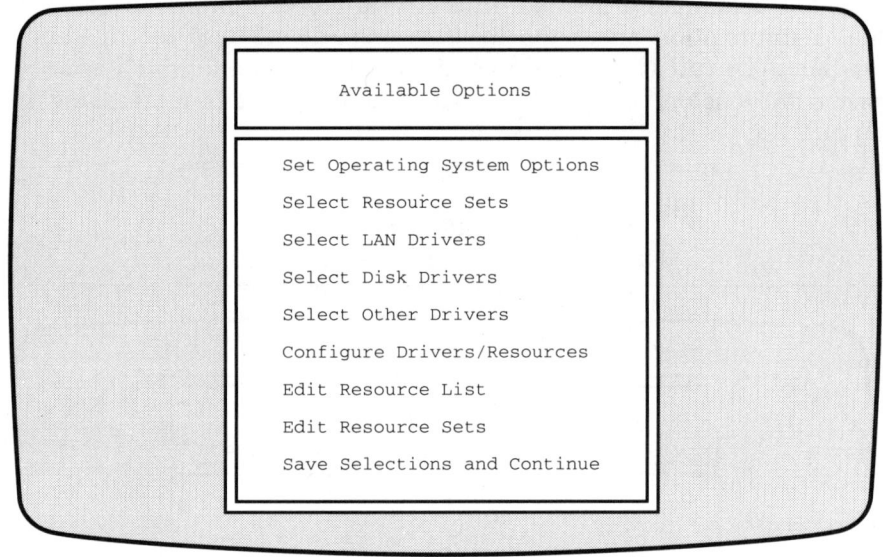

```
                    Available Options

            Set Operating System Options

            Select Resource Sets

            Select LAN Drivers

            Select Disk Drivers

            Select Other Drivers

            Configure Drivers/Resources

            Edit Resource List

            Edit Resource Sets

            Save Selections and Continue
```

SELECT NETWORK CONFIGURATION

Operating System Options

The first selection in the Available Options menu is *Set Operating System Options* (see Figure 7.5). This option enables transaction tracking (TTS) in SFT NetWare 286. (Transaction tracking is the feature that keeps a file or a set of files properly updated if a power interruption or system failure occurs.)

Once the selection is highlighted, another menu appears and asks if you wish to invoke transaction tracking (see Figure 7.6). When this menu appears, highlight the appropriate option and return to the "Available Options" menu.

FIGURE 7.6
Set Operating System Options Menu

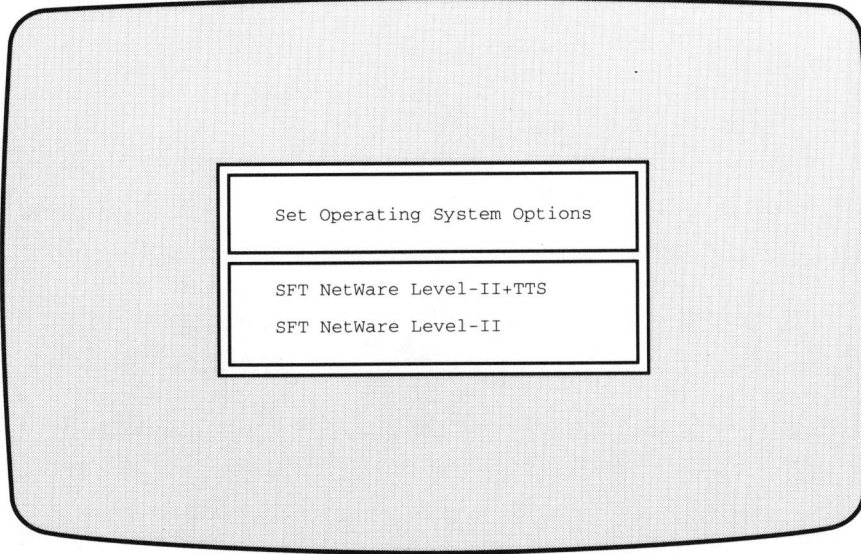

```
          Set Operating System Options

        SFT NetWare Level-II+TTS
        SFT NetWare Level-II
```

For those installing Advanced NetWare 286, the first option on the menu in Figure 7.5 is used to indicate if the server will be dedicated or nondedicated, rather than to indicate TTS. The nondedicated option means the file server can have other operating systems installed on the hard disk, such as DOS. This enables the file server to double as a workstation. By contrast, if the file server is dedicated, it is used exclusively for NetWare. The menu to select the dedicated and non-dedicated mode is shown in Figure 7.7.

FIGURE 7.7
Set Operating System Options Menu

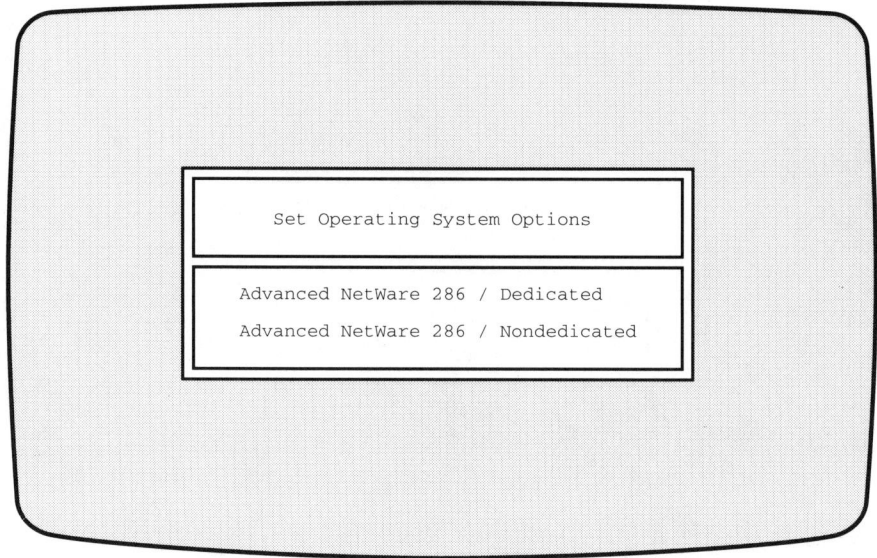

```
                   Set Operating System Options

              Advanced NetWare 286 / Dedicated
              Advanced NetWare 286 / Nondedicated
```

Resource Sets

The option *Select Resource Sets* in the "Available Options" menu in Figure 7.5 permits you to tell the NETGEN process what hardware is in the server, which enables you to avoid conflicts. For example, your server may have two communication ports, two parallel ports, and an ESDI disk controller. You can specify these as one resource set. When you configure the server, NETGEN will look for hardware conflicts. For instance, a conflict is present if two devices use the same interrupt (the interrupt is used to communicate with the CPU). If NETGEN finds a conflict, it will report the conflict. It also will prevent you from going ahead until the conflict is resolved.

Conflicts are most likely to occur between a NIC and a communication port or the disk controller. For example, the NIC may come set to use interrupt 3 (IRQ3). On many computers, IRQ3 also is used by communication port 2 (COM2). This conflict can be resolved by setting the NIC to use another IRQ, such as IRQ2.

Any hardware in the file server can be defined as a resource or resource set. The Novell installation guide has an extensive description of resources and resource sets (a resource set is a list of one or more resources).

Appendix A in the Novell installation guide provides information on how to establish new resource sets not provided with the Novell system disks.

When the *Select Resource Sets* option is used, a window of the available resource sets appears. Below the window is a small menu from which you select and load the resource sets. Or you can choose to load and select a different group of resource sets (see Figure 7.8).

FIGURE 7.8
Selected Resource Sets Menu

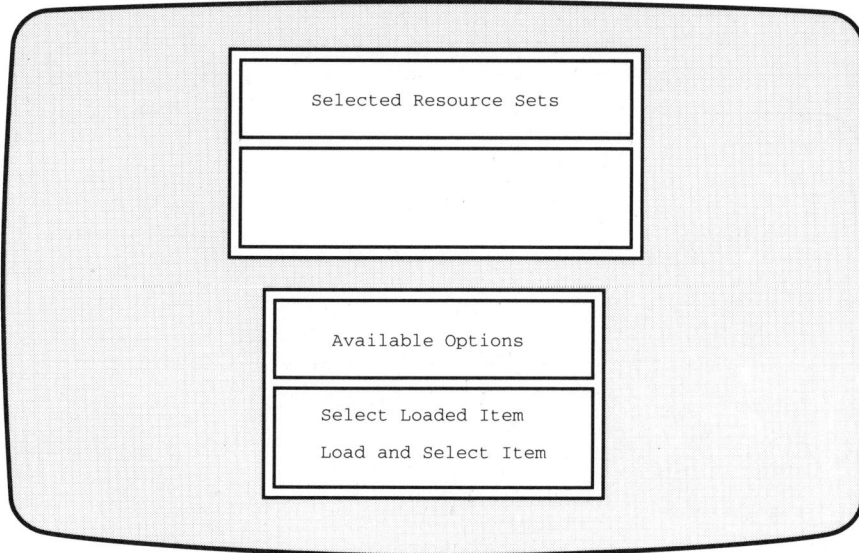

LAN Drivers

The *Select LAN Drivers* option on the menu in Figure 7.5 permits you to select a network interface card driver from the set included with the operating system diskettes. The drivers that come with the operating system are located on two diskettes:

- LAN_DRV_.001
- LAN_DRV_.002

Additional drivers can be obtained from manufacturers of inter-face boards and placed on supplementary diskettes. Normally, these diskettes have a volume ID such as LAN_DRV_.003, LAN_DRV_.004, and so on. However, other volume IDs may be used. This makes it advisable to follow the manufacturer's instructions for implementing the drivers. When a driver set is obtained from a manufacturer, there is often a .LAN file that contains configuration information regarding the driver files. The .LAN file is copied to a backup of the Novell AUXGEN diskette.

When you choose this option, you get a window of the currently selected LAN drivers and a window that permits you to use the au-tomatically loaded LAN driver(s) or to load and select additional LAN drivers (see Figure 7.9).

FIGURE 7.9
Selected LAN Drivers Menu

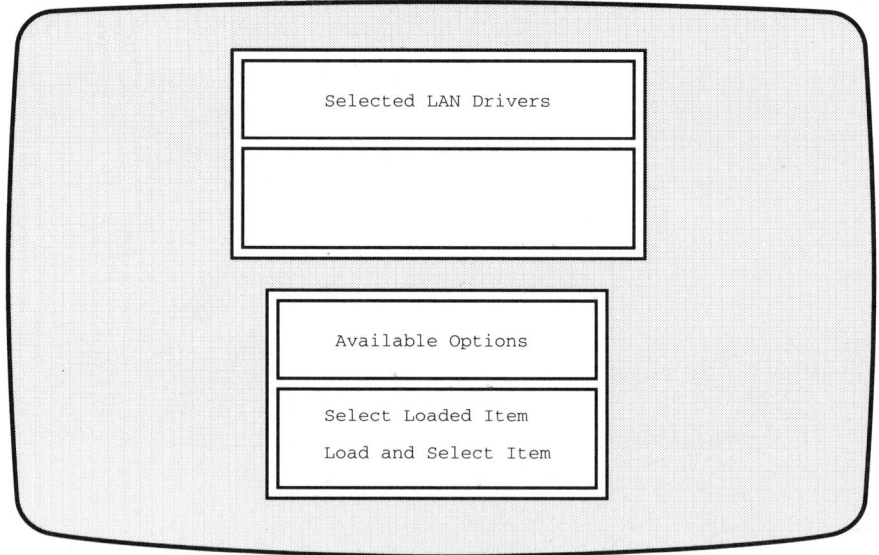

Disk Drivers

The fourth option on the Available Options menu in Figure 7.5, *Select Disk Drivers*, is used to specify hard disk drivers. In most instances, if the file server has an AT or AT-compatible disk controller, the correct driver is already selected. But if a more specialized disk controller is used, such as an ESDI or SCSI disk controller, it may be necessary to select an appropriate disk driver for the controller that accompanies the hard disk. It is necessary to obtain the driver for the disk drive and controller from the vendor who supplies the equipment. The vendor will give instructions indicating where the driver files should be located. Frequently, they will be copied onto a diskette with the volume label, LAN_DSK_.002.

Once you choose the menu option, the automatically selected disk drivers appear. A two-selection menu is displayed where you can select to use any automatically loaded disk driver(s) or to load and select a different list of disk drivers (see Figure 7.10).

The *Select Disk Drivers* option also requires you to specify which disk channel to use. There are five possible **disk channels,** numbered 0, 1, 2, 3, and 4. The channel selected depends on the number of controllers in the server. The first controller is an internal hard drive, which is designated as channel 0. The second is channel 1, and so on.

FIGURE 7.10
Selected Disk Drivers Menu

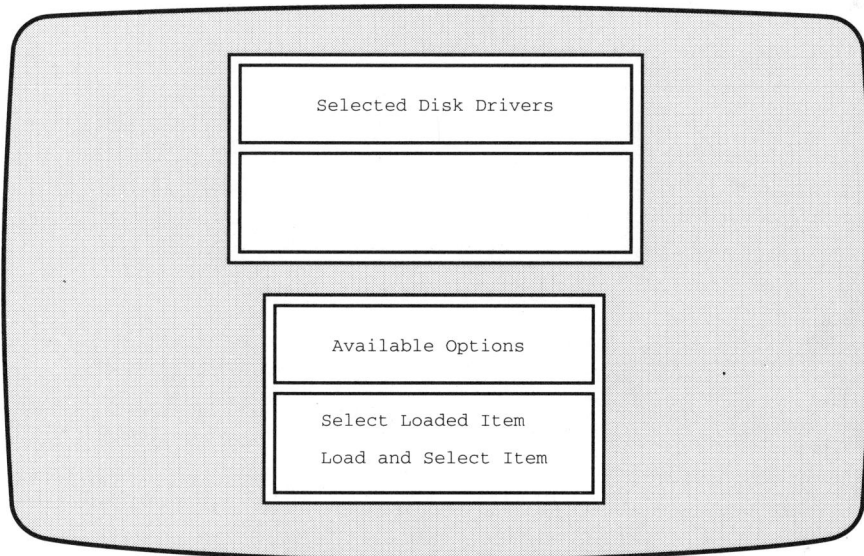

Other Drivers

The fifth selection on the menu in Figure 7.5, *Select Other Drivers*, permits you to add drivers other than LAN and disk drivers. These might be drivers for a tape subsystem, a specialized communications device, or other add-on equipment that comes with its own software. These drivers are also loaded from diskettes provided by the vendor. Follow the vendor's instructions for copying the drivers into NetWare. Typically the drivers are copied to a diskette with the volume ID, OTH_DRV_.XXX. The "XXX" is an extension, such as .002, which is determined by the vendor.

As with the LAN and disk driver options, the *Select Other Drivers* option displays a window showing available drivers. Accompanying the window is a menu that allows you to use any of the automatically loaded drivers. The menu also permits you to load and select drivers that do not automatically appear in the window (see Figure 7.11). As with other file server hardware, be certain the hardware associated with the drivers is Novell compatible.

FIGURE 7.11
Selected "Other" Drivers Menu

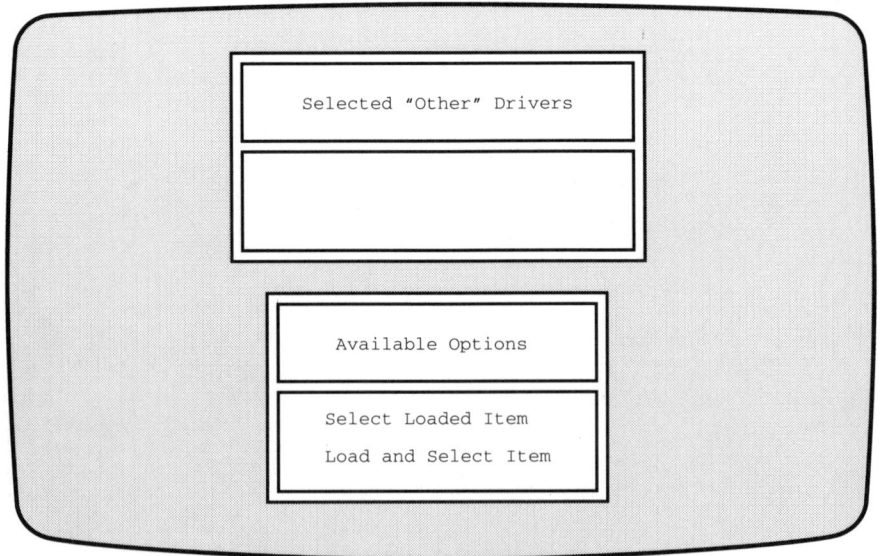

- Selected "Other" Drivers

- Available Options
- Select Loaded Item
- Load and Select Item

Configure Drivers

The *Configure Drivers / Resources* option on the menu in Figure 7.5 produces another menu, which enables you to review the options selected to this point. If there are hardware resources that have not yet been configured, this menu produces an option to configure these resources, such as LAN drivers, disk drivers, and other drivers. Configuring the drivers involves specifying the interrupts, I/O buffer locations, memory locations, and DMA channels. (See Figure 6.9.)

Edit Resources

In Figure 7.5, the next two options listed provide the ability to add more hardware resources to the resource list and to change what resources are in resource sets. The editing performed in these two options affects the selections you make from the *Select Resource Sets* option on the menu in Figure 7.5. Normally, it's not necessary to edit resource lists or resource sets. Appendix A in *NetWare 286 Installation* explains how to edit available resources.

Save Selections

Finally, the *Save Selections and Continue* option on the menu in Figure 7.5 is used to save the configuration information. This information is used to create the operating system. (The operating system is contained in the file, NET$OS.EXE, which is written to the file server.)

Once you invoke *Save Selections and Continue*, you are asked to provide the LAN board address, the network address, the number of communication buffers, and the serial number of the NetWare operating system. The LAN board address is the unique address for the LAN to which the file server is attached. Each file server and each interface board on the LAN must have a different address. The network address is a hexadecimal number up to eight characters in length. File servers that are on the same network segment must have identical network addresses; and file servers on the same internetwork, but not on the same network segment, must have different addresses. For many network interface boards, the system reads the address directory from the board. Consequently, the address does not have to be entered.

Communications buffers are used to store arriving packets from network stations temporarily. The number of communications buffers depends on the number of workstations that will access the server. There should be a minimum of forty communication buffers, plus one

additional buffer for each workstation. If there are forty-five workstations, the number of communication buffers will be eighty-five. The
formula for determining the number of communication buffers is the
following:

Communication buffers = 40 + number of workstations

The operating system serial number is printed on the label of the
GENDATA diskette. Normally, the operating system will automatically read the serial number from this diskette. Earlier versions of the
operating system required entry of the serial number.

NETWORK GENERATION OPTIONS

Link and Configure

The "Network Generation Options" menu is again represented in
Figure 7.12. Once the *Select Network Configuration* option is completed, select the *Link/Configure NetWare Operating System* option

FIGURE 7.12
Network Generation Options Menu

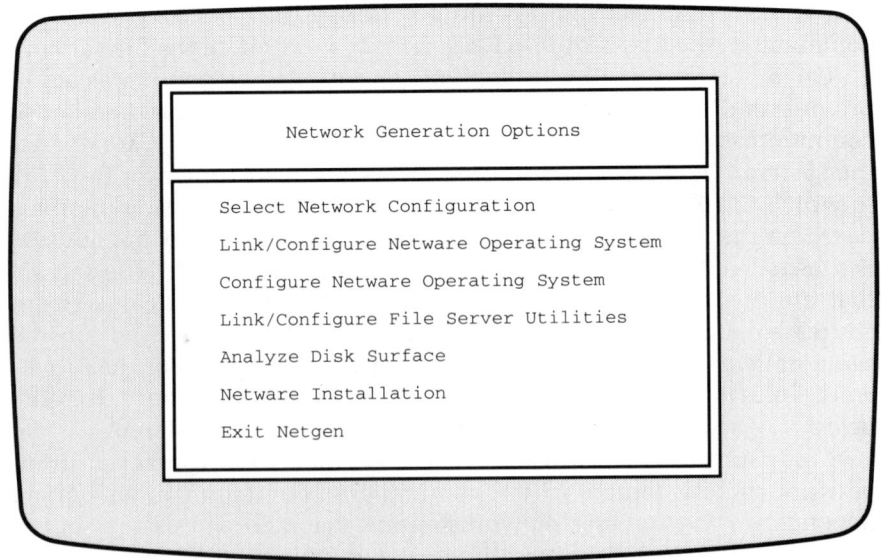

```
                   Network Generation Options


         Select Network Configuration

         Link/Configure Netware Operating System

         Configure Netware Operating System

         Link/Configure File Server Utilities

         Analyze Disk Surface

         Netware Installation

         Exit Netgen
```

from the menu in Figure 7.12. This option automatically links and configures the LAN, disk, and any other drivers selected.

After the operating system has been linked and configured, the *Link/Configure File Server Utilities* option is selected. The file server utilities that are generated from this action include VREPAIR, COMPSURF, DISKED, and INSTOVL. These utilities are linked and configured so they correlate with the disk driver or drivers that have been installed. Once the utilities are linked and configured, they are written to the UTILEXE-1, UTILEXE-2, and NETGEN diskettes.

HARD DISK ANALYSIS

The option to *Analyze Disk Surface*, should be run after the utilities are linked and configured. This option performs a comprehensive analysis of the disk surface (COMPSURF). It looks for any bad blocks on the disk and formats them so they are unused by the file server. Note that on many hard disks, the DOS low-level format executed by the MS-DOS PREP command should be performed on the hard disk prior to commencing the NETGEN process.

Some hard drive manufacturers, such as Storage Dimensions, ship drives that have already been prepared for operation. They use their own versions of PREP and COMPSURF. And they warn the user not to PREP or to COMPSURF the disk. If this is the case, follow the manufacturer's instructions and do not prepare the disk. Go to the next stage of NETGEN.

The COMPSURF utility can cause an error message on hard disks larger than 30 MB. The message indicates that the hard drive has more than the permissible number of bad blocks. This is because COMPSURF permits an upper limit of bad blocks that is appropriate to small disk drives. Large drives, such as those which hold 80-300 MB, can have a larger number of bad blocks. If you are using a drive larger than 30 MB, follow these steps in COMPSURF:

Step 1   To the question "FORMAT the disk?" answer "NO."

Step 2   To the question "Maintain the current media defect list?" answer "NO."

Step 3   To the question "Enter media defect?" answer "NO."

Step 4   When you are asked for the number of sequential passes, specify three passes.

Step 5   The number of I/O in random test should be answered with the default provided by COMPSURF. The default is determined by the parameters you have entered up to this point in NETGEN.

Step 6   Answer "YES" to COMPSURF's request to confirm what you have entered. The COMPSURF analysis of your disk will now begin.

Step 7   If a message is displayed showing there are too many bad blocks, exit COMPSURF and go to Step 8. If you do not get this message skip Step 8 and continue with the NETGEN.

Step 8   Start COMPSURF again. Repeat Step 1. In Step 2 answer "YES" instead of "NO." Repeat Steps 3–6.

COMPSURF can be run on any or all of the disk drives installed in the file server. If the manufacturer's specs indicate that COMPSURF can be performed on a disk drive, then the utility should be used. *COMPSURF is destructive to data on the disk drive, and must be performed before the operating system files are written to the disk.*

Install NetWare

The second-to-last option on the menu in Figure 7.12, *NetWare Installation*, is selected after all other options have been executed except *Exit NETGEN*, which is on the menu to permit you to leave the installation process at any time.

The *NetWare Installation* option signals that you have finished configuring the hardware. You are now ready to customize operating system parameters and copy NetWare onto the file server.

SPECIFYING NETWORK OPTIONS

The second level of the NETGEN installation process involves specifying options, such as the file server name, the number of simultaneous open files, the number of **bindery** objects, and so on. This level begins with a survey of the physical characteristics of the file server, such as the sizes and types of disk drives available. When the system finishes the survey, it will respond with a table showing the hard disks installed. Figure 7.13 shows an example table with one AT compatible hard drive and controller.

FIGURE 7.13
Disk Configuration Screen

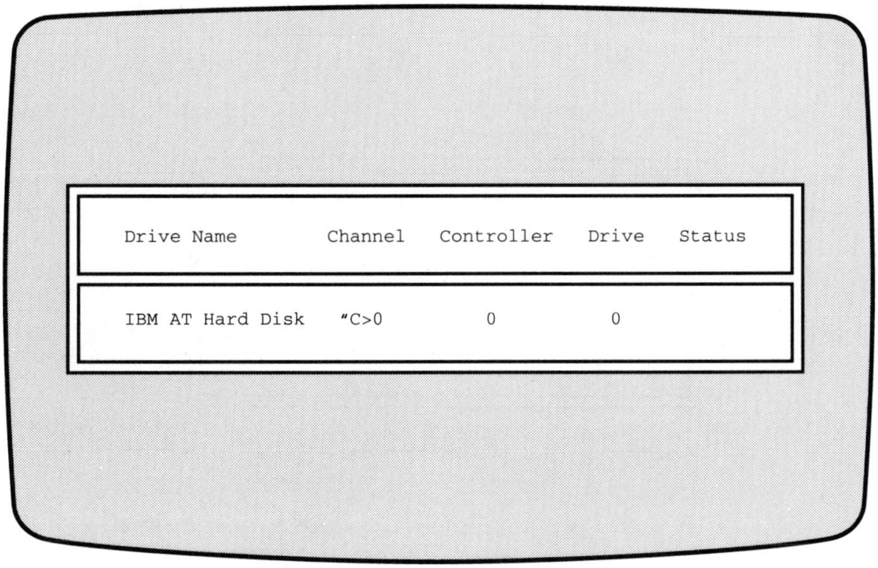

```
Drive Name          Channel   Controller   Drive    Status

IBM AT Hard Disk     "C>0         0           0
```

When the system completes the survey, it asks for verification of the hard drive information displayed. Once you verify the information, the Installation Options menu shown in Figure 7.14 is displayed.

FIGURE 7.14
Installation Options Menu

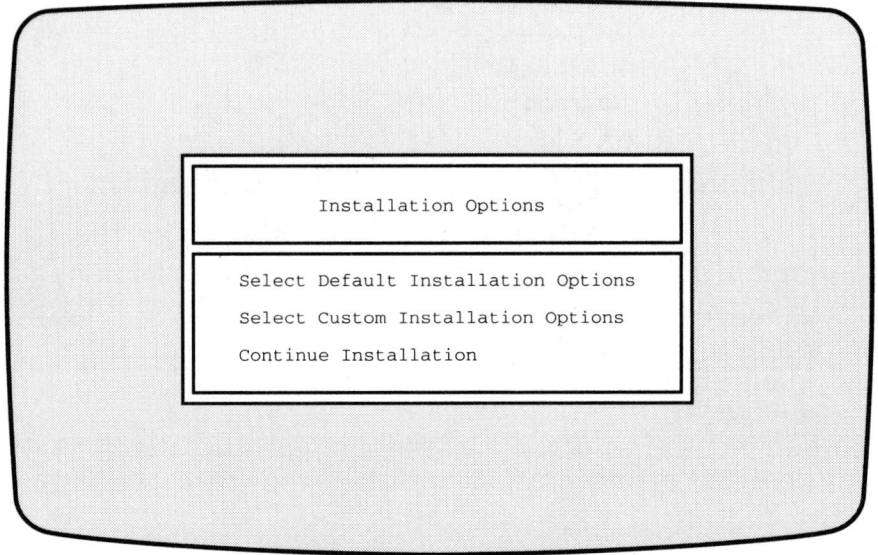

```
                    Installation Options

         Select Default Installation Options
         Select Custom Installation Options
         Continue Installation
```

From this menu, *Select Custom Installation Options* provides a broader range of alternatives than *Select Default Installation Options*. The default confines you to providing the file server name and defining parallel and serial printer options. Opting for *Select Custom Installation Options* produces the Custom Installation menu illustrated in Figure 7.15.

FIGURE 7.15
Custom Installation Menu

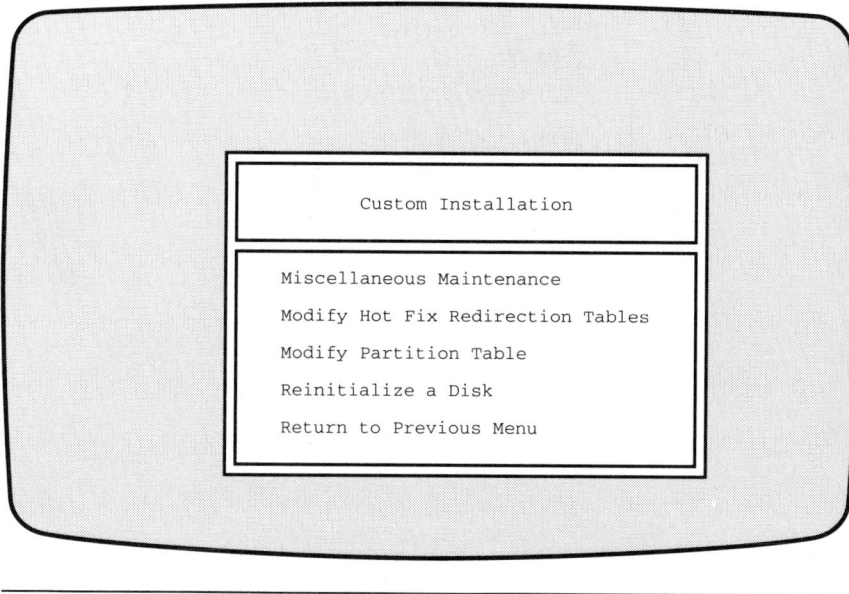

```
                    Custom Installation

         Miscellaneous Maintenance
         Modify Hot Fix Redirection Tables
         Modify Partition Table
         Reinitialize a Disk
         Return to Previous Menu
```

MISCELLANEOUS MAINTENANCE

The first selection on the Custom Installation menu is *Miscellaneous Maintenance*. This menu supplies options to set up system configuration information, volume information, and printer maintenance information as follows:

- File server name
- Number of open files
- Number of indexed files
- Disk volume names
- Printer port specifications (The file server can have up to three parallel ports and two serial ports for printing.)

When the *Miscellaneous Maintenance* option is selected, another menu appears with a range of six options. This menu is reproduced in Figure 7.16.

FIGURE 7.16
Miscellaneous Maintenance Menu

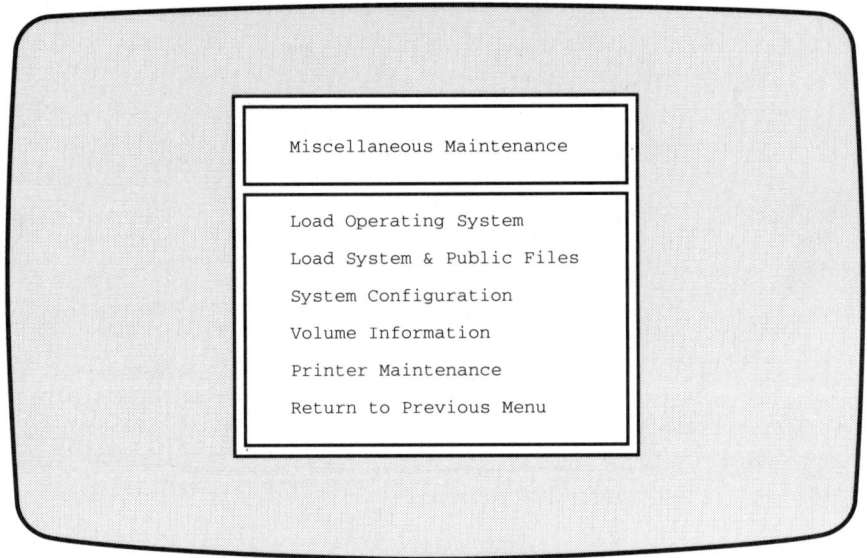

```
              Miscellaneous Maintenance


              Load Operating System
              Load System & Public Files
              System Configuration
              Volume Information
              Printer Maintenance
              Return to Previous Menu
```

Load Operating System

The *Load Operating System* option on the menu in Figure 7.16 is used to designate whether the operating system is to be loaded when the NetWare files are copied to the file server. When this option is selected, you are asked whether to flag the operating system to be loaded. The "Yes" answer should be highlighted here. This flags the operating system to be written to the file server disk.

Load System and Public Files

Likewise, the *Load System & Public Files* option should also be flagged "Yes" to load these files as well. These are the files that constitute the SYSTEM and PUBLIC directories on the file server.

System Configuration

The *System Configuration* selection on the "Miscellaneous Maintenance" menu produces a series of parameters to establish on the file server. These include the following:

- File server name
- Number of open files
- Number of indexed files
- Transaction backout volume
- Number of transactions
- Limit disk space
- Number of bindery objects

The length of the file server name can be from two to forty-five characters. Normally, it is advisable to choose a name that's not too long to type, but that is descriptive of the file server.

Number of Open Files The number-of-open-files parameter establishes how many files can be open at the same time on the file server. The installation process will automatically place a number in this parameter. If you select to override this number, the new entry must be between 20 and 1,000. Note that each open file consumes 100 bytes of the file server memory. File servers that will have large numbers of smaller files, such as word processing files, should allow for more open files. On the other hand, servers that are used to house large data files will require fewer open files. A viable number of open files to begin with will range between 250 to 400. If the estimate is too low, you can always change this number later through NETGEN.

Number of Indexed Files As mentioned earlier in this chapter, indexing is used to speed access to files larger than 1 MB. The maximum number of indexed files is 1,000. However, since the server reserves memory for this function, the number of indexed files should be set to match as closely as possible the number of anticipated large files. Begin with five to twenty indexed files.

Transaction Backout Volume If transaction tracking has been enabled and there are two volumes, the option to select a transaction backout volume is displayed. This volume is used to store information when transactions have to be backed out. Normally, NetWare designates the SYS volume as the transaction backout volume. The designated transaction backout volume should have at least 1 MB of free storage. The server will operate more efficiently if the transaction backout volume is not the same as the volume containing the actual transaction data.

Number of Transactions   The number-of-transactions parameter is displayed only where transaction tracking has been enabled. The value entered specifies the largest number of transactions that can be processed at one time. The number of transactions can range from twenty to 200. The NETGEN process enters 100 transactions as the default. The general rule of thumb is to estimate the largest number of users who may be on the network at the same time. Then double this number to generate the number of transactions.

Limit Disk Space   NetWare permits you to limit disk space per user. This is a useful feature. It enables you to control the total amount of disk storage allocated to users. Furthermore, if there is a bug or problem with a program, limiting disk space ensures the problem will be contained to the disk space permitted for the user. For these reasons, it is advisable to enter "Yes" to the limit-disk-space parameter.

Number of Bindery Objects   If disk space is designated as limited, then NETGEN will ask you to establish the number of bindery objects. This number pertains to the total number of users, groups, and print servers that will be created on the file server. One bindery object is created for each user, group, and print server. The default number of bindery objects is normally set at 500; and this default is generally sufficient for most installations. The number that appears here can range from 500 to 5,000.

Volume Information

The selection on the "Miscellaneous Maintenance" menu in Figure 7.16, which appears after *System Configuration*, is the *Volume Information* option. When this option is selected, a small window appears with the names of the volumes (hard drives) that have been established. If a volume name is highlighted and you press the ENTER key, information about the volume appears on the screen. This information includes the volume name, the number of directory entries, and the answer to whether the directory is cached (see Figure 7.17).

The "Volume Definition" menu enables you to change the volume name. However, the first volume, the one containing the PUBLIC and SYSTEM files, should always be named SYS. Subsequent volumes are named VOL1, VOL2, and so on. The number of directory entries is automatically determined by the system, according to the size of the hard disk. This is the maximum number of files, directories, and subdirectories that can be on the volume. If the volume is destined to

FIGURE 7.17
Volume Definition Menu

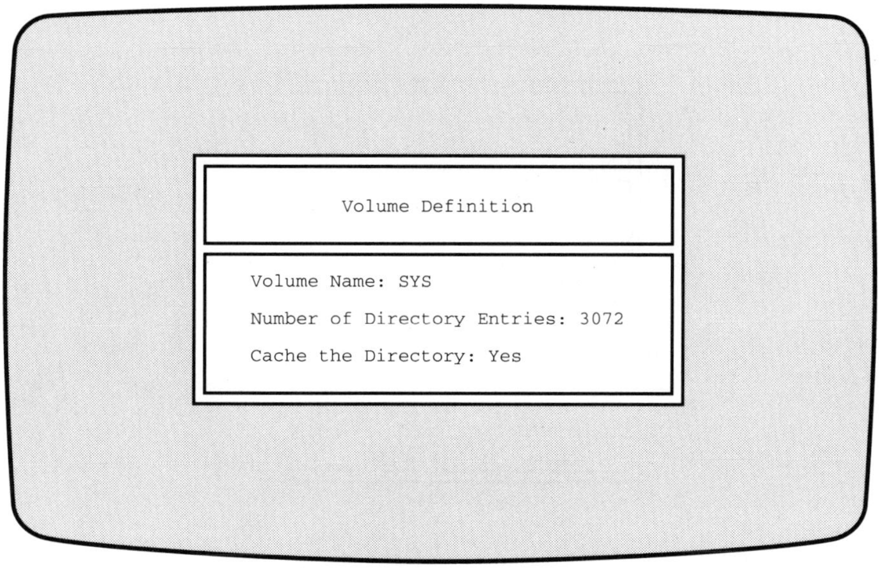

```
                    Volume Definition

      Volume Name: SYS
      Number of Directory Entries: 3072
      Cache the Directory: Yes
```

have a large number of small files, it may be necessary to increase the number of directory entries. This can be done at a later date, once file utilization has been monitored after the file server is in use. It is important to monitor the maximum number of files because, if the limit is reached, users will not be able to use programs or menus that necessitate creating new files. Finally, the parameter to cache the directory should be set to "Yes." Directory caching will significantly speed file access on the server.

Printer Maintenance

The *Printer Maintenance* option on the "Miscellaneous Maintenance" menu in Figure 7.16 is used to specify printer information. For example, the file server may have one parallel and one serial printer port. **Network printers** can be connected to these ports, if the ports are established so NetWare recognizes them. (Network printers can be shared by users.) This is accomplished through the *Printer Maintenance* option. In this example, the parallel printer connection might be designated as Printer 0 and the serial printer designated as Printer 1.

FIGURE 7.18
Spooled Serial Printer Menu

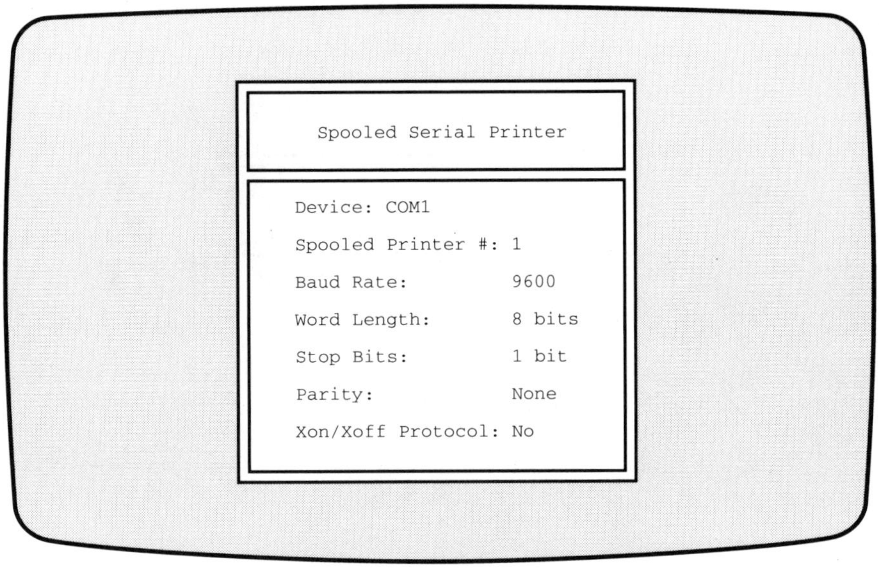

```
            Spooled Serial Printer


   Device: COM1

   Spooled Printer #: 1

   Baud Rate:        9600

   Word Length:      8 bits

   Stop Bits:        1 bit

   Parity:           None

   Xon/Xoff Protocol: No
```

When the *Printer Maintenance* option is selected, a menu to define the serial port will appear, much like the parameter menu in Figure 7.18.

Figure 7.18 displays typical parameters for a serial printer. The device parameter is used to specify the serial port, COM1 or COM2. The printer number in this figure is 1. Since there are two printers in our example, the serial port has been designated as Printer 1, or the second printer attached to the file server (printer number starts at 0). The baud rate should be set on the file server port to match the setting on the printer. The word length, too, must be set to match the capabilities of the printer. Most printers use an 8-bit word length. Like word length, the number of stop bits is based on the printer's capabilities. One stop bit is typical for many printers. The printer may be set to check data using even or odd parity; or the printer may be set for no parity. Last, Xon/Xoff protocol refers to printer/computer communications. Some printers are capable of telling the computer to stop sending data when the computer sends faster than the printer can process it. If Xon/Xoff protocol is enabled, this means the printer will tell the server when the server is sending characters too fast. Not all

FIGURE 7.19
Spooled Parallel Printer Menu

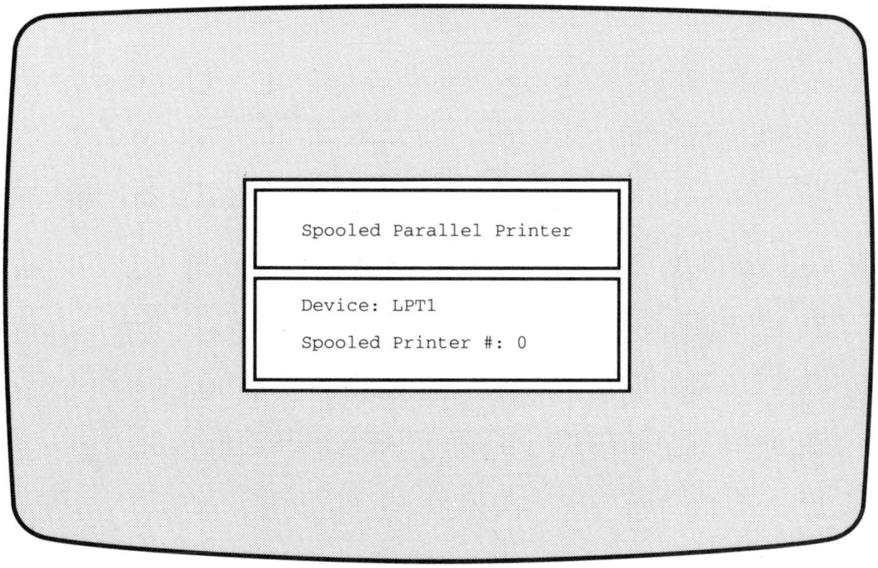

```
Spooled Parallel Printer

Device: LPT1

Spooled Printer #: 0
```

printers have this capability. Check the printer documentation before entering "Yes" for Xon/Xoff protocol.

Since parallel communications are different from serial communications, the menu for setting the parallel port is much shorter. Transmission speed and communications protocol do not have to be set for parallel interfaces. Figure 7.19 shows the menu used to establish parallel printing. Note that in this menu the device corresponds to the parallel port designation, LPT1, LPT2, or LPT3. The other parameter to set is for the printer number. In our example, the parallel printer is set as the first network printer, which is Printer 0.

Once the printer information is provided, the NETGEN process asks whether to use the printer definitions. A "No" answer gives you the option to change the printer definitions. A "Yes" answer retains the definitions you supply, and NETGEN continues to the next step in the installation.

Return to Previous Menu

Finally, the "Miscellaneous Maintenance" menu in Figure 7.16 contains the option, *Return to Previous Menu*. Once you are finished with

FIGURE 7.20
Custom Installation Menu

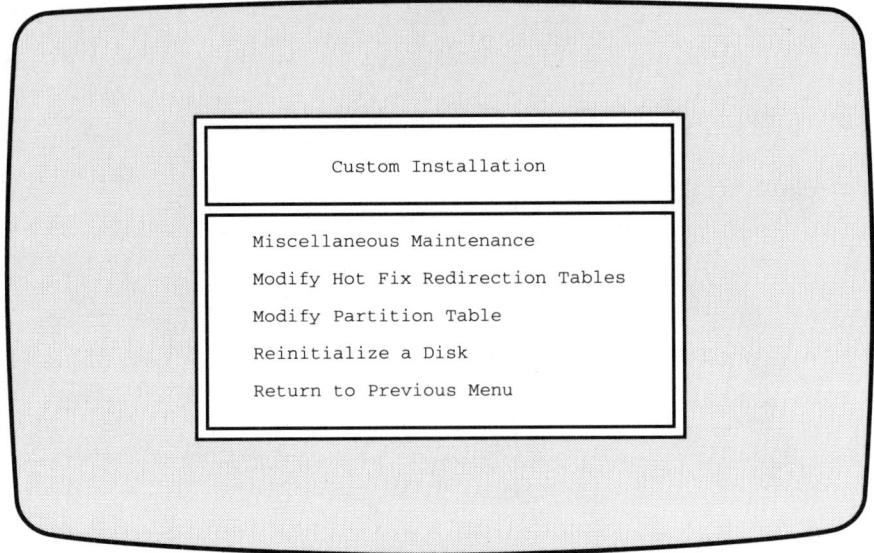

```
                    Custom Installation


   Miscellaneous Maintenance

   Modify Hot Fix Redirection Tables

   Modify Partition Table

   Reinitialize a Disk

   Return to Previous Menu
```

the other options on the menu, this one is selected to save the parameters that have been specified; and the option transfers back to the "Custom Installation" menu shown in Figures 7.15 and 7.20.

CUSTOM INSTALLATION

Modify Hot-Fix Redirection Tables

Following the *Miscellaneous Maintenance* option on the menu in Figure 7.20 is the option to *Modify Hot-Fix Redirection Tables*. The NETGEN process automatically establishes hot-fix redirection for each hard drive. This means that if a bad portion of the disk is detected, data is redirected so it is written within the portion of the disk designated as the hot-fix area.

NetWare automatically allocates 2 percent of the disk storage area to hot-fix redirection. This amount of disk space should prove sufficient for most disk applications. If not, this is usually an indication the disk is failing and should be replaced. It's better to replace a bad disk than to modify the automatic hot-fix allocation so it is larger than 2 percent. If a disk is failing to the extent that it has consumed most of its hot-fix area, it is likely to soon fail entirely. The NetWare statistics in the FCONSOLE utility (see Chapter 8) provide a way to monitor the hot-fix situation. Plan to replace a disk when 75 percent or more of the hot-fix redirection blocks are used. Do not increase the portion of disk the hot-fix redirection table uses.

Modify Partition Table

The option to *Modify Partition Table* has two functions. First, it can be used to ensure that any pre-existing partition table is overwritten by the one created by NetWare. During the NETGEN process, NetWare automatically establishes a default partition table to write onto the disk. Selecting the *Modify Partition Table* option with the pre-established defaults ensures the partition table is written onto the disk.

For Advanced NetWare users, this option makes it possible to use the file server also as a workstation. A portion of the hard disk can be partitioned for DOS or other operating systems in addition to NetWare. When a portion of the hard disk is partitioned for another operating system, this entails specifying the operating system name, whether the partition is to be bootable or nonbootable, and the starting and ending cylinder locations for the partition. This is illustrated in Figure 7.21.

Once changes are specified for the partition table, NetWare automatically asks whether to save the partition table changes.

When establishing other partitions, make certain NetWare is on the first partition, starting from cylinder 0. Only one partition can be the bootable partition. Consult the NetWare installation manual for further instructions about establishing additional partitions.

You should partition all of the file server disk for NetWare. Therefore, you must use the default partition table that is established in the NETGEN process. If you need an extra workstation to run DOS, UNIX, PICK, OS/2, or another operating system, purchase an extra workstation for this purpose. Most file server installations will quickly become too important to an organization to have the server doubling as a workstation.

Reintialize a Disk

Following the *Modify Partition Table* option on the Custom Installation menu in Figure 7.20 is the *Reinitialize a Disk* option. When installing NetWare for the first time on a file server, each disk should

FIGURE 7.21
Partition Information Entry Menu

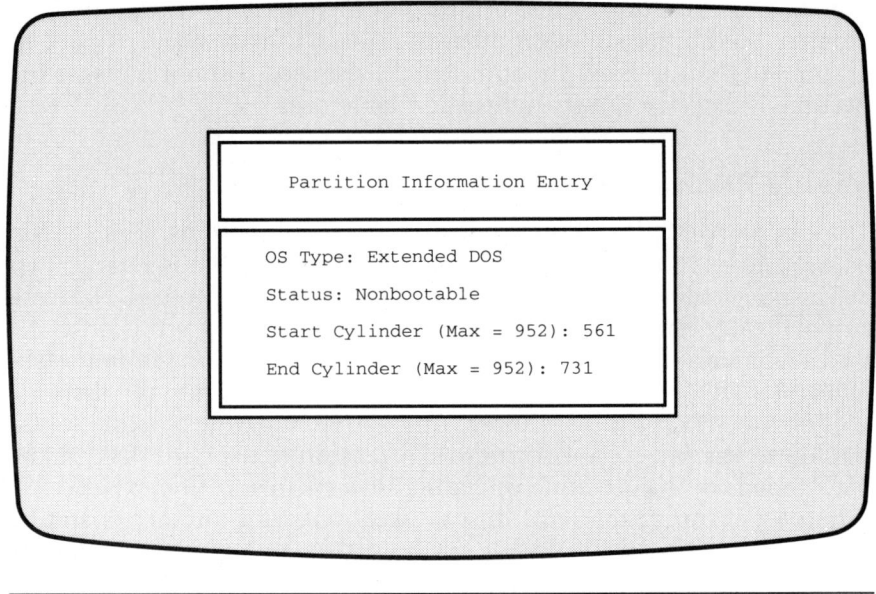

```
        Partition Information Entry


  OS Type: Extended DOS

  Status: Nonbootable

  Start Cylinder (Max = 952): 561

  End Cylinder (Max = 952): 731
```

be initialized for use by the NetWare operating system. Once the *Reinitialize a Disk* option is selected, each volume on the server is displayed. You should highlight each disk to be initialized. Note that the first disk highlighted for initialization is the disk that will be used as the system disk (with the SYSTEM directory files).

Return to Previous Menu

The last option on the Custom Installation menu is *Return to Previous Menu*. Use this option when you're completely finished with the custom installation options and are ready to continue with the installation. The option returns to the initial "Installation Options" menu shown in Figures 7.14 and 7.22.

FIGURE 7.22
Installation Options Menu

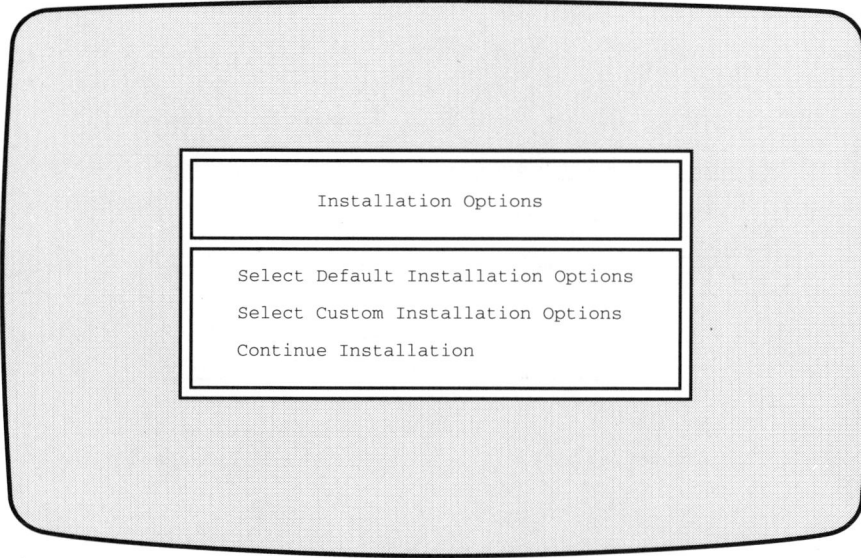

```
           Installation Options


   Select Default Installation Options
   Select Custom Installation Options
   Continue Installation
```

INSTALLATION OF NETWARE FILES

Continue Installation

When you select *Continue Installation* on the menu in Figure 7.22, the NETGEN process displays a small menu that asks whether to install the software on the file server. An example of this menu is shown in Figure 7.23.

A "No" answer to the menu in Figure 7.23 enables you to go back to a previous step and change a response. A "Yes" answer instructs NETGEN to begin writing files onto the SYS volume of the file server.

When the system begins writing files to the server, a message appears. The message instructs you to be patient while the files are loaded, since this can take several minutes. The first information loaded onto the server is the cold boot loader, which is used to boot the computer after it has been powered off. The following message is then displayed:

Installing the cold boot loader on track 0 of hard disk 0.

FIGURE 7.23
Install Networking Software on File Server Menu

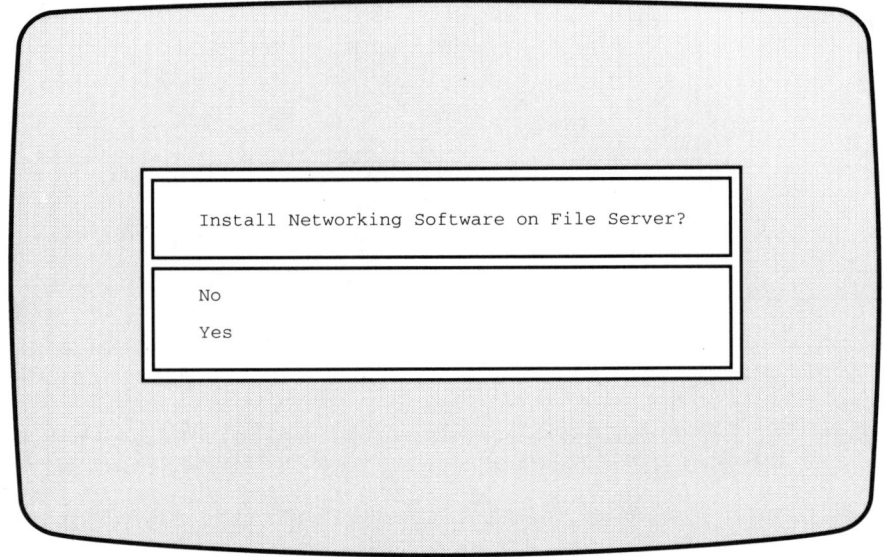

```
┌─────────────────────────────────────────────────┐
│  Install Networking Software on File Server?    │
├─────────────────────────────────────────────────┤
│  No                                             │
│  Yes                                            │
└─────────────────────────────────────────────────┘
```

As soon as the cold boot loader is installed, NETGEN displays another message instructing you to press a key to continue the loading process:

The Cold Boot Loader has been successfully installed.

Strike a key when ready . . .

The next step is to load the NET$OS.EXE file (the operating system file) into the SYSTEM directory:

Copying NET$OS.EXE to SYS:SYSTEM

Once this is complete, the following message is displayed:

NET$OS.EXE successfully installed

Strike a key when ready . . .

Finally, NETGEN copies the remaining SYSTEM files onto the file server. It then copies the PUBLIC directory files. Once all files have been copied, the NETGEN process displays the message:

System files successfully installed.

Strike a key when ready . . .

Exit NETGEN

When you reach this point, you're returned to a menu with the option to *Exit NETGEN*. If the network drive method has been used, NETGEN asks if you wish to download files to floppy disk. Downloading includes files on the following disks:

- NETGEN
- SUPPORT
- OSEXE-1
- OSEXE-2
- UTILEXE-1
- UTILEXE-2

Copies of the original disks should have been made prior to running NETGEN. The pre-made copies should now be used for the files that have been generated through the NETGEN procedures.

BOOTING THE FILE SERVER

When the NETGEN process is completed, power the file server off. Next, power it back on. Make sure the server is connected to the network before powering it on. The server will boot under the Novell operating system; and it is now ready for you to log on to the supervisor account.

SUMMARY

The NETGEN steps described in this chapter show what happens during initial installation of the operating system onto the file server. However, the same steps are applicable to those instances where you want to run NETGEN again to change a hardware or operating system setting on an existing Novell file server.

NetWare has built-in disk-error protection to ensure against file allocation table and directory data area corruption. There is also a hot-fix table feature, which enables data to be redirected from corrupt portions of a hard disk. The transaction tracking system permits NetWare to back out of a series of related file transactions, in case a power interruption should put several transaction files out of synchronization. And disk mirroring or disk duplexing provides backup insurance in the event of disk failure.

Another feature of the operating system is the ability to partition the file server disk for additional operating systems, such as DOS. (Advanced NetWare 286 and NetWare 386 have this option, while Net-Ware SFT 286 does not.) Furthermore, NetWare file servers can be interfaced with an uninterruptible power source to guard against power failures. Another feature of the operating system is the utility to cache the disk, which speeds access to data on the file server.

A large portion of this chapter has focused on the installation process for NetWare 286, particularly on how to perform a custom installation. The installation process itself is divided into two main levels:

- Hardware configuration
- Selection of operating system options

CHAPTER QUESTIONS

1. Explain the differences between dedicated and nondedicated file servers. Which is preferred? Why?
2. How is the number of open files determined when generating software for a file server? How much memory is consumed by one open file?
3. Explain the purpose of indexed files.
4. What is the hot-fix function?
5. What is the purpose of transaction tracking?
6. What are bindery objects?
7. Explain how the disk directory and file allocation table are protected on NetWare file servers.
8. What are the two main levels of installation performed in the process of generating a NetWare file server? Explain the general steps involved in each level.

8

Novell Utilities and Commands

INTRODUCTION

This chapter discusses Novell menu utilities and commands for NetWare 286. Chapter 9 provides similar information and additional details for NetWare 386.

Once the operating system has been generated, Novell makes a variety of utilities available to the network manager. Most of these utilities are located in the SYS:PUBLIC and SYS:SYSTEM directories. They address a range of needs from creating user IDs to monitoring file server performance statistics.

The Novell utilities come in three general formats: menu utilities, command line utilities, and console commands. This chapter is organized according to these groupings. At the end of the chapter you will find cross reference tables to the utilities. The cross reference tables enable you to locate an activity, such as setting up a printer or creating a new user. The utilities required to complete each activity are also presented in the table. The table uses the chapter section numbers as reference points.

Menu and Command Line Utilities

Menu and command line utilities are accessed by logging onto the file server from a workstation, using the supervisor user ID or regular user ID. Those with supervisor privileges have more options available in both the menu and command line utilities.

Menu utilities are started by typing a single command. Once the menu is displayed, selections are made by highlighting a specific option and pressing the ENTER key. On-line documentation on a selection is available by pressing the F3 key when that selection is highlighted on the menu. Documentation on an individual work-station keyboard is accessed by pressing the F3 key twice.

Command line utilities are accessed by typing the individual command along with appropriate parameters used with the command. Some of the commands are self-documenting by typing a "?" after the command. Both the menu utilities and the command line commands are documented in the FOLIO program, which provides on-line access to the Novell manuals.

Console Commands

The console commands are accessed only from the file server console keyboard. These utilities are designed to permit the console operator to monitor server activities and to manage print operations.

Note: The information contained in this chapter summarizes menu, command line, and console information available in the NetWare *Supervisor Reference* manual, the *Menu Utilities* manual, the *Command Line Utilities* manual, and the *Console Reference* manual. Consult these manuals for more detailed reference inquiries.

MENU UTILITIES

The menu utilities are designed for use by the network manager, authorized operators, and general users. However, the highest privilege level for menu operations resides at the supervisor or network manager level. The menu utilities enable the network manager to create new users, to add or alter trustee rights, to create and modify login scripts, to create print queues, to monitor connection data, and so on. The available menu utilities include the following:

- **SYSCON**   This utility enables the network manager to install and manage user and group information.
- **FCONSOLE**   This utility manages log-on activities of users and keeps statistics on the file server's performance.
- **MAKEUSER**   The system manager uses this to create a number of users with a single batch process.
- **SESSION**   This menu permits users to modify paths (mappings) to file-server directories.
- **FILER**   This is used to view and modify access to volumes, directories, subdirectories, and files.
- **PCONSOLE**   This utility provides access to print-queue and print-server information.
- **PRINTDEF**   This enables the user to control printer functions, such as compressed printing.
- **PRINTCON**   This utility establishes print job information, such as whether to print a banner page.
- **VOLINFO**   Disk volume information is displayed by this utility, such as storage and directory entry information.

8.1   SYSCON

The SYSCON menu is a valuable tool for the network manager. It is used to manage user and group information. To display the menu, type SYSCON at the NetWare command level. An example of the SYSCON menu is shown in Figure 8.1.

This menu is available to users with and without supervisor privileges. However, the options available to those without supervisor privileges are limited to information pertaining to their individual accounts and not to other users' accounts.

Accounting   The first option on the menu is *Accounting*, which is used to establish accounting on a server. When this option is selected, it provides the network manager with the ability to establish accounting. The charging methods include:

- **Blocks Read**   This option allows the charge rate to be based on the number of 4 KB blocks that are read by a user.
- **Blocks Written**   With this selection, the charge rate is determined by the number of 4 KB blocks of data that are written to the server.
- **Connect Time**   Through this option, the user is charged per minute.

FIGURE 8.1
Available Topics Menu for SYSCON

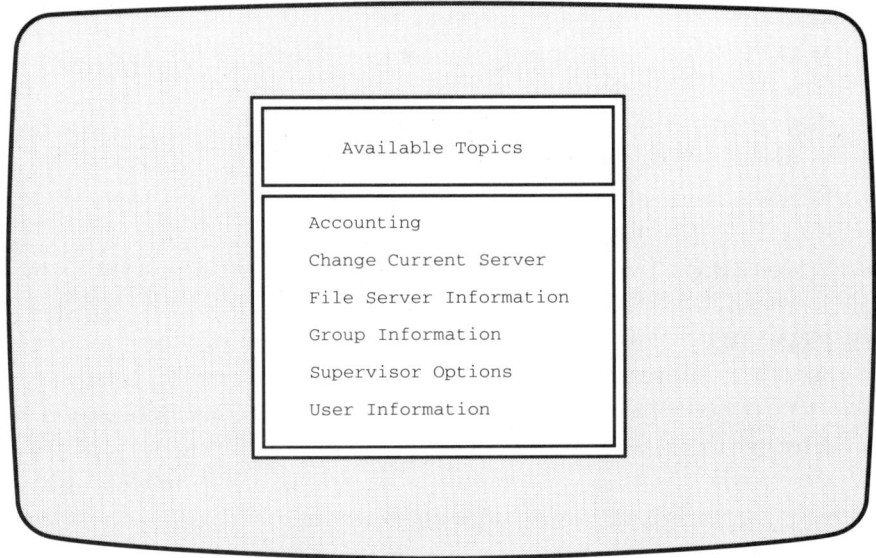

```
                    Available Topics

          Accounting

          Change Current Server

          File Server Information

          Group Information

          Supervisor Options

          User Information
```

- **Disk Storage** With this selection, the user is charged by the number of 4 KB blocks of data stored on the file server each day.
- **Service Requests** This charge rate is based on the number of server requests made.

The *Supervisor Reference* for NetWare 286 contains several formulas for assigning a dollar value to charge rates.

In addition to establishing charge rates, the network manager can create account balances for individual users. Each new user starts with a balance, such as 100. The account balance is based on charges, with each user allowed a given number of charges. For each log-in session, the number of charges used is automatically subtracted from the user's account balance.

To provide users with a grace period when their account balance is exhausted, the network manager can elect to assign credit to accounts. Credit can be based on the number of negative charges; certain users can even be given unlimited credit. Establishing such accounting services is reserved for supervisors.

Change Current Server Selection The *Change Current Server* selection on the SYSCON menu enables the user to view a list of all servers attached to the internetwork. The selection is also used to:

- Select a server as the current server
- Attach to one or more servers
- Log into the current server, but use a different user ID
- Log into another server
- Log out of one or more servers

The ability to attach to one or more servers means that a single user can access information and run programs from several servers during one log-in session. The main server is highlighted as the current server on the list. When one or more servers are highlighted to be attached, SYSCON asks for a user ID and password. Once another server is attached, it is necessary to map one or more drives of that server in order to access data and programs.

For example, SR1 might be designated as the main server. Next, the user might attach server SR2. At this point, there is no way to access information on SR2. However, SR2 may have a WordPerfect text file that the user needs to access in the directory, SYS:APP\WP51\DP. To access the directory, the user could type the following MAP (path) command:

MAP L:=SR2/SYS:APP/WP51/DP

In this example, the MAP command is used to establish a logical drive. The drive is L:. If you type this drive letter, NetWare switches to the directory SYS:APP/WP51/DP (where SYS: is the name of the volume). The command line section on the MAP command in this chapter explains more about how this command is used.

File Server Information Another option on the SYSCON menu in Figure 8.1 is *File Server Information*. Like the *Change Current Server* selection, this option displays a list of the servers connected to the internetwork. When a server on the list is highlighted and selected, SYSCON displays the following information about that server:

- The name of the file server
- The version of NetWare on the file server
- The level of the operating system on the file server
- Whether transaction tracking is enabled on the file server
- The maximum number of connections supported

- The number of connections currently in service
- The total number of disk volumes the server supports
- The network address of the server
- The node address of the server

Group Information   The fourth SYSCON menu option is titled *Group Information*. When selected, this option displays a list of all **groups** that have been created. (Groups are lists of users who are assigned the same access privileges on the file server.) Additional groups can be added to the list by pressing the INSert key and entering the name of the group. Or a group can be deleted by highlighting the group and using the DEL key.

Whenever a group is highlighted for examination, a submenu of options is displayed, such as the one in Figure 8.2. The *Full Name* selection here is used to enter an extended name for the group. For instance, if the group name is "ESTAFF," the extended name may be "Engineering Staff." Next, the *Member List* selection produces a list of

FIGURE 8.2
Available Options Submenu for GROUPS

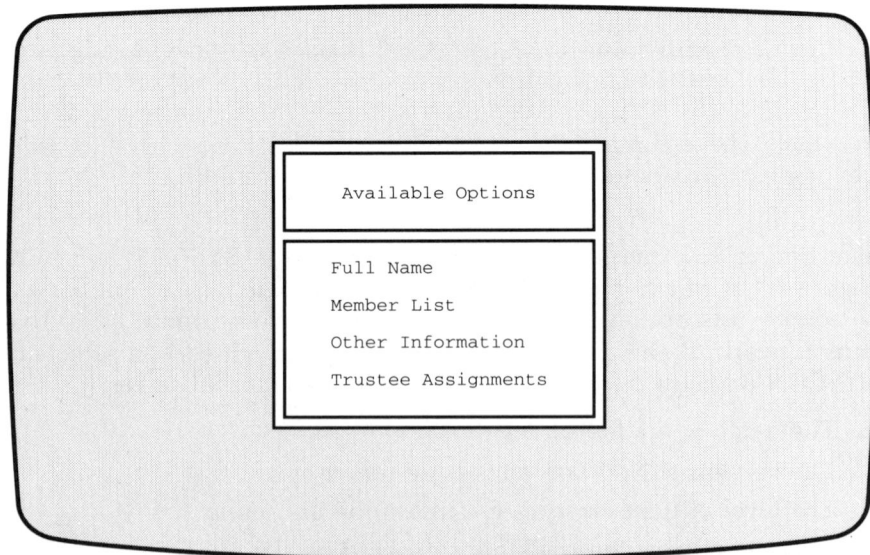

```
                 Available Options

            Full Name

            Member List

            Other Information

            Trustee Assignments
```

members who belong to the group. New members can be added here via the INSert key.

The third selection, *Other Information*, provides the ID number for the group. And the *Trustee Assignments* option displays the user rights that have been set for the directories and subdirectories the group might access. These user rights are also called **trustee rights**. Available trustee assignments are to:

- Open any files
- Read from any files that have been opened
- Write to any open files
- Create and open new files
- Delete any files
- Give parental authority (to create, rename, and delete subdirectories, as well as modify trustee and directory rights)
- Search the directory and display the file names
- Modify file attributes of any file in a directory or subdirectory

To create new trustee rights for a specific directory or subdirectory:

1. Select the *Trustee Assignments* option
2. Press the INSert key
3. Enter the desired path for the directory or subdirectory

Supervisor Options The fifth option on the SYSCON menu in Figure 8.1 is *Supervisor Options*. It produces another menu, illustrated in Figure 8.3.

On this menu, the *Default Account Balance/Restrictions* option enables the network manager to establish restrictions on all new accounts that will be created. The restrictions that may be established are based on decisions including whether:

- The account is disabled
- There is an expiration date for the account, at which time the account will be disabled
- A user can establish more than one connection
- The user can change his or her password
- A password is required for a user to log onto an account
- Periodic password changes are required
- Unique passwords are required
- The user's available disk space is limited

FIGURE 8.3
Supervisor Options Menu

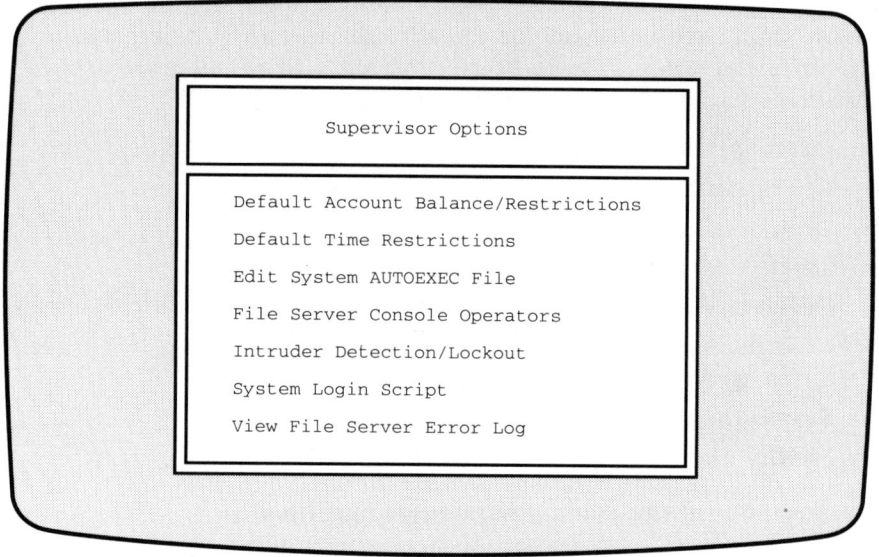

```
                    Supervisor Options

         Default Account Balance/Restrictions

         Default Time Restrictions

         Edit System AUTOEXEC File

         File Server Console Operators

         Intruder Detection/Lockout

         System Login Script

         View File Server Error Log
```

Normally, the default will not specify that accounts should be disabled, since most or all new accounts will be used immediately. A date can be set for which time-specified accounts are to be disabled (and are therefore no longer available for active use).

In most instances, only one person per user ID will be allowed to access the network at any one time. (The situation where there are multiple users is called concurrent connections.) Many versions of commercial software will not work properly when there are two or more concurrent connections using the same account. Users should be given the option to change their passwords, as a security precaution. It is also good management to require users to change their passwords periodically. The restrictions menu provides the ability to specify the required time between password changes. It also allows a given number of grace log-ins before the account becomes inaccessible to the user if the password is not changed.

Finally, it is a good precaution to limit each user's available disk space. This protects against the number of unused (residual) temporary files from menus and programs becoming inordinately large.

The *Default Time Restrictions* option permits the network manager to specify times of the day and days of the week when the file server is unavailable to users. This is done for security and maintenance. For example, the network manager might establish four hours a week for maintenance, during which time users are not allowed on the system. Or security needs might necessitate making the server available only during work hours.

The *Edit System AUTOEXEC File* option enables the network manager to create an AUTOEXEC.SYS file, which is stored in the SYS:SYSTEM directory. The function of this file is to feed commands to the file server console when it is booted up. Commands that might routinely be entered when booting the server include the (P) command to add print queues to a printer, and the (S) command to establish spool mappings.

The supervisor option, *File Server Console Operators*, is used to authorize specific users as console operators. Console commands, which enable operations management of the server, are available in the FCONSOLE menu. Only authorized users have access to FCONSOLE (see the FCONSOLE section in this chapter).

Intruder Detection/Lockout is an option that allows the network manager to enable detection of possible intruders, or individuals who attempt to log onto an account unsuccessfully. If intruder detection is enabled, the system can be told to track intruder information, after a specified number of unsuccessful log-in attempts, to an account. The system can also be told to lock the account upon detection of an intruder. This prevents anyone from logging into that account.

System Login Script is used to create a system login script that's run for all users when they first log in. The system login script establishes user controls for search and network drive mappings, break key authorization, establishment of home directories, and so on. Chapter 12 explains system login scripts and provides an example of a system login script.

The last selection on the supervisor's menu is *View File Server Error Log*. When operation errors are detected by the file server, they are recorded in an error log. The contents of the log can be viewed by selecting this option from the menu. Once the error log has been examined, the network manager has the option to delete the log.

User Information The last SYSCON option on the menu in Figure 8.1 is *User Information*. When this option is selected, a list of existing users is displayed. From here, new users can be added to the list via the INSert key, or information about existing users can be displayed and modified. The information available on individual users is presented in the menu in Figure 8.4.

FIGURE 8.4
User Information Submenu

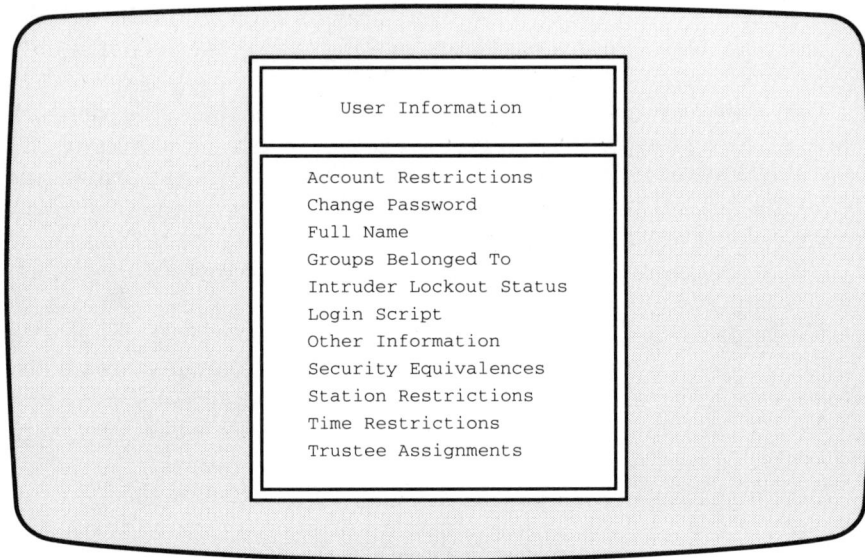

```
                    User Information

          Account Restrictions
          Change Password
          Full Name
          Groups Belonged To
          Intruder Lockout Status
          Login Script
          Other Information
          Security Equivalences
          Station Restrictions
          Time Restrictions
          Trustee Assignments
```

The first option in the "User Information" menu enables account restrictions to be set. The same account restrictions appear here as appear from the *Default Account Balance/Restrictions* option on the Supervisor Options menu in Figure 8.3. These options determine whether:

- The account is disabled
- There is an expiration date for the account, at which time the account will be disabled
- Concurrent connections will be allowed a single user (if so, how many)
- The user can change his or her password
- A password is required in order to log onto an account
- Password changes are to be forced
- Unique passwords are required
- The user's available disk space is limited

(The only difference between the options displayed in the account restrictions and those in the "Supervisor Options" menu is that the "Supervisor Options" menu sets defaults for creating new users.)

The *Change Password* option on the "User Information" menu in Figure 8.4 is used to establish or change a password. When this option is selected, the system asks that the password be entered twice for verification.

Next, the *Full Name* option enables the network manager to associate a full name with the user name. If the user name is PJONES, then the full name might be entered as Paul Jones. Guidelines for creating user names are discussed in Chapter 12.

The *Groups Belonged To* option enables the network manager to view the user's membership groups. The user can also be added to a new group via the INSert key.

Intruder Lockout Status permits the network manager to view whether an unauthorized user has attempted to log into a specific user account. Selection of this option displays:

- Whether the account has been locked because of unsuccessful log-in attempts
- The number of unsuccessful log-in attempts
- When the account was last reset
- The network address of the workstation where the last unsuccessful log-in was attempted

The sixth option, *Login Script,* creates a login script for an individual. This script is run just after the system login script, and establishes a log-in sequence for a user. Chapter 12 contains more information about user login scripts, including guidelines for their creation and a sample login script.

Next *Other Information* displays such information as the last log-in date, whether the user is a console operator, the maximum disk usage permitted, the amount of disk space currently used, and the user ID.

The *Security Equivalences* option displays the group or individual security equivalences of a given user. For example, normally the network manager will have an individual account, in addition to access to the supervisor account. The network manager's individual account should have supervisor equivalence, so there is someone else who has these privileges in addition to the supervisor. Security equivalence privileges can be added by pressing the INSert key to display the available groups and users. Privileges can be removed by highlighting the one to be removed and by pressing the DEL key.

The ninth option, *Station Restrictions,* makes it possible to restrict which physical workstations can log on using a particular account. Through this option important information can be restricted to access by office or room location. The system uses log-in addresses assigned to workstations in order to restrict log-ins. Likewise, access to the server can be restricted by time of day or day of the week via the *Time Restrictions* option.

The last option on the "User Information" menu is *Trustee Assignments*. Trustee assignments, which can be made here, are the same as those that can be made at the group level. The difference is that the trustee rights will apply only to the specified individual, not to an entire group. The trustee rights list enables you to:

- Open any files
- Read from any files that have been opened
- Write to any open files
- Create and open new files
- Delete any files
- Give parental authority to create, rename, and delete subdirectories, as well as modify trustee and directory rights
- Search the directory and display the file names
- Modify file attributes of any file in a directory or subdirectory

Remember that trustee rights are assigned to directories and subdirectories. If trustee rights are set for a directory, they will apply to all subdirectories under that directory, unless they are changed for a specific subdirectory.

8.2 FCONSOLE

The FCONSOLE menu is used to manage daily operations activities on the file server. These include monitoring server statistics, connections information, and locks on files. System messaging and the ability to shut down the file server are also available from FCONSOLE.

The FCONSOLE menu is displayed by entering FCONSOLE from the command level of the workstation. Only users who have been authorized to access FCONSOLE via the SYSCON menu can display the FCONSOLE menu. The FCONSOLE menu is illustrated in Figure 8.5.

A message can be sent to all system users through *Broadcast Console Message*. The message, for example, could warn users that the system will soon go down for maintenance activity.

The *Change Current File Server* option enables the operator to log onto another file server. When this option is selected, a list of available file servers on the internetwork is displayed. The server the operator wishes to access is then highlighted, and the log-on user name is provided by the operator.

FIGURE 8.5
Available Options Menu for FCONSOLE

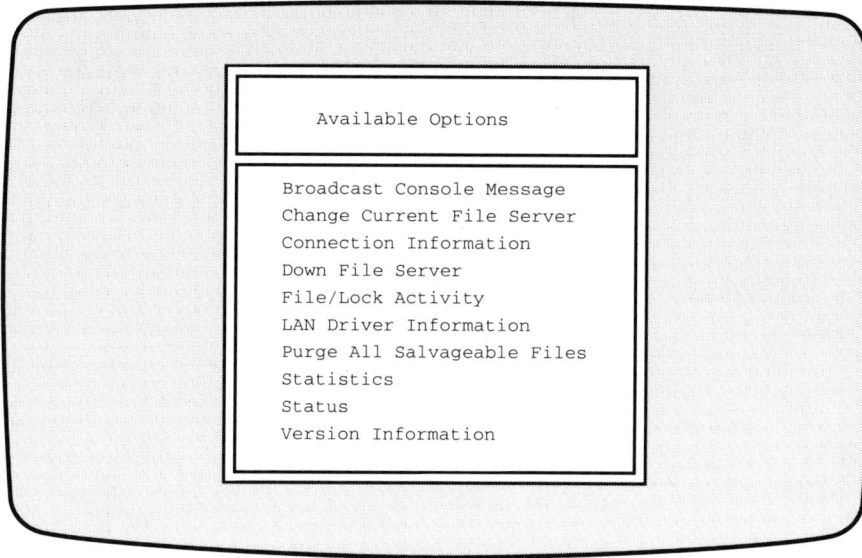

```
                    Available Options

            Broadcast Console Message
            Change Current File Server
            Connection Information
            Down File Server
            File/Lock Activity
            LAN Driver Information
            Purge All Salvageable Files
            Statistics
            Status
            Version Information
```

The *Connection Information* option provides a list of all users currently logged on to the file server and their connection number. If one or more of the logged-on users is highlighted, a second menu appears displaying further options to view connection information. These options include:

- The ability to broadcast a message to the user or users who have been highlighted
- The option to clear connections
- The logical record locks of users
- The open files and open physical records of users
- General information about a user's connection
- Semaphores
- Task information
- Usage statistics

The *option to broadcast a message* enables the operator to send a message to a specific user or to several users. Likewise, the *option to clear a connection* can be exercised for one or more users. The users affected are those marked or highlighted before the "Connection Information" menu is entered.

If a user is in a program that accesses a data file, then the *logical record lock* information will display any records currently locked in the data file. The system will display any files currently in use by a connection. These are shown under the *option to view open files and open physical records.*

The *general information* available about a connection includes the user name, the connection number, the full name of the user (if any), the log-in time and date, and the network address of the user.

Semaphores limit the number of tasks that can use a resource at the same time. Or they limit the number of workstations that can access a program at the same time. When this option is selected, it shows the resource and program availability, as well as the number of connections waiting to use a resource or program.

The *task information* selection shows the number of active tasks for a connection. It also shows when a connection is awaiting a physical record lock, a logical record lock, a file lock, or a semaphore. When a specific task is highlighted for display, the system shows information about the status of in-progress locks and transactions.

Finally, the *usage statistics* report:

- Amount of connection time elapsed since log-on
- Number of requests issued to the file server since the connection was established
- Total number of disk reads in bytes since the user logged in
- Total number of bytes written to disk since the user logged in

The *Down File Server* option on the FCONSOLE menu in Figure 8.5 is used to down the file server. The system automatically warns the operator if files are still open when this selection is made. There is an option to retract the request if files are still open.

File/Lock Activity provides information about locks and semaphores. When this option is selected, a second menu appears, which contains options to view current transactions, file/physical records information, logical lock information, and semaphore information. The option to view current transactions shows the transactions affected by transaction tracking. Similarly, the option to view file/physical records information shows which files are in use and their file status.

The logical record lock information shows which records are locked, and the number of connections using the record. The option to view semaphore information displays the number of connections using a semaphore and the number waiting to use the resource or program represented by the semaphore. It is necessary to know the semaphore name in order to view information pertaining to specific semaphores.

The sixth option on the FCONSOLE menu in Figure 8.5 is *LAN Driver Information*. This option displays the LAN address for each NIC in the file server. It also shows the board type, the configuration, the IRQ, the I/O, the DMA, and the memory addressing of the board.

Next on the list of FCONSOLE options is *Purge All Salvageable Files*. When files are deleted from the file server, they can still be recovered; they still occupy disk space. The disk space is released only when the files are purged. Once files are purged, they can no longer be recovered. The option to purge files should be executed on a regular basis, such as once a week or once a month, depending on the demand for available disk space.

The *Statistics* option is used to display a broad range of server statistics, including statistics that gauge server performance. When this option is selected, a second menu is displayed, showing categories of available statistics. The categories include:

- Cache statistics
- Channel statistics
- Disk-mapping information
- Disk Statistics
- File system statistics
- LAN I/O statistics
- Summary statistics
- Transaction-tracking statistics
- Volume information

The *Supervisor Reference* manual, which accompanies NetWare, contains a valuable section that describes the statistics available. We recommend monitoring these statistics, because they provide critical information about the need for more memory in the file server, disk performance, communications performance, and overall use of the file server.

The ninth option on the FCONSOLE menu is *Status*. This option supplies information on:

- The server date and time
- Whether users can log into the server
- Whether transaction tracking is enabled (for SFT NetWare)

The last option is *Version Information*. This is the version of Net-Ware installed on the file server, as well as the copyright date.

8.3 MAKEUSER

The network manager can create a large number of new users on the file server by initiating the MAKEUSER menu. This menu enables the network manager to create customized .USR files needed to establish users in a batch mode.

The MAKEUSER menu is started by entering MAKEUSER at the command level. This menu is reserved for use by the system supervisor and individuals who have supervisor privileges. A reproduction of the menu is presented in Figure 8.6.

The *Create New USR File* option on the menu is used to start a new .USR file. The *Edit USR File* selection is available for the purpose of editing an existing .USR file. The *Process USR File* option executes the commands in a .USR file to generate new-user information.

When the *Create New USR File* option is selected, MAKEUSER displays a blank editing screen. MAKEUSER commands are entered on the screen and saved in ASCII format. Normally, a .USR file is

FIGURE 8.6
Available Options Submenu for MAKEUSER

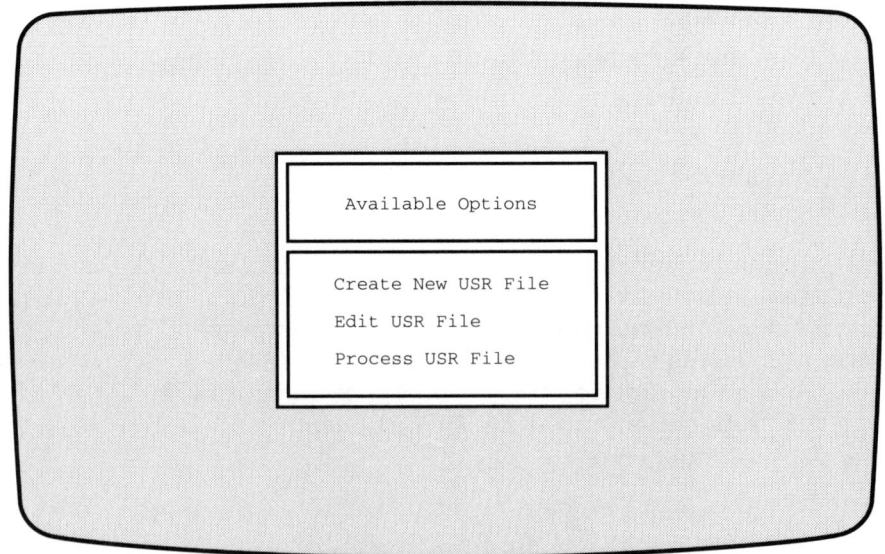

```
            Available Options

            Create New USR File
            Edit USR File
            Process USR File
```

stored in an appropriate user subdirectory. For example, if there is a
SYS:USER directory for all users and a SYS:USER\STAFF subdirectory, then the .USR file created to generate staff users will be stored in
the SYS:USER\STAFF subdirectory. This subdirectory will also contain home directory entries for each user. For instance, if one of the
user names is PJONES, then there will be a SYS:USER\STAFF\PJONES
subdirectory that will serve as the home directory for user PJONES.
Chapter 12 contains more information about establishing home directories.

If the *Edit USR File* selection is taken, MAKEUSER displays a box
for the path and file name of the .USR file to be edited. Editing is
performed in a full-screen edit mode.

Once a .USR is ready to be run, the *Process USR File* selection is
made. A .USR file is then specified and MAKEUSER proceeds to generate the specified users. Figure 8.7 contains a sample MAKEUSER file.

The MAKEUSER command selection includes options to specify
account restriction information, to create groups, and to create individual users. Each command is prefaced by a pound sign (#) in the
.USR file. The following is a summary of the MAKEUSER commands:

FIGURE 8.7
Example MAKEUSER File Listing

```
                    Example MAKEUSER File


        #REM ** ESTABLISH RESTRICTIONS **
        #PASSWORD_REQUIRED
        #PASSWORD_LENGTH 7
        #PASSWORD_PERIOD 30
        #MAX_DISK_SPACE 500
        #GROUP STAFF

        #REM ** LOGIN SCRIPT
        #LOGIN_SCRIPT SYS:USERS/STAFF/STAFF.LOG

        #REM ** HOME DIRECTORY **
        #HOME DIRECTORY SYS:USERS/STAFF

        #REM ** CREATE USERS
        #CREATE PJONES;PAUL JONES;PASS1;;SYS:USERS/STAFF/PJONES
        #CREATE RANDERS;RON ANDERS;PASS2;;SYS:USERS/STAFF/RANDERS
        #CREATE LSMIT;LANCE SMIT;PASS3;;SYS:USERS/STAFF/LSMIT
        #CREATE TJONES;TOME JONES;PASS4;;SYS:USERS/STAFF/TJONES
        #CREATE LTHOMAS;LIN THOMAS;PASS5;;SYS:USERS/STAFF/LTHOMAS
```

- **ACCOUNT_EXPIRATION**   Specifies date when the account is to be disabled.
- **ACCOUNTING**   Establishes the account balance and credit limit.
- **CLEAR** or **RESET**   Clears keyword instructions that have been specified before the CLEAR or RESET instruction.
- **CONNECTIONS**   Establishes the maximum number of simultaneous connections for an account.
- **CREATE**   Creates specified accounts including the user name, full name, password, group membership, and trustee rights.
- **DELETE**   Deletes one or more existing accounts.
- **GROUPS**   Assigns designated users to a group.
- **HOME_DIRECTORY**   Creates the user's home directory.
- **LOGIN_SCRIPT**   Specifies what script file (.LOG) is to be used as the user login script for one or more users.
- **MAX_DISK_SPACE**   Establishes the maximum disk space to be available for one or more users.
- **PASSWORD_LENGTH**   Sets the minimum length for a user password.
- **PASSWORD_PERIOD**   Specifies how often (in days) the password must be changed.
- **PASSWORD_REQUIRED**   Specifies that one or more users must have a password on their account.
- **PURGE_USER_DIRECTORY**   Deletes the user's home directory.
- **REM**   Prefaces a comment line to provide information about the contents of the .USR file.
- **RESTRICTED_TIME**   Sets the times and days specified users cannot access the file server.
- **STATIONS**   Restricts the physical workstations from which a user account can be accessed.
- **UNIQUE_PASSWORD**   Specifies the user cannot reuse old passwords when changing the current password.

8.4 SESSION

The SESSION utility enables a user to connect to another file server, to display and modify drive mappings, to send messages to other users, and to view a list of users connected to the file server. SESSION is started by entering SESSION while you are in the command mode on a server. An example of the SESSION menu is shown in Figure 8.8.

FIGURE 8.8
Available Topics Menu for SESSION

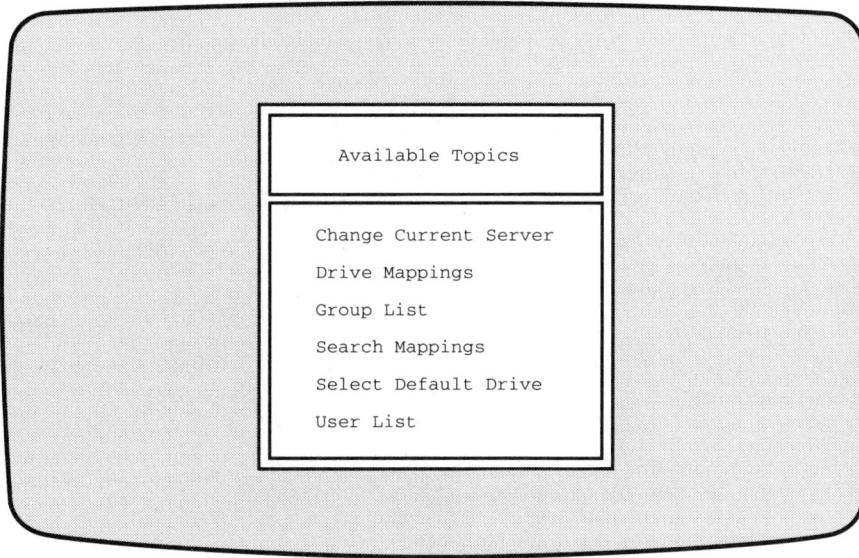

```
                    Available Topics

              Change Current Server

              Drive Mappings

              Group List

              Search Mappings

              Select Default Drive

              User List
```

The option *Change Current Server* is used to connect an additional server or to log out of one or more servers. Once the selection is made, a list of available servers on the internetwork appears. Any of these servers can be highlighted to connect it. Similarly, if a logged-on server is highlighted, it can be logged out by using the DEL key. A drive must be mapped to any connected servers to access data from those servers.

Next, the *Drive Mappings* option is used to display existing drive mappings, including network and local drive mappings. A new drive mapping can be created by pressing the INSert key and entering the new mappings; or an existing drive mapping can be deleted by highlighting the mapping and pressing the DEL key. If one of the existing network drive mappings is highlighted, and the ENTER key is pressed, then information about the user's effective rights in that directory is displayed.

The third option, *Group List*, displays a list of existing groups. A message can be broadcast to all users in one or more of these groups by highlighting the desired groups and pressing the ENTER key.

A box appears into which a message can be entered. The message is limited to forty characters.

The next option on the SESSION menu is *Search Mappings*. When this selection is made, a list of all existing search drive mappings is displayed. The list shows the search drive number, the drive letter, and the path. From this menu, search drives can be added, modified, or deleted in the same way as network drive mappings. Furthermore, the rights information associated with a search drive can be displayed by highlighting a search drive and pressing ENTER.

Fifth on the SESSION menu is the option *Select Default Drive*. This option displays the complete list of drives and allows the user to switch to any of the drives displayed. To mark it for selection, highlight the new default drive and press the ENTER key.

The last option in the SESSION menu is *User List*. This option displays a list of users currently connected to the file server. One or more users can be highlighted for receipt of the message from the SESSION user. Once the ENTER key is pressed, a box appears into which the message can be entered. As with messages sent to members of a group, the length is limited to forty characters.

8.5 FILER

The FILER utility enables the network manager to view and modify information about volumes, directories, subdirectories, and files. FILER allows files to be copied, renamed, or deleted. The same applies for subdirectories. In addition, FILER facilitates modification of file attributes and directory rights.

To start FILER, enter the name FILER from the command level. An illustration of the FILER menu is presented in Figure 8.9.

When the *Current Directory Information* option is selected, FILER makes available data on the directory from which it was initially invoked, or the directory to which it is currently pointing. The *Select Current Directory* option is used to change the directory to which FILER is pointing. Once the *Current Directory Information* selection is made, FILER displays another menu with the following options:

- Creation date
- Current effective rights
- Maximum rights mask
- Owner
- Trustees

FIGURE 8.9
Available Topics Menu for FILER

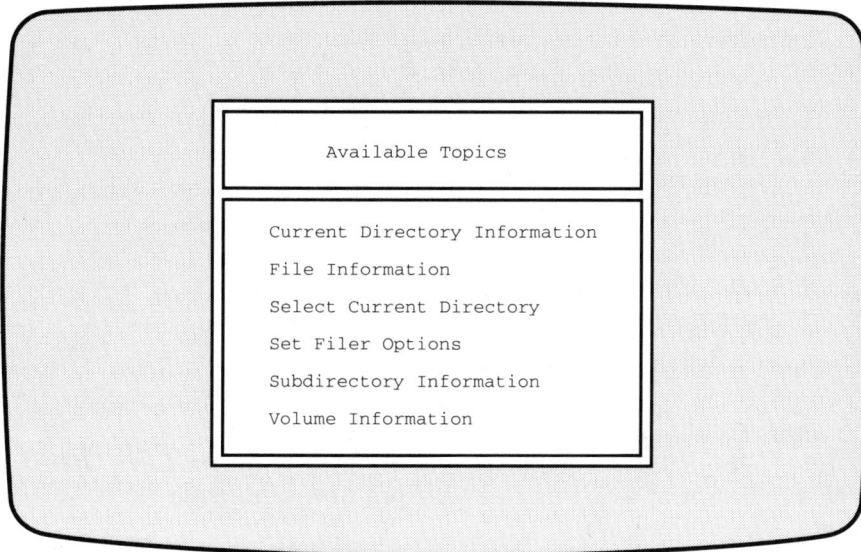

```
                    Available Topics


       Current Directory Information

       File Information

       Select Current Directory

       Set Filer Options

       Subdirectory Information

       Volume Information
```

The *Creation Date* option displays the date the directory was first established. Next, the *Current Effective Rights* option shows the user's trustee rights to the directory. The *Maximum Rights Mask* displays the maximum rights anyone can have in accessing the directory. Users who have parental rights to a directory can add or delete maximum rights from that directory. (Parental rights enable the user to create, rename, and delete subdirectories, and to modify trustee and directory rights.)

The *Owner* option under *Current Directory Information* enables the user to view the owners of the directory. The owner is who created the directory, such as the supervisor. Finally, the *Trustees* option lists all users and groups who have trustee rights in the directory. If the FILER user has parental rights to the same directory, he or she can add or delete trustees.

The second option on the FILER menu in Figure 8.9 is *File Information*. This option displays a list of all files contained in the directory or subdirectory to which FILER is pointing. If a file is highlighted and the ENTER key pressed, a submenu containing options to display file information is produced. This menu permits the user to view or execute the following:

- The file attributes
- The option to copy the file
- The creation date of the file
- The date when the file was last accessed
- The last archive date of the file
- The date the file was last modified
- The owner of the file
- The size of the file
- The contents of the file

Third on the list of selections on the FILER menu is *Select Current Directory*. This option is used to switch to another directory or subdirectory from which the FILER options can be executed.

Next, the FILER menu contains the selection, *Set Filer Options*. The FILER options that can be set from here are displayed on a submenu. The options are:

- **Confirming deletions**   A default parameter can be set so each time a file is deleted, the system asks for confirmation of the deletion before deleting the file.

- **Confirming file overwrites**   Whenever a file is copied over a file with the same name, this default can be set to verify whether the user wants to overwrite the file.

- **Directories exclude pattern**   This can be established so subdirectories matching a specified pattern are not displayed on a listing of subdirectories. For example, all subdirectories that begin with the letter *F* can be excluded from the listing of subdirectories. The pattern specified in this case will be F*.

- **Directories include pattern**   This option enables the user to include only specific patterns for a subdirectory display. For instance, the include pattern might be specified to display *only* subdirectories that begin with the letter *F*. The pattern specified here will also be F*.

- **File exclude pattern**   Just as the exclude option can be used for directories, it can also be used for files. Files that fit a given pattern can be excluded from a listing of files.

- **File include pattern**   Only files that match a specified include pattern can be displayed on a file listing by using this default setting.

File search attributes With this option, search file attributes can be set so system files and hidden files are displayed on a listing of files.

The fifth selection on the FILER menu in Figure 8.9 is *Subdirectory Information*. When this option is selected, a listing of subdirectories in the current directory is displayed. From here, new subdirectories can be created by using the INSert key. One or more subdirectories can be deleted by highlighting an individual subdirectory or by specifying a subdirectory pattern to delete, such as all subdirectories that begin with the letter R (in which case the pattern R* will be specified). Note that whenever one or more subdirectories are deleted, the system will ask: "Delete Entire Subdirectory Structure" or "Delete Subdirectories Only." This option on the FILER menu is also used to rename one or more subdirectories.

Trustee rights and the maximum rights mask are also modified using the *Subdirectory Information* option. And the ownership of a subdirectory can be displayed.

The final selection on the FILER menu is *Volume Information*. This option displays the name of the server, the name of the volume, the type of volume (such as fixed disk), the total number of bytes in storage, and the total number of bytes used. It also shows the total number of allowed directory entries and the number of directory entries that have not yet been used.

8.6 PCONSOLE

The PCONSOLE utility supplies information about, and access to, **print queue** and **print server** information. A print queue is a way to manage printing tasks. The queue directs printouts to certain printers, and establishes a priority list to determine which print jobs are printed first. A print server is software that enables users to share printers connected to a network.

Through PCONSOLE, users can add or delete print queues. Users can also monitor print jobs, delete print jobs, and specify which users have access to given queues.

The utility is entered by executing PCONSOLE from the command line in NetWare. Once PCONSOLE is executed, the menu in Figure 8.10 appears.

The first option on the menu, *Change Current File Server*, enables the user to attach other file servers. By using this option, it is possible to print files from more than one file server. Before a file server can be attached, a valid user name and password must be specified.

FIGURE 8.10
Available Options Submenu for PCONSOLE

```
                    Available Options

         Change Current File Server
         Print Queue Information
         Print Server Information
```

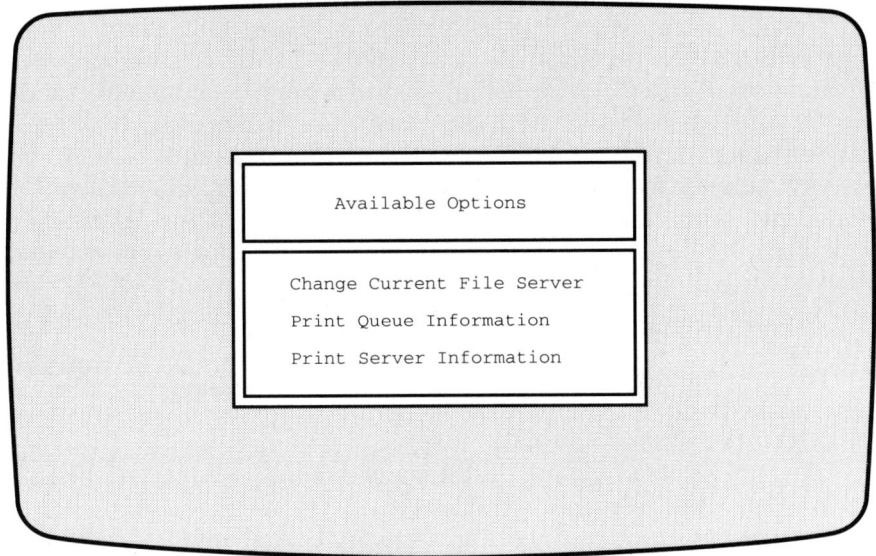

Besides attaching file servers, this first option also provides the ability to log out of one or more file servers or to log into a different account on the same file server.

The second option on the PCONSOLE menu is listed as *Print Queue Information*. When selected, this option displays the print queues on the current server. From here, a new print queue can be created by pressing the INSert key. A print queue can be deleted as well.

Additional information about a print queue is available by taking the *Print Queue Information* option and highlighting a specific queue name. When this is done, a Print Queue Information menu appears listing several options, which include:

- **Current print job entries** This option lists all current print jobs waiting in the queue. When the option is selected, the PCONSOLE operator can place print jobs on hold, change the priority of printing, or delete print jobs.

- **Current queue status** This displays the number of entries in the specified queue, and the number of servers attached to the queue.

- **Currently attached servers** This option displays the list of file servers attached to the print queue.

- **Print queue ID** Every print queue is associated with an object ID number, which this option displays.

- **Queue operators** Besides the supervisor, a user must be authorized as a queue operator to access PCONSOLE and manipulate entries in the queue. This option is used to authorize given users as operators.

- **Queue servers** This option specifies other servers who can access the print queue.

- **Queue users** Besides the supervisor, only users who have been authorized can send a print job to a specific queue. This option enables the PCONSOLE operator to authorize users to use the print queue.

The last option on the menu in Figure 8.10 is *Print Server Information*. Several third-party software companies have written print server utilities for NetWare. Utilities like these enable one or more remote workstations to act as print servers. Printouts can be routed to printers attached to these workstations, as well as to network printers attached to the file server. In this way, it is not necessary to obtain all printouts from the room containing the file server. Specialized printing applications can be localized at a given workstation. As an aid to print server utilities, Novell has created the *Print Server Information* option. When a print server utility is purchased, it can be integrated with this option. It's necessary to consult the print-server vendor's documentation to establish a print server utility on the network.

8.7 PRINTDEF

PRINTDEF is used to define and associate specific characteristics with a print device. For example, printer pitch, tabbing characteristics, landscape printing, and specific fonts can be set up for use with a certain printer. Once print characteristics are established for a printer, they can be associated with a print job configuration definition through the PRINTCON utility.

To start PRINTDEF, enter the PRINTDEF command at the file server command level prompt. The menu in Figure 8.11 is displayed.

The first option in the menu, *Print Devices*, produces a second menu that supplies three options. The second menu is illustrated in Figure 8.12.

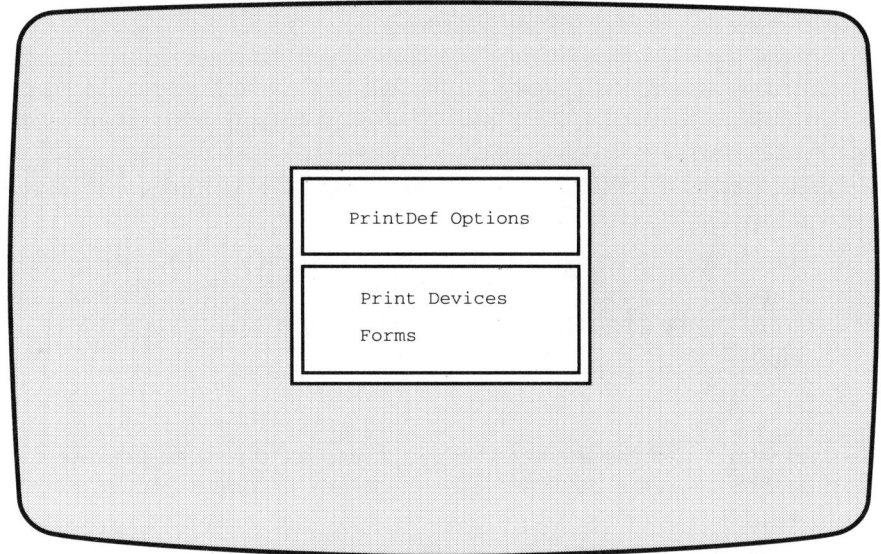

```
                    PrintDef Options

                    Print Devices
                    Forms
```

Before any print device options are available, they must be imported into PRINTDEF or created from scratch through the *Edit Print
Devices* selection. The *Import Print Device* option is used to import
existing print device files. The print device files are supplied with
some versions of the operating system on one of the PUBLIC diskettes.
They normally are loaded into the SYS:PUBLIC directory and have
the extension ".PDF," for "printer device file."

Before importing a printer device file into PRINTDEF, list the .PDF
files in the PUBLIC directory and determine which files to import.
Next, enter PRINTDEF and take the *Import Print Devices* option from
the Print Devices submenu. A box will appear into which the name of
one of the selected print device files can be entered. The path to the
PUBLIC directory must be entered, as well as the name of the print
device file. The *Import Print Device* option must be used for each
printer device file to be incorporated into PRINTDEF.

Once a print device file has been imported, it can be edited using
the *Edit Print Devices* option. When this option is selected, a list of
the imported print devices is displayed. Any of these devices can be
highlighted for editing. When one is highlighted to be edited, a sub-

FIGURE 8.12
Print Device Options Submenu

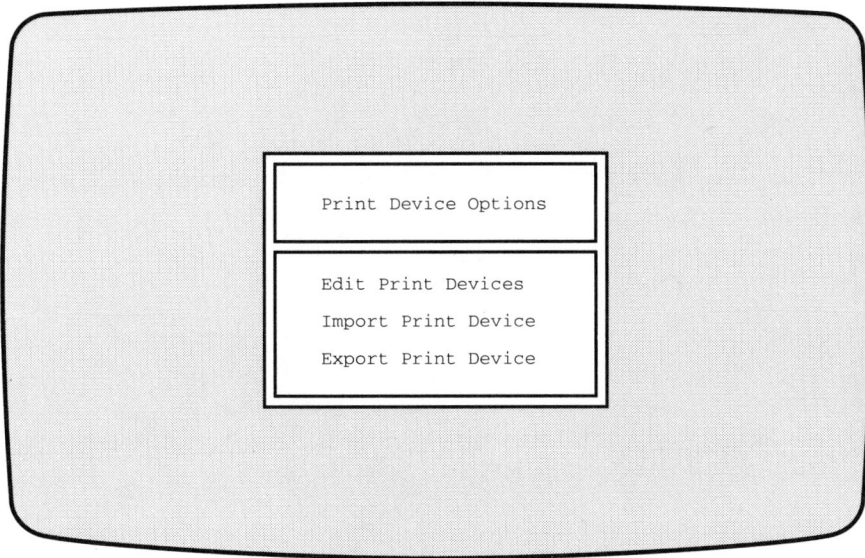

```
┌─────────────────────────────────────┐
│                                     │
│     ┌─────────────────────────┐     │
│     │  Print Device Options   │     │
│     │                         │     │
│     ├─────────────────────────┤     │
│     │  Edit Print Devices     │     │
│     │  Import Print Device    │     │
│     │  Export Print Device    │     │
│     └─────────────────────────┘     │
│                                     │
└─────────────────────────────────────┘
```

menu appears offering two selections: *Device Modes* and *Device Functions*. This submenu is reproduced in Figure 8.13.

If *Device Functions* is selected from the menu, a list of the printer functions appears along with the printer control codes used to elicit each function. Information about printer control codes is contained in the individual printer manuals. Consult the manual for your printer or printers before editing any printer control codes. Also note that if there is no predefined printer device file for a particular printer, a new file can be created by specifying a device name on the Defined Print Devices list, which appears when the *Edit Print Devices* selection is made from the menu in Figure 8.12. Then select the *Device Functions* option on the menu in Figure 8.13 to add the desired printer functions and their corresponding control codes.

The *Device Modes* selection on the "Edit Device Options" menu in Figure 8.13 is used to establish specific print modes, such as condensed printing, landscape (sideways) printing, letter quality printing, and so on. The predefined print device files imported into PRINTDEF come with a set of preestablished device modes. When *Device Modes* is viewed for one of these print files, a list of modes is displayed. This

FIGURE 8.13
Edit Device Options Submenu

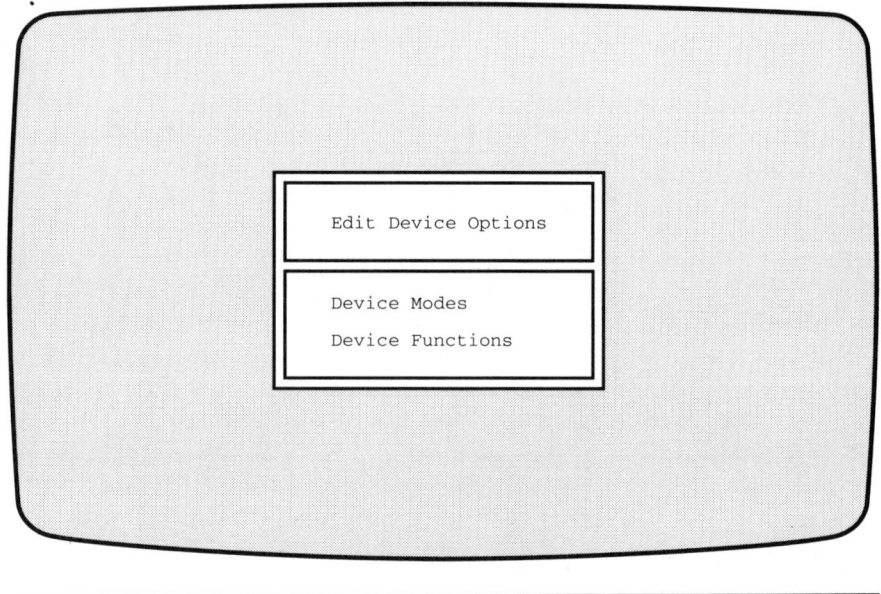

```
Edit Device Options

Device Modes
Device Functions
```

list is also made available to the PRINTCON utility to specify a device and mode in a print job configuration. Each device mode is a set of one or more printer control codes that accomplish a given function. For example, a mode to perform landscape printing will have the given printer's landscape control code built into the mode.

The last option on the menu in Figure 8.12 is *Export Print Devices*. This option is used to export a device definition to another directory or to another file server. This is a useful option for those who wish to use a printer on another file server, and to make the appropriate device definitions available for that printer. Normally, the device definition is exported to the SYS:PUBLIC directory on the other file server. The export procedure requires having supervisor privileges on both file servers.

This last item on the "PrintDef Options" menu in Figure 8.11 is titled *Forms*. This option permits the user to create form specifications for use with the PRINTCON utility. When this option is selected, the system asks for the name of the form, such as "Checks" or "Grades." A number is then assigned by the user to the form to distinguish it from other forms. Forms can be numbered from 0 to 255. Next, the length of the form in terms of lines per page is specified. Forms have a maximum of 255 lines. Finally, the width of the form is specified in characters. The maximum width is 999 characters wide.

8.8 PRINTCON

PRINTCON is a utility menu that enables the user to establish print job configuration information. Print job information can be associated with specific print queues and printer numbers. The print job information that can be specified includes the number of copies to be printed, tabulation information, timeout count, and the decision to print a banner.

PRINTCON is begun by entering PRINTCON at the command level prompt in NetWare. At the start, PRINTCON displays the menu shown in Figure 8.14.

The first option in the PRINTCON menu, *Edit Print Job Configurations*, is used to edit existing print job configurations and to create new ones. Since print job configurations are not automatically created by NetWare at the time the system is generated, the network manager must create the first configurations. It is not mandatory a print job

FIGURE 8.14
Available Options Menu for PRINTCON

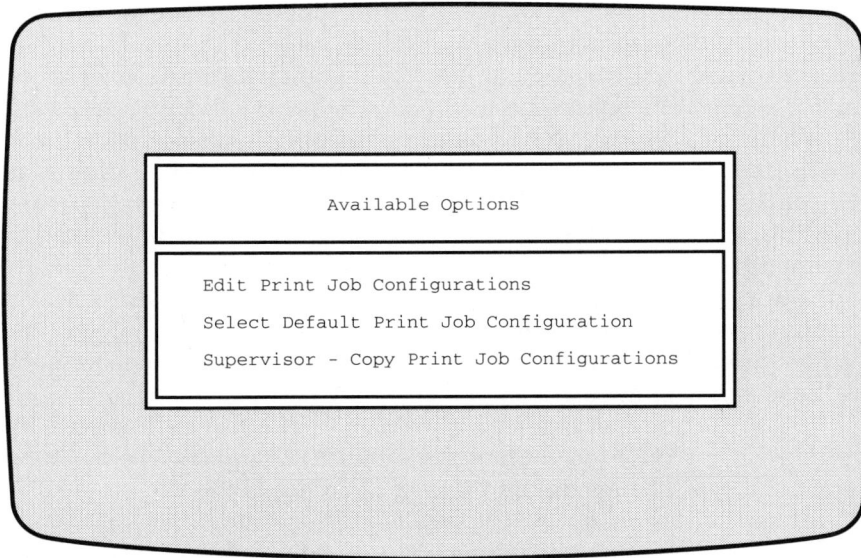

```
                        Available Options

    Edit Print Job Configurations

    Select Default Print Job Configuration

    Supervisor - Copy Print Job Configurations
```

FIGURE 8.15
Edit Print Job Configuration Submenu

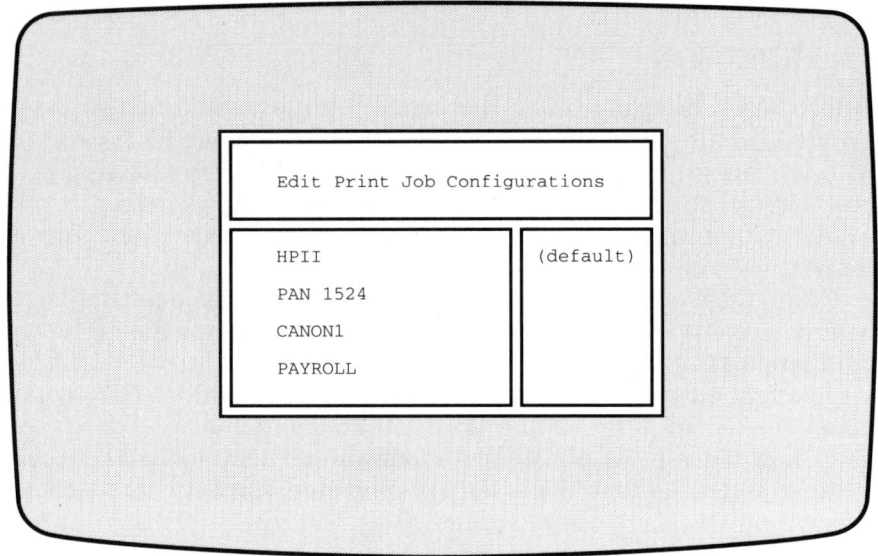

```
Edit Print Job Configurations

HPII                          (default)

PAN 1524

CANON1

PAYROLL
```

configuration be created for each printer and each queue. Creating print job configurations is simply a tool available to enable the network manager and the user to have more precise control over printouts. Figure 8.15 illustrates a list of sample print job configurations.

When the *Edit Print Job Configurations* option is selected, a list of existing configuration names is displayed, as in Figure 8.15. Any print job configuration can be edited by highlighting the configuration, then pressing the ENTER key. Similarly, configurations can be deleted or renamed by using the DEL or F3 keys.

New configurations are created by pressing the INSert key and specifying a name for the new configuration. Once the configuration name is specified, an Edit Print Job Configuration menu appears, such as the example shown in Figure 8.16.

The first option shown in Figure 8.16 is *Number of Copies*. This option enables the user to enter the number of copies to be made for each print job. The maximum number of copies is 65,000.

Second on the menu is *Suppress Form Feed*. Whether this parameter is set to "Yes" or "No" depends on whether the form feed is set by the individual application or the printer. Some applications auto-

FIGURE 8.16
Edit Print Job Configuration "HPII" Submenu

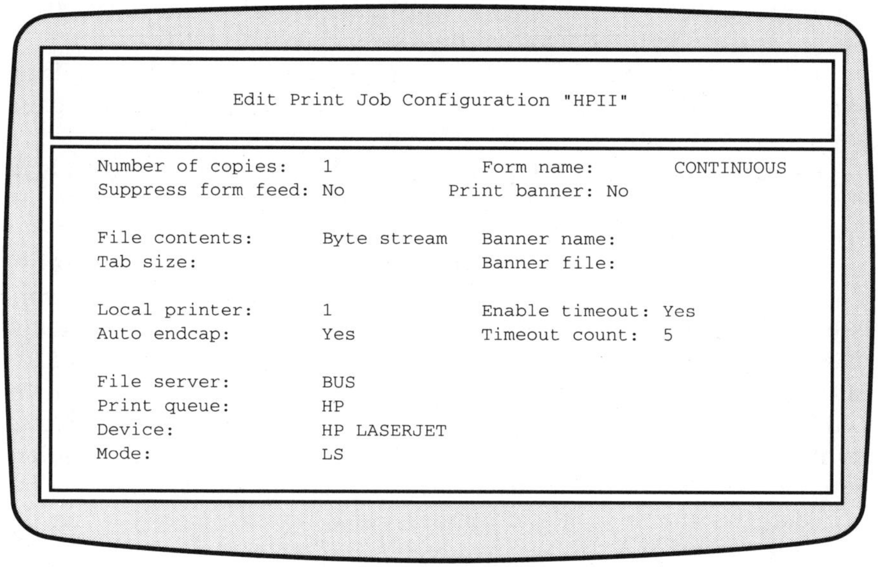

```
                Edit Print Job Configuration "HPII"


   Number of copies:   1           Form name:       CONTINUOUS
   Suppress form feed: No          Print banner: No

   File contents:      Byte stream Banner name:
   Tab size:                       Banner file:

   Local printer:      1           Enable timeout: Yes
   Auto endcap:        Yes         Timeout count:  5

   File server:        BUS
   Print queue:        HP
   Device:             HP LASERJET
   Mode:               LS
```

matically send a form feed, or blank form, after each print session.
Some printers can be set to do the same thing. If the form-feed option
is turned on in the software application or is set on the printer, then
Suppress Form Feed should be set to "Yes." Otherwise, the form feed
is set to "No."

The *File Contents* parameter presents two options: text and byte
stream. The *Text* option is used when printing outside an application
to send tabbing and any formatting characters within the document
directly to the printer. The *Byte Stream* option is used when printing
from within an application, such as WordPerfect or WordStar. This
option ensures that the formatting characters established by the application are used.

Tab Size sets the tabbing to a number from 1 to 18 at the user's
discretion. This applies only to documents sent in the text mode.

The *Form Name* option is used to specify a form created via
PRINTDEF. For example, in a school setting there might be special
forms for printing grades and other forms for printing credit memos.

The sixth option, *Print Banner*, provides the ability to specify that
a banner page will be printed at the beginning of each printout. The

banner page contains the name of the user and the name of the file that is printed. In this way, individual printouts can be identified.

The next option, *Banner Name,* enables the user to create a specific name on the banner. The banner can include twelve characters. If no banner is specified, the name of the user appears.

Banner File enables the user to change the banner file name. If no name is provided, the name of the file being printed is used. Again, the banner file name is limited to twelve characters.

The *Local Printer* option is used when the Capture command is in effect for the print session. This option specifies the workstation printer port from which the file will be captured (Ports 1–3).

The tenth option, *Auto Endcap,* specifies when the file will print. If this parameter is "Yes," the printout is sent as soon as the program is exited, or as soon as the printer file is closed. If the parameter is marked "No," the job is printed as soon as an Endcap command is invoked, or when the printer timeout occurs (the "TI" option in the CAPTURE command). Note that this parameter is not in effect for local printouts. Set auto endcap to "Yes" if you plan print data that requires frequent searches of the hard disk, such as a spreadsheet file.

Next, the *Enable Timeout* option is also used to specify when the file will be printed. If this parameter is marked "Yes," the file is printed at the end of the timeout parameter specified in the CAPTURE command. If it is marked "No," the time at which the file is printed is based on the *Auto Endcap* parameter. Like *Auto Endcap,* this option does not apply to local printouts.

The *Timeout Count* is used to specify the number of seconds to wait until the file is printed. The possible range is 1 through 1,000. For programs that pause to perform a data search, the range should be set relatively high, such as sixty seconds. This helps to ensure that all pages of the file are printed as a single group.

File Server is an option used to specify which server will receive the printout. Viable servers are presented in a displayed list.

The *Print Queue* option is used to specify which print queue will receive the printout.

Finally, the *Device* and *Mode* options are related to what has been defined through PRINTDEF. The *Device* option presents a list of pre-defined printer devices. And the *Mode* parameter is used to specify which device mode will be used, such as compressed printing or landscape printing.

Once the print job information has been completed, the user presses the ESC key to save it and return to the menu in Figure 8.14.

The second option on the PRINTCON menu in Figure 8.14, *Select Default Job Configuration,* is there so an existing print job configuration is designated as the default. If a print job configuration is not specified (for instance, when you're using the CAPTURE or NPRINT commands), the default is used. When the *Select Default Print Job Configuration* option is selected, a list of print job configurations is displayed. The default is designated by highlighting the desired configuration and pressing the ENTER key.

The last option in Figure 8.14 is *Supervisor—Copy Print Job Configurations*. This is used to copy a user's defined configurations to another user. If one user creates a print job, it is not seen by other users. This is because print jobs created by users are stored in association with the specific user. However, the network manager can allow a user to use another's print job definition. This is done by copying one user's configurations to another user.

8.9   VOLINFO

The last menu utility is VOLINFO, which is accessed by entering VOLINFO. This utility displays information about each disk volume on a file server. The information is presented in pages, with up to eight volumes displayed per page.

The information provided by this utility includes the volume name, the total number of kilobytes of storage compared with the number of available kilobytes, and the total number of directory entries allowed compared with the number available.

In addition to displaying volume information regarding the logged-on server, the option also offers the opportunity to attach to other servers. In this way, volume information can be viewed on those servers as well.

COMMAND LINE UTILITIES

Several command line utilities can be used to accomplish some of the tasks performed through menu utilities, as well as many other tasks. The command line utilities, however, are executed from the command prompt and not from a menu. The command line utilities are explained in the following sections. Many of these utilities include a variety of options. Only the most commonly used options are outlined here. Consult the Novell *Command Line Utilities* manual for extensive information on these utilities. Note that utilities designed for use by the network manager are marked with "M."

8.10   ATOTAL (M)

The ATOTAL command resides in the SYS:SYSTEM directory. This command processes accounting records and provides daily and weekly totals for account services. Once the totals are processed, they can be stored in a file by using the DOS redirection command: ATOTAL>File. (File is the name of the file that will contain the information.)

8.11   ATTACH

This command enables the user to connect to additional file servers on the internetwork. When the command is used, it is necessary to specify the server that will be attached, the user ID, and the password. For example, to attach to the server ENGIN using account GUEST, the following command line is entered:

ATTACH ENGIN/GUEST

If there is a password associated with account GUEST the server will prompt for the password. Once a server is attached, it must also be mapped. For instance, after attaching to server ENGIN, the SYS:PUBLIC directory is mapped as follows:

MAP L:=ENGIN/SYS:PUBLIC

8.12   CAPTURE

CAPTURE is used to redirect print requests from the workstation printer ports to the network printers. A series of parameters can be used with this command to control options, such as:

- Print queue
- Network printer number
- Print job configuration
- Number of copies to print

  The most commonly used parameter options include:

- **P=n**   This option specifies the number of the network printer to receive the printout.
- **S=server**   This indicates which server is to receive the printout.
- **Q=queue name**   This determines which print queue is to receive the printout.
- **F=form**   This indicates which form name or form number is to be used (forms are created through the PRINTDEF utility).

- **C=n** This option specifies the number of copies to print per print request.

- **J=job** This option associates a print job configuration created through PRINTCON with the print request.

- **NB** This is used to suppress the generation of a banner page at the beginning of the printout.

- **FF** This parameter indicates a form feed should be issued after the printout.

- **NFF** This suppresses the form feed after the printout.

- **T=n** This option sets tabbing for applications which do not have tabbing instructions included.

- **NT** This option ensures that the tab characters in a document are printed. NT should always be used for word processing and desktop publishing software. Also use NT whenever you print fonts.

- **TI=n** This parameter specifies the length of time needed for the print job to get to the print queue before timing out. The timeout should be set higher for print requests which take longer than others to process, such as desktop publishing files and database files. For these types of printouts, the timeout may need to be as high as thirty or sixty seconds or more. The timeout parameter can be set up to 1,000 seconds.

- **SH** This option shows what CAPTURE parameters are currently in effect.

Once the CAPTURE command is invoked, it remains in effect until another CAPTURE command is issued or until an ENDCAP command is used.

8.13 CASTOFF

The CASTOFF command is used to prevent messages from reaching the workstation from which the command is issued. If the "A" option is used, messages sent from the file server console, as well as messages from other workstations, are blocked. The two forms of this command are:

CASTOFF (block workstation messages)

CASTOFF A (block workstation and console messages)

8.14   CASTON

CASTON reverses the effect of the CASTOFF command, so messages can be received from other workstations and the file server console.

8.15   CHKVOL

This command enables the user to display disk volume information on one or more volumes. The data supplied includes:

- Name of the volume
- Total number of bytes
- Number of bytes used
- Number of files
- Number of bytes remaining for use
- Number of bytes available to the user
- Number of directory entries remaining

8.16   ENDCAP

The ENDCAP command discontinues the capture of printer output at a workstation. It reverses the CAPTURE command, so a print request can be directed to a local printer connected to the workstation.

8.17   FLAG

The FLAG command is used to display or modify attribute designations for one or more files in a directory. The attribute parameters that can be set using FLAG are:

- **RO**   Read only
- **RW**   Read write
- **S**   Shareable
- **NS**   Nonshareable
- **N**   Normal or nonshareable read write
- **T**   Transactional (for SFT NetWare)
- **I**   Indexed
- **SUB**   Flag all subdirectories in the directory

The FLAG command can be used, along with a path designation, to set attributes in a specified directory. When the FLAG command is used with no parameters, the current attributes are displayed. Note

that the FLAG command can be used with the wildcard character (*).
For example, if all .TXT files in the SYS:DATAWP directory are to be
flagged "Shareable Read Write," the following command line would
be entered:

    FLAG SYS:DATAWP *.TXT SRW

8.18   GRANT (M)

The GRANT command is used to modify trustee rights in a directory.
The parameters that can be used with this command include:

- **S**   Search
- **O**   Open files
- **R**   Read files
- **W**   Write to files
- **C**   Create new files
- **D**   Delete existing files
- **M**   Modify file attributes
- **P**   Give parental rights
- **ALL**   Grant all rights
- **NO RIGHTS**   Remove all rights

When the command is used, modifiers such as FOR and TO can be
included. The FOR modifier is used to specify a directory; the TO
modifier specifies a group or individual user. For example, to grant
read, open, and search rights to the group SALES in the directory
SYS:APP/LOTUS/DATA, the user would enter:

    GRANT R O S FOR SYS:APP/LOTUS/DATA TO SALES

8.19   HIDEFILE (M)

One or more files can be flagged so they are hidden from view through
the help of the HIDEFILE command. Files marked with this attribute
cannot be copied over via a COPY command. However, the TYPE command in DOS can still be used to display the contents of hidden files.
HIDEFILE can include drive and directory paths. As an example, to
hide the file MY.DAT in the directory SYS:APP/LOTUS/DATA, the
system manager would enter: ·

    HIDEFILE SYS:APP/LOTUS/DATA MY.DAT

HIDEFILE resides in the SYS:SYSTEM directory, and is normally run from that directory. Use the SHOWFILE command to reverse the HIDEFILE attribute on a file.

8.20   HOLDOFF (M)

The HOLDOFF command reverses the effect of the HOLDON command. It is accessed from the SYS:SYSTEM directory.

8.21   HOLDON (M)

HOLDON is used to ensure that files are held open until the user is finished with a software application. This guarantees no one has access to the application files, even if they are closed while the application program is still in process. Consequently, others who have access to the same application and files cannot access or update those files. Once it is no longer necessary to prevent access to the files, the HOLDOFF command should be run to release the files.

8.22   LISTDIR

LISTDIR allows the user to view all subdirectories in a given directory. This command has four parameters:

- **S**   Lists all subdirectories, and the subdirectories within each subdirectory
- **R**   Shows the maximum rights mask of the subdirectories
- **D**   Shows the creation date of each subdirectory
- **A**   Combines the functions of the S, R, and D parameters

8.23   LOGIN

This command enables users to log in to a file server. If there are two or more servers on the internetwork, the server and user ID can both be specified. A log-in where there is only one server would look like the following:

LOGIN ANDERS

If there is more than one server, and the user ANDERS wishes to access server ENG, the log-in would be:

LOGIN ENG/ANDERS

8.24 LOGOUT

LOGOUT permits the user to log out from one or more servers. If LOG-OUT is used alone, the primary and all attached servers are logged out. However, if a server name is specified with LOGOUT, only that server is logged out. For instance, if the user is logged on to servers ENG and LIB, and wishes to log out of server LIB, he or she enters:

LOGOUT LIB

8.25 MAKEUSER (M)

When a .USR file is created to generate or delete a group of users, the MAKEUSER command can be used to process the .USR file. As an example, if there is a .USR file titled, STUDENTS.USR, the file can be processed by entering:

MAKEUSER STUDENTS.USR

If MAKEUSER is entered without a filename, the MAKEUSER menu utility is run automatically.

8.26 MAP

MAP is used to display, modify, and create drive mappings. When MAP is typed alone, the current drive mappings are displayed. There are two general types of drive mappings: network drives and search drives. Network drives are drive paths associated with a letter. Drives F: through Z: can be mapped as network drives (see Chapter 12 for more information on establishing standards for mapping drives).

When a network drive is mapped, this means the user can switch to the designated drive to access any programs or data files on that drive. For example, a subdirectory containing LOTUS 1-2-3 might be mapped as drive R:. Once the user switches to drive R:, he or she can run LOTUS 1-2-3 programs and the printer and setup files in LOTUS 1-2-3. If the LOTUS 1-2-3 subdirectory has the path SYS:APP/LOTUS, the mapping is established by the following command:

MAP R:=SYS:APP/LOTUS

Search drives work like network drives. In both, subdirectories are mapped to specific drive letters. The difference, though, is that programs with .EXE and .COM extensions can be accessed without switching to the network drive that has the path containing the programs. For example, if a search drive is established for WordPerfect, the WP command to start WordPerfect can be used from any drive. Search drives are mapped this way:

MAP S3:=SYS:APP/WP51

In this instance, search drive 3 (S3) becomes drive X:. This is because search drive mappings begin with the last letter of the alphabet. Search drive 1 is mapped to drive Z:, search drive 2 is mapped to drive Y:, and so on. Up to sixteen search drives can be mapped. The Novell manual *Command Line Utilities* contains instructions showing how to map drives.

8.27 NCOPY

The NCOPY command works in a fashion similar to that of the COPY command in DOS. It is used to copy files. NCOPY, however, displays source and destination locations of the file copy. As with COPY, NCOPY will accept wildcard designations (*). NCOPY can also use TO as a modifier. For example, the command to copy WORDS.TXT from the SYS:APP/WP51 directory to the VOL1:DATA directory is:

NCOPY SYS:APP/WP51/WORDS.TXT TO VOL1:DATA

To verify the data copied in the above NCOPY sequence, the /V switch is added:

NCOPY SYS:APP/WP51/WORDS.TXT TO VOL1:DATA /V

8.28 NDIR

NDIR is a NetWare command used to display the contents of a directory. This command is accompanied by a variety of parameters for displaying specific directory information. Information routinely displayed using just the NDIR command includes file ownership, file access dates, file update dates, file creation dates, and file attributes. Furthermore, NDIR displays rights and ownership information for subdirectories within the displayed directory.

8.29 NPRINT

Individual files can be printed by using the NPRINT command. Like CAPTURE, this command comes with many print options that can be set by parameters. When you use the NPRINT command, first type NPRINT. Next type the name of the file to print. Last, type the parameter you wish to use. The parameters include:

- **P=n** This option is used to specify the number of the network printer that will receive the printout.
- **S=server** This option indicates which server receives the print-out.
- **Q=queue name** This option sets the print queue to receive the printout.
- **F=form** This indicates which form name or form number is to be used.
- **C=n** This option specifies the number of copies to print per print request.
- **J=job** This option associates a print job configuration created through PRINTCON with the print request.
- **NB** This suppresses the generation of a banner page at the beginning of the printout.
- **FF** This parameter indicates a form feed should be issued after the printout.
- **NFF** This suppresses the form feed after the printout.
- **T=n** This option is used to set tabulation for applications that do not have tabulation instructions included.
- **D** This deletes the file after it is printed.

To print the file YEARLY.RPT, on Printer 1 with no banner and using print job configuration HPII, enter this command statement:

NPRINT YEARLY.RPT P=1 NB J=HPII

8.30 PAUDIT (M)

The PAUDIT command is used by the network administrator to view system account data. The displayed data contains a record of log-in information on users.

8.31 PSTAT

PSTAT shows information about network printers. The information displayed includes the printer number, on-line status, active status, and form number and form names currently associated with the network printers.

8.32 PURGE

Once files are deleted or erased, the disk space they occupy is still allocated for those files. This means the files can still be retrieved. The

PURGE command is used to release the disk space; and as a consequence, the files can no longer be retrieved.

8.33   REMOVE (M)

This command enables the user to remove a group or user from the list of trustees for a given directory. If no directory is specified, the trustee rights are removed from the current directory. In the following example, the user ANDERS is removed as a trustee from the directory SYS:APP:

    REMOVE ANDERS SYS:APP

8.34   RENDIR

The RENDIR command permits the user to rename a directory. For instance, if the directory SYS:WPROCESS is to be renamed SYS:WP, the following two commands would work equally well:

    RENDIR SYS:WPROCESS TO SYS:WP

    RENDIR SYS:WPROCESS SYS:WP

8.35   REVOKE

REVOKE can be used to revoke specific trustee rights for users or groups in a directory. The REVOKE options are:

- **S**   Search
- **O**   Open files
- **R**   Read files
- **W**   Write to files
- **C**   Create new files
- **D**   Delete existing files
- **M**   Modify file attributes
- **P**   Give parental rights
- **ALL** Revoke all rights

In addition to these parameters, REVOKE uses the modifiers FOR and FROM. The modifier FOR is used to specify the directory path. The modifier FROM specifies the group or user. The following example revokes write, modify, and parental rights for the user group SALES in the directory SYS:APP.

    REVOKE W M P FOR SYS:APP FROM SALES

8.36 RIGHTS

The RIGHTS command enables the trustee rights to be viewed for the current user in a given directory. For instance, if a user wishes to view trustee rights for the directory SYS:DATA, he or she would enter:

RIGHTS SYS:DATA

8.37 SALVAGE

When files are deleted using the DEL or ERASE commands in DOS, they can still be retrieved, should the user have a change of heart. Files are retrieved via the SALVAGE command. The SALVAGE command will not work if the PURGE command has been executed just after the files were deleted. Furthermore, the files cannot be retrieved if the user logs off the server before running SALVAGE.

8.38 SECURITY (M)

Security is always an important concern in the administration of a file server. Some accounts may not have passwords, and other accounts may have inappropriate security equivalences. The SECURITY command generates a report showing possible security problems. It shows if an account is not passworded, if the password is too short, if users have supervisor privileges, and if accounts do not have login scripts. It also shows the directories where trustee rights are inappropriate.

8.39 SEND

The SEND command enables users to send short, one-line messages to other users. A message can be sent to another logged-on user or to all currently logged-on members of a group. As an example, a message can be sent to the user STEVENS and to the group SALES in the following way:

SEND "THE ORDERS ARE IN!" STEVENS SALES

8.40 SETPASS

SETPASS enables the user to establish a new password. When SETPASS is entered at the command prompt, the system returns with a prompt to enter the current password. Next, the user is requested to enter a new password. Finally, the system asks the user to retype the new password for verification.

8.41   SETTTS (M)

It is unlikely that the SETTTS command will be used. It is designed to permit the user to establish record locks that the transaction tracking system should ignore before starting to track a transaction. The network manager should consult the application program documentation to determine if SETTTS is required.

8.42   SHOWFILE (M)

This command enables the network manager to remove the hidden attribute from files. SHOWFILE is located in the SYS:SYSTEM directory. The command permits entry of a path statement to remove the hidden attribute. For example, if the file RPT.DAT is flagged as hidden in the SYS:DATA directory, the following command removes the hidden attribute:

SHOWFILE SYS:DATA/RPT.DAT

8.43   SLIST

SLIST enables a user to display a list of all file servers connected to the internetwork. The information shown includes the server names, their network addresses, and the node address of each server.

8.44   SMODE

The SMODE command is used to establish a search mode for application files with .EXE and .COM extensions. Often, executable application files must have access to overlay, library, or data files in order to run properly. The additional necessary files may be in the same directory as the executable file or in a different directory. SMODE enables the user to tell the system how to search for these additional files in the directory structure. There are six search modes that can be used:

- **0** No search path is established. Instead, the search path can be specified in the SHELL.CFG file.
- **1** The search path is the same path used to invoke the executable file. If no path is specified with the executable file, the default directory is searched, along with all search drives.
- **2** The default directory is the only path searched.
- **3** The search path for the executable file is used; or if the data files are flagged RO, the system searches default and search directories.

- **4**   This number is not used.
- **5**   The default and search drives are searched, no matter what path is used by the executable file.
- **6**   This number is not used.
- **7**   If the data files are opened RO, it searches the default and search directories, regardless of the path used by the executable file.

For example, if the additional needed files exist in the default directory, a program such as TRIALB.EXE might use the following search mode command statement line:

SMODE SYS:PROGRAMS/TRIALB.EXE 2

8.45   SYSTIME

This command displays the day of the week, date, and time of day on a file server on the network. To view the system time information on any file server, you name that server in the command. If you do not name a server, the currently logged-on server information is displayed.

8.46   TLIST

TLIST displays the trustee information in a directory. It shows user trustees, group trustees, and the trustee rights associated with each. For instance, to display trustee information for the directory SYS:DATA, the user enters:

TLIST SYS:DATA

By adding the modifiers GROUPS or USERS the display can be limited to group or user information.

8.47   USERLIST

The USERLIST command presents a list of currently logged-on users. The display of information includes the connection number, each user's name, and his or her log-in time. If the /A option is used with this command, it adds information about each network address and each user node address.

8.48   WHOAMI

The WHOAMI command is used to show log-on information about the user. The information shown includes the file server name, user name, connection number, and log-in time. If more than one server is attached, information is produced for each server.

CONSOLE COMMANDS

Network managers, along with operators who participate in management of the network, have several specialized commands, which are available only from the file server console. Many of these commands are similar to options contained in the FCONSOLE menu utility, available from any workstation. They include commands to broadcast messages to users, down the server, and observe the status of server volumes. The following sections offer a summary of many of the available console commands.

8.49   BROADCAST

BROADCAST is used from the file server console to send a message to all users. For example, this message warns that the server will soon be downed:

BROADCAST Please log off immediately for system maintenance.

8.50   CLEAR MESSAGE

This command is used to clear messages that have been sent to the server console.

8.51   CLEAR STATION

A connection can be cleared by using the CLEAR STATION command from the console. The station number to be cleared is typed just after the CLEAR STATION command is given.

8.52   CONFIG

The CONFIG command displays file server configuration information. This includes the server name, number of processes, network address, manufacturers of network interface boards in the server, and hardware settings on the interface boards.

8.53   DISABLE LOGIN

By entering DISABLE LOGIN at the console, the operator can prevent users from logging on to the server. Users who have already logged on, however, are not cleared. This command is reversed by entering the ENABLE LOGIN command.

8.54 DISK

The DISK command permits the console operator to view information about all disk drives that are mounted. The information displayed includes the channel number, controller number, drive number, and hot-fix status of each drive. The display also shows I/O errors and hot-fix table usage.

8.55 DOWN

DOWN is used to shut down the server in preparation for powering it off. Avoid turning off the server before entering the DOWN command. If the server is turned off first, file allocation table errors are likely to occur. Also, make certain all users are logged off before you down the server.

8.56 ENABLE LOGIN

The ENABLE LOGIN command resumes log-in permission after DISABLE LOGIN has been entered at the console.

8.57 MONITOR

The MONITOR command permits the console operator to monitor connection activity on the server. Connection activity for up to six connection locations is displayed on the screen at one time. When the operator wishes to view a specific connection, he or she types the connection number following the MONITOR command.

8.58 OFF

OFF is used to clear the console display.

8.59 PRINTER

Each printer connected to a file server is assigned a number at the time the server is generated (beginning with Printer 0). The PRINTER command displays the number of each printer connected to the server. It also shows the print queues serviced by each printer, along with which printers are on-line.

8.60   PRINTER ADD

The PRINTER ADD command permits the console operator to add print queues to a printer. The priority of added queues can also be set. For example, to add the queue HPII to Printer 1 with a priority of 1, the operator enters the following statement at the console:

    P 1 ADD HPII AT PRIORITY 1

8.61   PRINTER DELETE QUEUE

A queue can be deleted from use by a printer by using the PRINTER DELETE QUEUE console command. To delete the queue, EPSON from Printer 1, the operator enters:

    P 1 DEL EPSON

8.62   PRINTER FORM

The type of form to be used on a given printer can be specified through the PRINTER FORM command. For instance, to assign form type 10 to Printer 1, the operator enters:

    P 1 FORM 10

8.63   PRINTER QUEUES

The existing print queues assigned to a specific printer can be displayed through the PRINTER QUEUES command. For example, the queues associated with Printer 1 are displayed by typing the following command:

    P 1 QUEUES

8.64   PRINTER START

The PRINTER START command restarts a given network printer after the PRINTER STOP command has been issued.

8.65   PRINTER STOP

The PRINTER STOP command is used to stop a printer briefly, as for ribbon or paper maintenance. For instance, to stop Printer 2, the operator enters:

    P 2 STOP

8.66   QUEUE

The QUEUE command permits the console operator to display a list of all print queues on a file server.

8.67   QUEUE CHANGE PRIORITY

The priority of a print queue is changed through the QUEUE CHANGE PRIORITY command. For example, to change the priority of queue HPII to a priority of 2, the operator would enter:

Q HPII C TO 2

8.68   QUEUE CREATE

New print queues can be created using PCONSOLE or the QUEUE CREATE command at the file server console. For instance, if the operator wishes to create the queue HPII at the file server console, he or she enters:

Q HPII CREATE

8.69   QUEUE DELETE

Print jobs in a given queue can be deleted through the QUEUE DE-LETE command. For example, to delete job 10 in queue PAN1091, the operator enters:

Q PAN1091 DEL 10

To delete all jobs in the queue PAN1091, the entry is:

Q PAN1091 DEL *

8.70   SEND

The SEND command is used to send a message to specific server users. The connection number is used to direct the message to a user. For example, to send a message to users at connections 4 and 10, the operator enters:

SEND "PLEASE LOG OFF IMMEDIATELY" 4,10

8.71   SET TIME

The SET TIME command permits the console operator to reset the server date and/or time.

8.72   SPOOL

If the console operator wishes to view all spooler mappings, he or she can do so by entering the SPOOL command at the console.

8.73   SPOOL TO

Spool mappings can be changed or redirected to different queues via the SPOOL TO command. For example, the queue STAFF can be redirected to Spooler 1 by using the following command:

S 1 TO STAFF

8.74   TIME

The TIME command is used to display the file server time and date information.

FUNCTION TABLES

This section presents three types of tables that show commonly used NetWare functions, such as printing to the network printer. With each function is a list of commands used to perform the function. The commands include menu, command line, and console commands. If there are two commands, such as a menu and a command-line command that can be used, both are listed. If two commands of the same type will perform a function, both are listed too. For example, there are two menu commands that display volume information: FILER and VOLINFO (see Table 8.2).

Some functions require that two commands be executed to complete the task. For example, customizing print codes and associating them with a print job configuration is a two-step function (see Table 8.1). The first step is to create the codes in the PRINTDEF menu utility. The second step is to incorporate a PRINTDEF mode into a print job configuration by using PRINTCON. To show that this is a two-step process, PRINTDEF and PRINTCON are both listed. A (1) appears after PRINTDEF to indicate that it's the first step, and a (2) appears after PRINTCON to show that it's the second step.

Table 8.1 lists printer control commands, Table 8.2 has supervisor control commands, and Table 8.3 shows commands for users.

TABLE 8.1
Printer Control

Function	Menu Utilities and Section	Console and Command Line Utilities and Section
Print to a local printer		8.16 ENDCAP
Print to a network printer		8.12 CAPTURE
Print the contents of a file as with the DOS Print command		8.29 NPRINT
Print to a print server		8.12 CAPTURE
Delete a print request	8.6 PCONSOLE	8.69 QUEUE DELETE
Delete all print requests in a print queue	8.6 PCONSOLE	8.69 QUEUE DELETE
Hold a print request	8.6 PCONSOLE	
Customize printer codes and associate them with a print queue and print job	8.7 PRINTDEF (1) 8.8 PRINTCON (2)	
Customize a print configuration, such as the banner and number of copies to print	8.8 PRINTCON	
Create a form length for printer forms, such as invoices or paychecks	8.7 PRINTDEF (1) 8.8 PRINTCON (2)	
Print using custom printer codes and print job configurations		8.12 CAPTURE
Create new print queues	8.6 PCONSOLE	8.60 PRINTER ADD
Set a default print queue and print configuration	8.8 PRINTCON	
Delete print queues	8.6 PCONSOLE	8.61 PRINTER DELETE QUEUE
Stop the printer to change a ribbon or adjust the paper feed		8.65 PRINTER STOP
Change the priority of a print request	8.6 PCONSOLE	8.67 QUEUE CHANGE PRIORITY

TABLE 8.2
Supervisor Control

Function	Menu Utilities and Section	Console and Command Line Utilities and Section
Create a system login script	8.1 SYSCON	
Create new users	8.1 SYSCON	
Create user login scripts	8.1 SYSCON	
Create groups	8.1 SYSCON	
Create new users in a batch mode	8.3 MAKEUSER	
Create new directories	8.5 FILER	
Delete one or more directories	8.5 FILER	
Assign file attributes	8.5 FILER	8.17 FLAG
Assign trustee rights	8.1 SYSCON	8.18 GRANT
Remove trustee rights	8.1 SYSCON	8.35 REVOKE or 8.33 REMOVE
Assign maximum rights mask to a directory	8.5 FILER	
Change a user's password	8.1 SYSCON	
Change a user's restrictions	8.1 SYSCON	
Delete a user	8.1 SYSCON	
View file server performance statistics	8.2 FCONSOLE	
Send a user a message	8.2 FCONSOLE	8.39 SEND or 8.70 SEND
Send a message to all users	8.2 FCONSOLE	8.49 BROADCAST
Disconnect a user	8.2 FCONSOLE	8.51 CLEAR STATION
View user connection activity	8.2 FCONSOLE	8.57 MONITOR
Down the file server	8.2 FCONSOLE	8.55 DOWN
Establish file server accounting	8.1 SYSCON	
View information about volume use	8.5 FILER or 8.9 VOLINFO	
Examine security holes		8.38 SECURITY
Prevent all users from logging on to the file server	8.2 FCONSOLE	8.53 DISABLE LOGIN
Permit all users to log on to the file server	8.2 FCONSOLE	8.56 ENABLE LOGIN
Assign FCONSOLE operators	8.1 SYSCON	
Assign print queue operators	8.6 PCONSOLE	

TABLE 8.3
Common User Functions

Function	Menu Utilities and Section	Command Line Utilities and Section
View the file servers connected to a LAN	8.4 SESSION	8.43 SLIST
Log in to a file server		8.23 LOGIN
Connect to more than one file server	8.4 SESSION	8.11 ATTACH
Log off from a file server		8.24 LOGOUT
View the contents of a directory or subdirectory	8.5 FILER	8.28 NDIR
List all subdirectories in a directory	8.5 FILER	8.22 LISTDIR
Create new logical drive maps or search paths	8.4 SESSION	8.26 MAP
Delete a directory or files in a directory	8.5 FILER	
Copy one or more files	8.5 FILER	8.27 NCOPY
View your directory rights	8.5 FILER	8.36 RIGHTS
Print the contents of a file		8.29 NPRINT
Determine who is logged in to a file server	8.4 SESSION	8.47 USERLIST
Send a message to another user	8.4 SESSION	8.39 SEND
Recover a deleted file		8.37 SALVAGE
Rename a directory or subdirectory		8.34 RENDIR
Display information about your log-in session		8.48 WHOAMI

SUMMARY

Three general types of NetWare utilities have been reviewed in this chapter. First, menu utilities combine a variety of functions into one menu system for the user. The menu utilities span such activities as creation of user information, file and directory maintenance, performance statistics monitoring, manipulation of printer functions, and log-on session control.

The second type of NetWare utilities consist of the command line utilities. Some of these utilities, such as HIDEFILE, SECURITY, and HOLDON, are only for use by the network manager. Other utilities have a broader user base. They include CAPTURE, LOGIN, NCOPY, and NDIR. Many of the command-line functions are replicated in the menu utility functions.

File-server console commands represent the third type of utility discussed in this chapter. These commands are entered only from the console keyboard. They provide queue and spooler mappings, printer activities, and access to the file server. In addition to these functions, the console commands permit monitoring connection and server information.

CHAPTER QUESTIONS

1. Which menu utility permits the user to delete print jobs in a print queue?

2. Write a .USR file that creates ten users. Include the following characteristics:
   a. Disk space limited to 500 KB
   b. Membership in the group, STAFF
   c. Home directories in the SYS:USERSTAFF directory
   d. Home directory rights consisting of read, search, open, write and create
   e. Passworded accounts

3. What utility is used to rename a directory?

4. How would you prevent users from accessing a file server?

5. What utilities are available to create a new print queue?

6. Describe each of the rights that can be associated with a directory.

7. Explain the function of each of the file attributes that can be assigned to a file.

8. Explain the difference between the DOS COPY command and the NetWare NCOPY command.

9. Network Printer 1 will not print jobs routed to it. Describe the steps you would take to troubleshoot this problem.

9

NetWare 386

INTRODUCTION

Novell has surpassed the capabilities of NetWare 286 by introducing NetWare 386. Although NetWare 286 can be loaded onto an 80386 file server, it does not take full advantage of the potential of the 80386 CPU. NetWare 386 takes advantage of 80386 CPU capabilities, and uses the new 80486 CPU capabilities as well.

NetWare 386 can operate faster and uses the server's memory more efficiently than NetWare 286. With NetWare 386, the actual limit of concurrent users is 250. (The 80386 increases the theoretical limit of concurrent users to 4,000.)

NetWare 386 allows up to 100,000 open files, and uses a dynamic memory configuration for routing buffers, cache blocks, and maximum number of open files. Dynamic memory configuration is the ability to adjust the number of routing buffers, cache blocks, and maximum open files as the server is running. NetWare 386 adjusts these parameters automatically, without user intervention.

NetWare 386 is also capable of mounting thirty-two disk volumes. Each volume has the capacity of thirty-two hard drives. (The 80386 has a theoretical limit of 4 GB of memory.)

Complementing the 80386 CPU capabilities is a host of new and enhanced features not available in NetWare 286. Some of these new features include:

- An operating system that is easier to generate and maintain
- The option to reconfigure the server without regenerating it
- New and enhanced disk and RAM handling
- Improved salvaged file options
- New file and directory security options
- New bindery structure
- NetWare Loadable Modules (NLMs)
- A print server NLM
- Open Data-Link Interface
- New command line and menu utilities
- New console utilities

GENERATING THE OPERATION SYSTEM

Generating a NetWare 386 server is a five-step process. In the first step, you establish the hardware to be used for the server. This involves installing disk drives and network interface cards, and otherwise preparing the hardware in the server. Also in this step you run the file-server vendor's setup program, along with procedures to define the drive types, boot sequence, parallel and serial port configuration, monitor configuration, and memory.

In step two, you boot the server. It can be booted from a floppy diskette that's been formatted with DOS and which contains the Novell SYSTEM Disk files. Or the server can be booted from its hard drive with a DOS partition. When the server is booted from the hard drive you run FDISK or PART (depending on the version of DOS) to partition the hard drive. A 1 MB bootable DOS partition is then created, and SYSTEM Disk files are copied to this partition.

Step three is to run the SERVER utility. This utility performs the tasks below. SERVER:

- Establishes the server's name
- Sets the internal network number
- Loads the disk driver module
- Loads the LAN driver module

- Loads other driver modules
- Binds the IPX to the network driver
- Assigns the network number

In step four, you run the INSTALL utility. INSTALL performs these tasks:

- Creates the NetWare disk partition tables
- Establishes mirrored drives
- Creates and mounts volumes
- Copies system and utility files onto the file server
- Creates AUTOEXEC.NCF and STARTUP.NCF files to be placed on the DOS partition or the DOS boot diskette

The AUTOEXEC.NCF and STARTUP.NCF files provide startup information and contain a series of console commands that are executed when the NetWare operating system is loaded (see Console Utilities in this chapter).

Step five is to down the server, then create an AUTOEXEC.BAT file. This file is used to boot the server from the DOS partition or the boot diskette. When this is completed, reboot the server for live operation.

UPGRADING NETWARE 286 TO NETWARE 386

Novell has a utility that can be used to upgrade from NetWare 286 to NetWare 386. This menu-driven utility is called UPGRADE, and provides two ways to upgrade a server. The first method is to run UPGRADE from a DOS workstation. When you use this method, all of the existing server data is saved to a network directory or to a DOS-compatible device, such as a hard drive or tape unit.

Once the data is backed up, replace the NetWare 286 partition with the NetWare 386 partition, then place the NetWare 386 operating system on the server (following the steps outlined in "Generating the Operating System" in this chapter). Last, copy all of the saved data back onto the server. Trustee rights and passwords are translated and retained during the UPGRADE process.

The second UPGRADE option involves using a second server from the existing network. In this option, a new server is used for the NetWare 386 operating system. The new server is generated and then connected to the existing network. Both the old NetWare 286 and the new NetWare 386 servers are attached to your workstation. Use the UPGRADE utility to copy the files from the NetWare 286 server to the

NetWare 386 server. As in the first method, network security data is retained on the new 386 server.

An added benefit of attaching servers to the network for the upgrade is that two or more existing NetWare 286 servers can be combined into one NetWare 386 server. To do this, generate the NetWare 386 server, then connect it to the network. Also, connect the NetWare 286 servers that are to be upgraded. Use the UPGRADE utility to copy files from the NetWare 286 servers to the NetWare 386 server.

RECONFIGURING THE OPERATING SYSTEM

Several features are built into NetWare 386 so you don't have to regenerate the file server to add new disk drives, partitions, volumes, load modules, or to change configuration information. Most of these options are described in the following sections. For instance, you use the console LOAD command to load NetWare Loadable Modules (see "NetWare Loadable Modules" and "Console Utilities" in this chapter). Modules can be loaded or unloaded while the file server is running. Configuration settings on the file server can be altered by using the SET console command (see "Console Utilities"). And the INSTALL command installs disk drives without regenerating the file server.

NEW DISK HANDLING

Up to thirty-two hard disks can be combined into one volume. And up to thirty-two volumes can be used on one server.

Besides volumes, NetWare 386 uses *disk segments*. A segment can represent an entire hard disk, or one hard disk can be divided into several segments. However, one segment cannot exist on more than one hard disk. One volume cannot have more than thirty-two segments. For example, if thirty-two hard disks are to be attached to one volume, each hard disk must have only one segment.

A DOS partition can coexist with a NetWare partition. Generally, a server is established so a 1 MB DOS partition is on the hard disk that is used to boot the system, with the DOS partition as the boot partition. The remaining disks are then partitioned only for NetWare. And each NetWare partition has an allocation for hot-fix redirection tables.

As in NetWare 286, disk access is accomplished by an elevator-seeking method. This method is designed to speed access of data and reduce wear on the disk drive. The elevator method involves the use of two queues, an "In" queue and an "Out" queue. Requests for data closest to the center of the disk are placed in the "In" queue. When the "In" queue is active, requests are processed, with each request moving the disk head closer to the center of the disk. Once the "In" queue requests are serviced, the "Out" queue is activated. The "Out" queue progressively moves the head toward the outer edge of the disk. Disk thrashing is kept to a minimum because the disk head is either moving progressively in toward the center of the disk or out toward the outer rim. This reduces wear created by other disk access methods, which cause the disk head to jump all over the disk while accessing information.

Disk data is stored in allocation blocks of five different sizes. These are: 4 KB, 8 KB, 16 KB, 32 KB, and 64 KB. Only one block size can be established per volume. You must decide how to store data most efficiently, which requires estimating the typical or most frequent size of files. For example, if the block size is set at 8 KB, then the highest frequency of files should fall between 4 KB and 8 KB. With an 8 KB block setting, 1 KB files will occupy an 8 KB block. Likewise, 9 KB files will occupy two blocks.

FILE ALLOCATION AND DIRECTORY TABLES

Every server volume contains a file allocation table or **FAT**. The FAT holds information about each file showing which allocation block or blocks contain the file. If more than one allocation block is used, the table contains pointers that point from the first block to the next block and so on in sequence.

When there are more than sixty-four entries or pointers for a given file in the file allocation table, NetWare switches to a "turbo-file allocation table" or **Turbo-FAT** for that file. The Turbo-FAT is used for large files and replaces the file indexing used by NetWare 286. The Turbo-FAT builds a one-table index of the file allocation blocks. Through the Turbo-FAT, any portion of a file can be quickly accessed. Thus NetWare does not rely on examining the entire FAT for a portion of data in a large file. Instead, it goes directly to the Turbo-FAT and finds the needed pointer from the Turbo-FAT index.

Besides FAT and Turbo-FAT tables, each volume has a directory table. The directory table holds information about workstation operating systems, file trustee entries, directory trustee entries, and other data pertinent to system operation.

The directory table also contains the name of each file on a given volume, the file attributes, the length of the file, the file owner, and the creation date and time. NetWare 386 provides "multiple name spaces," which permit file names from different operating systems to be stored in the directory table. Multiple name spaces store two directory entries for file names that come from non-DOS systems, such as OS/2, UNIX, and Macintosh. One directory entry holds the non-DOS file name and supporting data. The other directory entry holds a DOS name for the file, along with the accompanying data regarding file attributes, ownership, creation date, and so on.

SALVAGING FILES

With NetWare 286, a user who accidentally deletes one or more files can recover those files by using the SALVAGE command. However, only the files that were last deleted can be recovered. Files deleted one or two days earlier are not available for recovery. NetWare 386 enables the user to recover any previously deleted files, as long as they have not been purged. Deleted files are saved in the default directory until they are purged or until the file server runs out of disk allocation space. When the server runs out of disk allocation space, salvageable files are automatically purged so the space they occupy is returned for use by existing and new files.

The SALVAGE command enables a user to view a list of deleted files and to recover files on the list. Even when the default directory has been deleted, the files in that directory can be recovered. In this situation, the deleted files are retained in a file called DELETED.SAV, which resides in the root directory of the volume.

RAM

Since the 80386 memory is not segmented, NetWare 386 can configure memory allocation dynamically. This allocation includes all kinds of memory for routing buffers, cache buffers, and FAT tables.

NetWare 386 requires at least 2 MB of memory in the server. But server performance is improved as more memory is available.

Because cache buffers are necessary for fast server operation, it is desireable to have as much memory for cache as possible. Under NetWare 386, you can set the cache buffer size to 4 KB, 8 KB, or 16 KB. Also, the cache buffers are used to cache Network Loadable Modules (see the section in this chapter on Network Loadable Modules) and to cache the FAT.

Memory is also used for other processes, which include:

- Directory table
- Turbo-FAT tables
- Routing buffers
- Disk elevator size
- Directory hash tables
- Maximum number of files
- File locks
- Kernel processes
- TTS transactions
- File service processes

Memory is allocated dynamically to each process. Thus, if more routing buffers are needed, NetWare 386 creates more. If the maximum number of files is too small, the number is automatically increased. It is unnecessary to down the server and re-generate it to establish more routing buffers or a higher number of maximum files.

FILE AND DIRECTORY ATTRIBUTES

With NetWare 386, several new attributes are available, as shown in Table 9.1.

TRUSTEE RIGHTS

With NetWare 386, the maximum rights mask from NetWare 286 is replaced by the inherited rights mask. Some new rights have been added while the open file right has been eliminated.

At the directory level, the inherited rights mask works like the maximum rights mask in NetWare 286. A trustee will have only rights that are allowed by this mask. For example, if a user has trustee rights to write to a directory, but not inherited rights to write to the directory, then he or she cannot write to that directory. However, unlike the maximum rights mask, inherited rights can be modified for specific files. For example, the inherited rights mask to the directory, DATA, might be R and F, where R permits the user to read the files and F permits him or her to display the files (file scan) in the directory. The directory might contain the following files: BUDGET.DAT, PAY.DAT, PERSONS.DAT, and CHECKS.DAT. The supervisor has the option to grant W (write) rights to a specified user for only the BUDGET.DAT

TABLE 9.1
File and Directory Attributes

Attribute	Full Name	Description
A	Archive needed	This attribute is automatically assigned to files that have been changed since the last backup. It applies only to files and not to directories.
C	Copy inhibit	This attribute prevents users from copying specific files. It is used for files only and not for directories.
D	Delete inhibit	This restricts users from deleting a file or a directory.
X	Execute only	The user can execute a file but not copy it. Note that files marked with this attribute cannot be backed up. The attribute is used only for files.
H	Hidden	This attribute prevents files from being viewed by a DIR command (but they can be viewed using NetWare's NDIR command). The attribute is assigned to directories and to files.
P	Purge	This attribute causes a file to be purged as soon as it is deleted. If it is applied to a directory, any file in that directory is purged when it is deleted.
RA	Read audit	This attribute is implemented in NetWare 386 version 3.1. It is used only on files to create an audit trail to show who has read the file.
RO	Read only	This attribute enables a user to read, but not write, to a file (or delete or rename the file). It is used only on files.
RW	Read write	This permits a user to read and modify a file, including the ability to delete or rename the file. This attribute applies only to files.
R	Rename inhibit	This attribute prevents a directory or a file from being renamed.
S	Shareable	This flag enables more than one user to access a file at the same time. This applies to files only.
SY	System	System files or directories are hidden from view of the DOS DIR command, but can be displayed with the NetWare NDIR command.

TABLE 9.1 *(Continued)*
File and Directory Attributes

Attribute	Full Name	Description
T	Transactional	Any file can be flagged for transaction tracking with this attribute. The attribute is used only for files and not for directories.
WA	Write audit	This attribute is available in Netware 3.1. It provides an audit trail for files that have been written to, showing who wrote to the file. The attribute applies only to files.

and PERSONS.DAT files. This user would then be able to modify these two files, but not the PAY.DAT or CHECKS.DAT files.

The directory and file trustee rights are presented in Table 9.2.

BINDERY

NetWare 286 contains the bindery files, NET$BIND.SYS and NET$BVAL.SYS. By contrast, NetWare 386 uses the bindery files, NET$OBJ.SYS, NET$PROP.SYS, and NET$VAL.SYS. The NetWare 286 bindery holds a maximum of 1,000 objects. Together, the NetWare 386 files can hold up to 16,777,216 objects and the same number of properties. An object is a user group, a user, a file server, a print server, and so on. Associated with each object is a set of properties. Each property is given a value.

For example, a user object will contain a set of properties, such as a password, a list of groups the user belongs to, and account balance information. Each property will have a value. For example, the value of groups belonged to might include the group name "Everyone."

The bindery automatically contains one object—supervisor—that has extensive rights and privileges. The supervisor can give supervisor rights to a work-group manager (wg-manager). For instance, the work group manager might be extended the right to create new users.

PASSWORDS

NetWare 386 permits encrypted passwords to be used both at the level of the workstation and over the network. This prevents others from finding a way to obtain a password without authorization.

TABLE 9.2
File and Directory Trustee Rights

Trustee Right	Full Name	Description
A	Access control	This trustee right enables the user to modify the trustee list of a directory or file, as well as the inherited rights mask.
C	Create	At the directory level, this means the user can create files and subdirectories. When assigned to a file trustee, it means the user can salvage a deleted file.
E	Erase	At the directory level, this means the user can delete the directory. At the file level, it means the user can delete the file.
F	File scan	For a directory, this right enables the user to view the names of files when scanning with the DIR or NDIR commands. For files, it means the user can view the file on a scan of a file.
M	Modify	This right enables a user to rename a directory/file or to change the directory/file attributes.
R	Read	The user has the right to open and read existing files in a directory. At the file level, he or she has the right to read and open a specific file.
S	Supervisor	This right gives the user all rights to the directory, its files, and all subdirectories within the directory. At the file level, the user has all trustee rights to the file.
W	Write	The user can open and write to all the files in the specified directory. At the file level, the user can open and write to the specified file.

FILE SERVER ACCOUNTING

NetWare 386 enables accounting charges to be made on the basis of the number of records accessed, number of service requests, and length of time connected. Charges can also be made according to the number of pages printed at a print server.

The system can keep an audit trail of all charges, as well as an audit trail of those persons who have read or written to specific files. A hold can also be placed on the account of a user who has an overdue balance.

NETWARE LOADABLE MODULES

NetWare Loadable Modules (NLMs) are used by NetWare 386 to replace the VAPs (Value Added Processes) used in NetWare 286. NLMs are separate modules that can be loaded or unloaded while the file server is running. They are loaded into memory and, when unloaded, release the memory allocated to them.

NLMs have direct access to the file server processes via a set of system calls known as the Application Program Interfaces. Together, the system calls represent the Loadable Module Interface. The APIs consist largely of various C-programming language libraries.

NLMs give the ability to add new functions to the file server operation. Likewise, third-party vendors can write powerful utilities that can be interfaced immediately with NetWare 386. The four kinds of NLMs are:

- Application modules and utilities, such as the VREPAIR utility and the print server utility
- LAN drivers, which consist of drivers for various network interface boards
- Disk drivers for disks, such as those using an ESDI controller
- Modules for including file system name spaces, such as the module for Macintosh file names

NLMs are easy to load. They are linked with the server's operating system by using the LOAD console command.

An example of an application NLM is the print server utility, included with NetWare 386. This application supports up to sixteen printers and is controlled through the PCONSOLE menu utility. Users can submit, modify, and delete print jobs on print servers. Queue operators can manage print jobs that are in specific print queues, and can request status information about print servers.

OPEN DATA-LINK INTERFACE

The **Open Data-Link Interface** allows NetWare 386 to handle a variety of network communication protocols, such as TCP/IP or AppleTalk, in addition to IPX/SPX.

NetWare 386 uses LAN adapters with LAN drivers, which will accept any kind of packet. These drivers are known as MLIDs, or Multi-Link Interface Drivers. When it receives a packet, the MLID sends it to the next layer, called the Link Support Layer (LSL). The LSL layer identifies the packet (IPX/SPX, TCP/IP, etc.), then passes it to the next layer, called the Protocol Stack layer.

The Protocol Stack layer contains stacks for different protocols, including IPX and TCP/IP. After the packet is placed onto the correct stack, it is passed to a higher network layer or sent back down through the previous layers to another LAN adapter on another network. The

TABLE 9.3
New and Enhanced NetWare Commands

Command	Description
ALLOW	This command-line utility enables you to change the inherited rights mask of a directory/file.
CHKDIR	This command line utility permits you to display the disk space limits of your volume and directory.
DSPACE	This menu utility enables you to view disk space restrictions, which apply to users for volume and directory.
FILER	This menu utility now incorporates all of the new attributes, trustee rights, and inherited rights mask options.
INSTALL	This menu utility is an NLM, which enables you to install partitions and hard disks while the file server is running.
MONITOR	This NLM is similar to the MONITOR console command and the FCONSOLE command in NetWare 286. This command is in a menu format.
NBACKUP	This menu command replaces the backup commands in NetWare 286. It replaces NetWare 286 commands, such as NARCHIVE, NRESTORE, LARCHIVE, and LRESTORE.
PCONSOLE	This menu utility now incorporates print server control. It also provides information about the printer status, such as when the printer is out of paper.
PSC	This is a command line utility which gives users quick control over printers.
RPRINTER	This command line utility connects and disconnects remote printers from the print server.
UPGRADE	This is a menu utility designed to upgrade a file server from NetWare 286 to NetWare 386.

Protocol Stack layer makes the packet available to the NetWare operating system.

NETWARE COMMANDS

NetWare 386 adds several utility menus and command-line commands to the user's repertoire. These commands are described in Table 9.3.

CONSOLE UTILITIES

In addition to the new command line and menu utilities, NetWare 386 contains several new console command features. These range from the option to add non-DOS files to the NetWare volume, to the option to turn off transaction tracking. A summary of these commands is in Table 9.4.

SUMMARY

NetWare 386 is a powerful file server operating system. It takes advantage of the 80386 CPU to make better use of file server memory and expanded access to available memory and disk storage. The operating system is easier to install than that of NetWare 286. It allows configuration changes without downing the server. Two significant additions to the NetWare 386 operating system include NetWare Loadable Modules and the Open Data-Link Interface. Additions to security management through attributes, trustee rights, and the inherited rights mask also provide important enhancements to the operating system.

CHAPTER QUESTIONS

1. Describe the disk-access method used by NetWare 386.
2. Explain disk volume, disk segment, and disk partition.
3. What is the Turbo-FAT in NetWare 386?
4. Discuss two ways in which NetWare 386 can be reconfigured without downing the file server.
5. How is memory allocated on a NetWare 386 file server?

TABLE 9.4
Console Commands

Command	Description
ADD NAME SPACE	This command enables you to add new file-naming conventions to a NetWare volume. For example, it is run to add Macintosh files to the server. However, the NLM, MAC.NAM must be run first.
BIND	This command is used to associate protocol stacks with LAN boards. As mentioned earlier, several protocol stacks can be associated with one LAN board.
CLS	This command is used to clear the console screen (same as the OFF command).
DISABLE TTS	This command enables you to turn off transaction tracking. Note that in NetWare 286, it is necessary to regenerate the file server in order to disable TTS.
DISPLAY NETWORKS	This command displays a list of the networks known to the router.
DISPLAY SERVERS	A list of servers known to the router is shown when this command is used.
ECHO OFF	This causes the server to suppress display of the console commands executed by AUTOEXEC.NCF or STARTUP.NCF files.
ECHO ON	When this is used, the commands executed by the AUTOEXEC.NCF and STARTUP.NCF files are displayed at the file server console.
ENABLE TTS	This command turns on transaction tracking if TTS has been disabled.
EXIT	This is used following the DOWN command. It returns the server to the DOS environment.
IPX INTERNAL NET	This command sets the internal network number used by the router to identify users who reside on the same server as the router.
LOAD	This command loads an NLM.
MODULES	This command shows a listing of the NLMs loaded on the file server.
REMOVE DOS	This command removes DOS from the file server's memory. DOS is no longer resident on the server until it is rebooted.

TABLE 9.4 *(Continued)*
Console Commands

Command	Description
RESET ROUTER	This command instructs the router to clear its tables of existing server and network information. It causes the router to rebuild its tables as it receives new information from communication packets it receives.
SEARCH	This command tells the server where to find NLM files and .NCF files. Search paths are entered with the command showing where to locate these files. When the command is used without search paths, it displays the currently established paths.
SECURE CONSOLE	This command enables the console operator to establish security options associated with the console, such as loading NLMs only from the SYSTEM directory, and limiting entry into the operating system debugger.
SERVER NAME	This command establishes the server name when the operating system is loaded. The command is only used from the AUTOEXEC.NCF file, and not directly from the console keyboard.
SET	This command enables the console operator to change configuration information on the server. For example, the command permits changing the cache buffer size, the minimum number of packet receive buffers, and so on.
SPEED	This command displays the server's CPU speed.
TRACK OFF	This turns off display of advertising packets from the network.
TRACK ON	This command enables the server to display advertising packets from the network.
UNBIND	This command is used to remove a given protocol stack from a LAN card.
UNLOAD	This command unloads an NLM that has already been loaded.
VERSION	This command shows the version of NetWare currently in operation.
VOLUMES	This command displays a listing of the server volumes.

6. How are NetWare 386 file attributes different from NetWare 286 file attributes?

7. What is the inherited rights mask?

8. What is the purpose of an NLM? Name the four kinds of NLMs.

9. What is the function of the Open Data-Link Interface?

10. Describe four new NetWare 386 utility commands.

11. You have been asked to design a LAN that will have one file server. The LAN is projected to have eighty active users. These users will be accessing the following software:

   • A word processor
   • A desktop publishing package
   • A package that makes charts and graphs
   • A computer-aided design package

   What microcomputer should be used for the file server? How much memory should the file server have? What NetWare operating system would you recommend? Justify your recommendations. What additional information about the LAN should you request to help in making recommendations?

10

Application Software: Supporting the User

INTRODUCTION

The guiding purpose of a LAN is to make a variety of applications available to users. Common applications are word processors, spreadsheets, databases, the DOS operating system, desktop publishing software, communications software, and other specialized software.

Some applications will be available only to a single user. Other applications will be available to all users (depending on licensing rights). The latter group of applications—those to be made available to many users—pose special challenges. In fact, the single most difficult aspect of establishing a LAN can be adapting application software to a multi-user environment.

This chapter focuses on how to install a variety of application software successfully, beginning with the step of setting up directories. Subsequent steps include testing the software on the LAN, installing software, creating menus, and establishing printer options.

ESTABLISHING DIRECTORIES

Before installing software, it is essential to develop a plan for organizing the directories on the file server. Without such a plan, directories

197

will quickly get out of hand. No one will know what software is where, which directory contains the most recent version of a program, or what software is mingled with other software in a given directory. Here are some simple rules for establishing directories and subdirectories:

- Limit your root directory to twenty or fewer entries.

- Avoid putting application software in the Novell-created directories: PUBLIC, SYSTEM, MAIL, LOGIN.

- Identify versions of the application software in the directory name.

- Establish major directories, such as APP, for applications; put specific applications in their own subdirectories under the major directory.

- Do not install two different applications in the same subdirectory.

- Keep a record of what software is installed on the LAN, including license authorizations.

A plan for organizing directories should include minimizing entries in the root directory. Entries in the root directory should not exceed what can be displayed on one screen. Think of the root directory as a master filing cabinet with a limited number of drawers. Each drawer represents a major area of work, with the drawers themselves

FIGURE 10.1
File Organization of a File Server

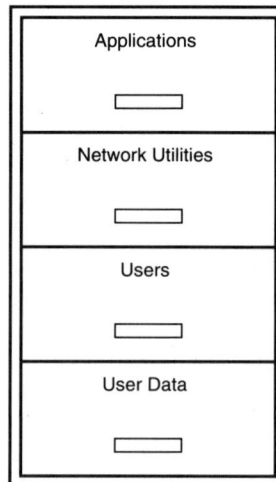

FIGURE 10.2
Sample Application Directory

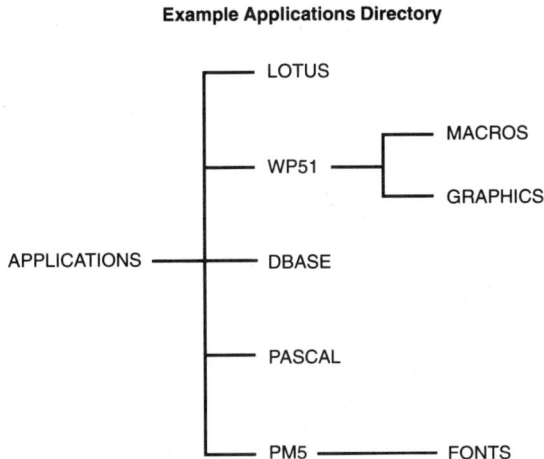

Example Applications Directory

```
                            ┌─── LOTUS
                            │                  ┌─── MACROS
                            ├─── WP51 ───┤
                            │                  └─── GRAPHICS
  APPLICATIONS ────────────┤─── DBASE
                            │
                            ├─── PASCAL
                            │
                            └─── PM5 ──────── FONTS
```

containing subareas of work. Major areas on a given file server might include software applications, network utilities, user directories, and user data (see Figure 10.1).

The applications directory, as an example, can be divided into a host of subdirectories, one for each software application. There might be a LOTUS subdirectory for Lotus 1-2-3, a DBASEIV subdirectory for dBase IV, a WP51 subdirectory for WordPerfect 5.1, and a PM4 directory for PageMaker 4.0.

Figure 10.2 shows how subdirectories might be allocated within an applications directory. Figure 10.2 illustrates with WordPerfect that specific files for an application can be placed in another subdirectory under the individual application subdirectory. Macros and set files (default settings) for WordPerfect can be placed in a WP51 MACROS subdirectory; and graphics files can be placed in a GRAPHICS subdirectory.

LICENSING AND COPY PROTECTION

When the purchaser buys an applications package, he or she is given a license to use the software only according to the vendor's stipulations. Normally the license does not include the option to alter the software, to make copies for use by others, or to run the software on more computers than the license authorizes.

When software is purchased, read the vendor's licensing restrictions and plan to follow these restrictions. Even when LAN- or site-licensed versions are purchased, know and follow the vendor's licensing restrictions. The same applies to shareware and public domain software.

Several Novell-compatible software products are available to help the network manager adhere to software licensing restrictions. When installed, these products will monitor the number of users of a particular software application. If there are only five licenses for a particular application, these packages will enable the network to prevent more than five people from accessing that specific application. Some monitoring packages even allow the network manager to gather data on how often applications are used. In this way, if there is a need to purchase more software licenses for a specific application, the network manager will know from the data.

Another good practice is to take steps to prevent software from being copied from the network. This is done by setting flags and trustee rights. Software not intended to be copied can be flagged "shareable read only" (SRO), and the trustee rights for users in that directory can be set at "read open search" (ROS). These flags and trustee rights permit several people to use the software, but not copy it from the network.

SOFTWARE INSTALLATION CONCERNS

Not all software is intended for a LAN or multi-user environment. Before installing a software application on a Novell LAN, find out if it is intended for LAN use. Some applications are written specifically to be used in a network environment. Some are not, but can be adapted to run on a LAN. And some software is not intended for LAN use, or even for adaptation to a LAN.

The considerations above are important, because a single software package can make a LAN act unpredictably. As a rule, software that is not intended for LAN use, or adaptation to a LAN, should not be put on the LAN. LAN use is likely to be in violation of the vendor's intention for that software, and the risk is simply not worth the effort.

A second rule to follow is always to test software applications before making them available in a production mode. Here are several guidelines to follow when testing software:

- Find out if the software can be used in a multi-user environment.

- Test the software when the LAN is not in a production mode, or at least when no critical user activities are taking place.

- Test the software by logging in several users simultaneously, and have them all try the software at the same time.

- Test the software on all of the workstation/printer configurations where it will be used.

- Test all menus involving the software before bringing them live to be accessed by users.

- Test the software by operating it as it was not intended to be operated; try to simulate common user mistakes.

One very important consideration while testing software is to determine how much memory is required for an individual workstation to use the software. Some applications, such as computer-aided design (CAD) packages, require a large amount of memory in the workstation. Use of these packages may have to be limited to specific workstations.

Another memory issue is whether the memory requirements of an application will interfere with the operation of the workstation. For example, the memory requirements of an application may cause the IPX.COM file on the workstation to fail, act erratically, or even hang the workstation. Often this means there is not enough memory for the IPX.COM file, any **terminate-and-stay-resident** (TSR) files, and the application itself. Or it may mean the application is addressing the same range of memory addressed by the IPX.COM file.

In the first case, where there is too much loaded into memory, the solution may be to clear any TSRs out of memory. Another approach is to experiment with the FILES and BUFFERS allocations in the CONFIG.SYS file. An additional step might be to increase the memory in the workstations where it will be used (if those workstations have less than 640 KB of memory).

Where there is an addressing conflict between the IPX.COM file on the workstation and the application, use the SHGEN utility to generate a new IPX.COM file. The new IPX.COM file should address another memory location.

MENUS

Installed software can be run from a NetWare menu or from a third-party menu system. The NetWare system combines Novell menu com-

TABLE 10.1
NetWare Menu Commands

Command	Description
%	This command is placed in the left-most margin. It indicates that the text that follows is the title of the menu.
n,n,n	Three numeric values separated by commas can be placed after the menu title. The first two values determine the horizontal and vertical placement of a menu. The third value specifies the color. If no values are given, the menu is placed in the center of the screen with no color palette. In Figure 10.3 the title of the menu will be *dBase Menu*, with a menu window centered on the screen.
Left-Justified Text	Left-justified text is interpreted as a menu option, which appears under the title of the menu. The menu created by the commands in Figure 10.3 will have two options, *dBase* and *dBase Applications Generator*.
Indented Commands	The menu system will attempt to execute any Novell or DOS command indented from column one. These include DOS commands, such as the clear-screen command (CLS). Or a DOS program can be run by giving the name of the program. A common Novell command is MAP INSERT. This command is used to create a search directory to a program file.
!logout	This command will log the user off. It must be indented from the left margin.

mands with DOS batch file commands. A list of frequently used menu commands is presented in Table 10.1.

Menu command files are created in ASCII format and have an ".mnu" extension. To run a menu, type the MENU command followed by the name of the menu.

INSTALLATION

The following sections describe important aspects of installing several popular applications packages. Use these examples as a guide for installing different software applications.

Each application installation section contains a sample NetWare menu for that application. The menus are simple and straightforward;

they illustrate each installation. As you design menus, you will likely want to add error checking and the ability to limit access, depending on the number of licenses for the software.

dBase

The dBase system is installed on the network by placing all of the dBase files in a dBASE subdirectory within the applications directory. Follow the vendor's directions to install dBase.

Once dBase is installed, change the dBase configuration file, CONFIG.DB. Add a statement to show where data files are to be written. For example, if the data is to be written to a diskette in drive A, then the CONFIG.DB file should have the following line:

DEFAULT = A

Figure 10.3 illustrates a sample dBase menu from within the Novell menuing system. Notice there is an option to run the applications generator in dBase. The applications generator is normally located in the same subdirectory as the dBase programs. In Figure 10.3 it is accessed from search drive 4.

FIGURE 10.3
NetWare dBase Menu

```
                Example NetWare dBase Menu


%dBase Menu
dBase
      echo off
      cls
      map insert s4:=sys:app/dbase >nul:
      dbase
      map rem s4: >nul:
dBase Applications Generator
      echo off
      cls
      map inserts4:=sys:app/dbase >nul:
      dbase v:appsgen
      map rem s4: >nul:
```

Lotus 1-2-3

Lotus 1-2-3 provides many installation possibilities on differing work-stations with various printer combinations. Information about driver sets is stored in a file called 123.CNF. Lotus uses this file to create another file, 123.SET, which contains the actual information or driver sets used for Lotus 1-2-3 to run on specific hardware.

To establish the LAN version of Lotus 1-2-3 on a file server, first install the software according to the vendor's directions.

Once Lotus 1-2-3 has been installed on the file server, it is necessary to create separate driver sets for each type of hardware configuration on the LAN. If the LAN has some workstations with EGA (Enhanced Graphics Adaptor) monitors, then their driver set needs to be created. If some HGA (Hercules Graphics Adaptor) workstations are used, then an HGA driver set needs to be created.

To generate driver sets, run the Install program that comes with Lotus 1-2-3. Once in the Install menu, choose the Advanced Options selection. Next, select "Modify the Current Driver Set." (If there are several driver sets, take the "Make Another Driver Set Current" selection.) Modifications that can be entered include:

- Text Display
- Graph Display
- Port Interface
- Text Printer
- Graph Printer

Consult the Lotus 1-2-3 documentation and select the options that need to be customized for one of the workstation combinations, such as an HGA workstation with an Epson network printer. Once all of the selections have been made, save the driver set, using the Install Menu's "Save" option. The save screen will ask for a name to give the driver set. Use names that are descriptive of the type of driver set. For instance, use HGA for Hercules compatible display adapters; or use EGA for enhanced graphics adaptor. In these two examples, an HGA.SET file would be created or an EGA.SET file would be created.

Repeat the installation process for each driver set that needs to be created. Once the driver sets are created, document what they are in a notebook or in a README file in the Lotus 1-2-3 subdirectory.

To run a specific driver set with Lotus 1-2-3, enter the name of the driver set just after the LOTUS command. (In some versions of Lotus, the LOTUS command is given as 123.) Thus, you enter "LOTUS HGA," to use the HGA.SET driver set. In a menu environment, a driver

FIGURE 10.4
NetWare Lotus 1-2-3 Menu

```
              Example NetWare Lotus 1-2-3 Menu

%Lotus 1-2-3
Lotus 1-2-3- Spreadsheets
     echo off
     cls
     map insert s4:=sys:app/lotus >nul:
     if P_Station = 123456 goto egal
     if P_Station = 456789 goto hgal
     :egal
          123 EGAL
         goto exit
     :hgal
           123 HGAL
          goto exit
     :exit
     map rem s5: >nul:
```

set can be invoked by identifying its unique station address, then invoking the driver according to its station address. For instance, if Station 123456 has an EGA display card and laser printer, it might use driver set EGAL.SET. Figure 10.4 illustrates how a Novell menu might be written for this environment.

An alternative to using physical station address, is to write a program to identify the display card, then invoke the correct driver set. Some versions of the C and Pascal compilers contain functions that will identify the type of display card in a workstation.

PageMaker

Before installing Aldus PageMaker on a network, create a CONFIG.SYS file on the workstation or workstations that will access PageMaker. Establish the CONFIG.SYS file with FILES = 20 and with BUFFERS = 30. Also, keep in mind two other factors regarding PageMaker. First, the workstation must have an 80286 or 80386 CPU to run PageMaker successfully.

Second, PageMaker runs under MicroSoft Windows. Both applications require large amounts of memory. PageMaker requires at least 640 KB of memory; and it runs 15- to 25-percent faster when used with expanded or extended memory. A memory manager program, called SMARTDrive, comes with MicroSoft Windows, and is available on the Windows Utility disk. If you intend to use SMARTDrive, add another line to the CONFIG.SYS file to load the smartdrv.sys file into memory as follows:

CONFIG.SYS
> files = 20
> buffers = 30
> device = \windows\ smartdrv.sys 1000

In this example, the 1,000 KB represents the amount of memory to allocate to SMARTDrive. Note that this discussion of memory pertains only to the workstation and not the file server. Adding memory to the file server will not make PageMaker run faster on the workstation.

During installation of PageMaker, the install process asks whether to install a path statement in the AUTOEXEC.BAT file. On most file server setups, NetWare will not recognize this path statement. Therefore, it is good practice to tell the installation procedure not to install the path statement.

Install and configure PageMaker for a specific workstation on the file server. It is necessary to have unique installations for EGA monitors, VGA monitors, CGA monitors, and HGA-compatible monitors. PageMaker can be installed with limited run-time Windows, which comes with the PageMaker diskettes. Or it can be installed with the full version of Windows, purchased separately from Microsoft. The advantage of a full version of Windows is that it allows access to clip-art, fonts, and graphics-design programs, which can be used with PageMaker.

If it is necessary to store preestablished defaults in PageMaker, then a PM.CNF file will be in the PageMaker subdirectory. To ensure access to this file, it is necessary to edit the WIN.INI file. WIN.INI is an initialization file stored in the Windows subdirectory if a full version of Windows is used with PageMaker. If the run-time version is used, this file is stored in the PageMaker subdirectory.

Contained within the WIN.INI file is the statement "defaults = ." The right side of the equals sign should reflect the full network path to the PM.CNF file if PageMaker is installed on the network. The default WIN.INI file reads:

[PageMaker]
Defaults = \app\pm\pm.cnf

Also contained within the WIN.INI file is a spooler control statement near the beginning of the file. The Windows spooler is not intended to work in the network environment; it must be turned off with this statement:

Spooler = no

Finally, when using the WIN.INI file for network installations, review it thoroughly to be certain all paths are correct. For example, if additional fonts are installed, the path statements must reflect the appropriate subdirectory containing the fonts.

Whether PageMaker is installed on the network or on a workstation, it is necessary to direct the PageMaker temporary files to the appropriate location. As work is performed in PageMaker, the software creates temporary files with the .TMP extension. For network installations, create a subdirectory under the PageMaker directory for these temporary files. Or direct the files to fixed drive C: or floppy drives A: or B:.

If the temporary files are directed to floppy drives, consider the access speed of the drives and the capacity. Writing to a fixed disk (if it has quick access) or to the network is considerably faster than writing to a floppy. Also, PageMaker temporary files can be quite large, and may be too large for smaller 360 KB and 720 KB diskettes. If the diskette is too small, this can cause PageMaker to fail when the software tries to write to a temporary file.

When you write temporary files to the network drive, it's good practice to delete these files routinely, since they lose their value once a PageMaker session is completed. (A utility to delete these files can be added to the network utility directory and can be run at regular intervals.)

One last factor regarding PageMaker installation involves establishing the CAPTURE command for network printing. Since PageMaker documents can be long and complex, set the time in the Novell CAPTURE command to 20 seconds or more to allow ample time for the document to be spooled. Here is a sample capture command:

CAPTURE NT NB Q = LASER TI = 20

Figure 10.5 provides an example of a NetWare menu for PageMaker.

FIGURE 10.5
NetWare PageMaker Menu

```
              Example NetWare Pagemaker Menu for
                  Run-time Windows Installation

%Pagemaker Menu
Pagemaker
      echo off
      cls
      set temp = c:
      map insert s4:=sys:app/pm >nul:
      pm
      map rem s4: >nul:
```

Paint Programs

There are many paint programs on the market that permit the user to draw images, set up type fonts, and design clip-art. Two examples of these paint programs are Microsoft's PC Paintbrush and Mouse System's PC Paint. Like most paint programs, PC Paintbrush and PC Paint use a drawing device, such as a mouse or roller ball.

Before accessing a paint program, it's necessary to have some means of loading the pointing-device driver into memory on the workstation. For PC Paint and PC Paintbrush, this is done in one of two ways. The mouse driver can be loaded at boot time onto the workstation via a "device=" statement in the CONFIG.SYS file. When using the Mouse System's Mouse with PC Paint, the device statement is:

DEVICE = MSMOUSE.SYS /1

In this statement, the 1 is used to specify COM1: as the port used to connect the mouse. To load the MSMOUSE.SYS file, you must put it on the boot diskette. For Microsoft's PC Paintbrush, the mouse driver is loaded in the same fashion, except that the name of the driver file is MOUSE.SYS:

DEVICE = MOUSE.SYS

The mouse driver can also be loaded after the workstation is booted and logged onto the network. This is done by executing a program. For PC Paint, the program is called MSMOUSE.COM; for PC Paintbrush, the program is MOUSE.COM.

Loading the program is the better method. When the mouse driver is loaded at boot time, it remains in memory, even if the paint program is not the first program to be accessed. If there is limited memory on the workstation, this may cause a problem when using programs that require a large amount of memory. (Keep in mind that the IPX and NETx files are also in memory.)

To avoid a possible memory shortage or memory conflict, it is simpler to load the mouse driver at the time the paint program is accessed. However, because the mouse driver stays resident after the paint program is exited, this may cause memory problems later. Thus, in some cases, it may be best to reboot the workstation after a paint session is completed.

The paint programs can be loaded into a subdirectory under the APP directory. Because the paint programs may need to access font and picture files from within the paint subdirectory, it is generally necessary to have the Novell calling menu switch to the subdirectory to access the paint program. Accessing the programs from the home directory via a map insert statement is generally not an effective way to access paint programs of this nature. If the paint program is licensed to only one or two people on the network, it may be better to put the paint files in a subdirectory under each user's home directory. The paint programs and data files can then be accessed from the user's own subdirectory.

Figure 10.6 illustrates a sample PC Paint Novell menu.

The paint program is often itself run from another program environment. PC Paintbrush runs from a memory-resident program called FRIEZE, and PC Paint runs from an INSET resident program. These program environments stay resident until they are removed. The programs are used to send graphics from the display screen to a printer. When the paint program is exited, these memory-resident programs are removed from memory automatically. In the process, the memory pointers that enable the return to the calling menu (such as the Novell menu) may be removed or deleted, too. The result may be that the menu is exited or aborted when the paint program is exited. One solution to this is to write a program, for instance in C language, to prevent

FIGURE 10.6
NetWare PC Paint Menu

```
               Example NetWare PC Paint Menu

     %Paint Menu
     PC Paint
          echo off
          cls
          map insert 1:=sys:app/pcpaint >nul:
          1:
          paint
          map rem 1: >nul:
```

the menu pointers from being lost. Another solution is to put a "#Log-out" statement in the user's login script to ensure that the user is logged out automatically if the menu call is aborted.

WordPerfect

WordPerfect is a widely used word processing package, which is also available in a version for networks.

Before you install WordPerfect, make certain the workstation boot diskettes or boot drives have a CONFIG.SYS file with two lines, FILES = 20 and BUFFERS = 5.

To install WordPerfect, create a subdirectory, such as APP/WP51. Install the WordPerfect diskettes into this subdirectory, including the WordPerfect program diskettes, the thesaurus, the speller, and the fonts/graphics diskettes. It is not necessary to copy all of the printer drivers onto the file server, since you will use only a few.

Once the WordPerfect files are copied onto the file server, you can establish one or more subdirectories under the WordPerfect directory. For instance, you can create a subdirectory for macros and keyboard files. You can create another subdirectory for graphics or clip-art. By doing so, you can retain previously-used macros or clip-art, if your version of WordPerfect is upgraded.

Start WordPerfect and establish the default setup options for users. The "Setup" menu is accessed via the Setup key, which is Shift-F1. You may wish to place WordPerfect macros, keyboard files, backup files, or dictionary files in separate subdirectories. If you do, select the Location of Auxiliary Files option on the "Setup" menu to establish search paths to these directories for WordPerfect. You may also wish to set up other defaults, such as screen display settings, keyboard layouts, or automatic backup options.

If you have 4.2 macros, they can be converted by using the MACROCNV.EXE program that comes with WordPerfect. WordPerfect also comes with a CONVERT.EXE program for converting other word processor text files, such as WordStar files, to the WordPerfect format.

WordPerfect setup information, including printer selections, can be saved to .SET files on the server. For instance, if there is a user who needs access to a network laser printer and his or her own local printer, a .SET file can be customized for this purpose. The network

FIGURE 10.7
NetWare WordPerfect Menu

```
                    Example WordPerfect Menu

        %WordPerfect Menu
        WordPerfect
                echo off
                cls
                map insert s4:=sys:app/wp51 >nul:
                a:
                wp/nc/nt=1/u-rmj
                map rem s4: >nul:
        WordPerfect Convert
                echo off
                cls
                a:
                map insert s4:=sys/wp51 >nul:
                convert
                map rem s4: >nul:
        WordPerfect Tutor
                echo off
                cls
                map insert s4:=sys/wp51/learn >nul:
                a:
                tutor
                map rem s5: >nul:
```

version of WordPerfect identifies the user by his or her initials. The initials are used for the .SET file name. If the user's initials are RMJ, then the file WPRMJ}.SET is created. Setup and printer options, which are installed during a WordPerfect session, are automatically saved under these initials. Every time users enter their initials when accessing WordPerfect, they automatically get their special setup defaults.

For general use, the network manager may want to establish a .SET file for users who do not need special setup options. This may be true for students who use WordPerfect in a student microcomputer laboratory. The set file they use may have the initials GEN (WPGEN}.SET).

To install given printer definitions for use with .SET files, access the "Print" menu by pressing Shift-F7. Install both network and local printer options via the *Select Printer* option from the "Print" menu. Consult the WordPerfect instructions for this process, noting that network printers use the queue name for the port selection. For example, a printer connected to network print queue 0 would be port 0.

WordPerfect comes with switches to reduce what the user must enter to invoke the program. For instance, the /U switch selects a given .SET file for the user; /NT is used to select the network type; /M tells WordPerfect to begin with a specified macro.

In some Novell network situations, WordPerfect's cursor speed option does not function well with all machines connected to the network. The /NC switch can be used to turn off the cursor speed facility. The menu in Figure 10.7 shows WordPerfect invoked with Network Type 1 for Novell, normal cursor, and a .SET file for user RMJ. Notice that the menu changes to drive A: before starting WordPerfect. This is to ensure that WordPerfect temporary files are not written on the network drive. Another alternative is to write a macro that directs the files to drive A: via the macro. This alternative entails using the /M switch to start the macro. Notice there are menu options to run the Convert program and the On-Line tutorial. And the files pertinent to the tutorial diskette are in the subdirectory LEARN.

WordStar

When WordStar is installed on a network, it is necessary to tell WordStar which drives to access. Once the WordStar files are copied to the file server, it is necessary to run a program called WSCHANGE, which sets up information WordStar needs, such as disk drive information and display adaptor information.

By using the WSCHANGE program, you can establish the valid disk drives for WordStar. Drives must be defined as hard or floppy.

FIGURE 10.8
NetWare WordStar Menu

```
              Example NetWare WordStar Menu

    %WordStar Menu
    WordStar
         echo off
         cls
         map insert s4:=sys:app/ws >nul:
         ws
         map rem s4: >nul:
```

The first drive defined is the search drive for WordStar. The search drive information allows WordStar to find its overlay files. For example, if WordStar files are to be saved on workstation drives A: or C:, these must be defined as valid drives to WordStar. If the network search drive for WordStar is drive R, this must be defined as the search drive in WordStar as well. The network search drive is always defined as a hard drive in WordStar.

Consult Figure 10.8 for a sample Novell menu used to invoke WordStar.

PRINTING

Most Novell networks contain a variety of printers connected to both the file server and to individual workstations. Because this is true, there must be options to permit users to direct their printouts to a desired printer.

Some application software permits the user to print on network or local printers from within the application. The network version of

WordPerfect is an example of application software where this flexibility exists. Many software packages, however, do not provide for this type of flexibility.

One way to give the user flexibility is to create a menu. The user's menu may have a printer routing option designed to enable users to control where their printouts go. The menu can make use of the CAPTURE and ENDCAP commands to ensure that print jobs go to the right printer. The menu can also contain a call to PCONSOLE, to give users the option to delete a print job from the queue.

For example, the network might have a laser printer and a plotter connected to the file server, which are designated as Printer 0 and Printer 1. Each user might also have his or her own 9-pin dot matrix printer, which might be used for rough drafts, while the laser printer is used for final copies, and the plotter used to plot formal graphs and charts. The user can go into a menu and select the appropriate option. The menu example in Figure 10.9 shows how a menu selection might be written to accommodate such options.

This menu can be made even more powerful if print queues are created via Novell's PRINTCON utility and if printer control modes are created via Novell's PRINTDEF utility. PRINTDEF enables you

FIGURE 10.9
NetWare Printing Menu

```
                   Example Novell Printing Menu


        %Printer Selections
        Print to the Laser Printer
              echo off
              capture p=0 nb nt ti=10
        Print to the Plotter
              echo off
              capture p=1 nb nt ti=10
        Print to Your Local Printer
              echo off
              endcap
```

to create specific control modes for a printer. For example, a mode can be created for the laser printer to put it into landscape mode and print at 16.6 pitch (small or compressed printing). This mode is appropriate for printing large spreadsheets sideways. Another mode can be created to print laser printer documents using a Helvetica font cartridge. These modes can then be associated with a specific print queue through PRINTCON. The landscape and 16.6 pitch mode might be used with a queue called LASER1. The Helvetica mode might be used with a queue called LASER2. With these options, two new capture commands can be added to the menu, resulting in the menu shown in Figure 10.10.

In addition to having network and local printers, it is also possible to establish remote printers in a Novell network. There are third-party software packages that make remote printing possible. Remote printing involves making one or more workstation printers available to anyone on the network. The workstation the remote printer is attached to can be dedicated or nondedicated as a print server. If it is dedicated, the workstation is used only for the print server functions. If it is non-dedicated, the print server functions run in the background, while the workstation is used as a normal workstation.

FIGURE 10.10
NetWare Printing Menu with Print Queue Options

```
              Example Novell Printing Menu
              with New Print Queue Options


%Printer Selections
Print to the Laser Printer Normal Mode
      echo off
      capture p=0 nb nt ti=10
Print to the Laser Printer Landscape Mode
      echo off
      capture p=0 nb nt ti=10 q=laser1
Print to the Laser Printer Helvetica Mode
      echo off
      capture p=0 nb nt ti=10 q=laser2
Print to the Plotter
      echo off
      capture p=1 nb nt ti=10
Print to Your Local Printer
      echo off
      endcap
```

Besides remote printing packages, memory-resident queuing packages are also available from third-party vendors. This software makes printer queue options memory-resident. When an application, such as Lotus 1-2-3, is entered, the user can invoke a specific key sequence and direct printouts to any desired queue. This is done without leaving the Lotus 1-2-3 application.

SUMMARY

A variety of software packages can be installed on a Novell network with good results. The key to successful software installation involves following some basic guidelines. First, decide on the directory and subdirectory structure. Second, each application package should be thoroughly tested on the LAN before it is made available to users. And last, care should be taken to follow each vendor's installation instructions, noting that individual software packages will require some special steps in the installation process.

CHAPTER QUESTIONS

1. List four guidelines for creating directories and subdirectories.
2. Develop an example directory structure for five applications: a compiler, two word processors, a database program, and a spreadsheet program.
3. What guidelines should be followed when testing software that is to be installed on a LAN?
4. What is the function of .SET files in Lotus 1-2-3?
5. What is the function of .SET files in WordPerfect?
6. Write a Novell menu that provides options to use Lotus 1-2-3, WordStar, WordPerfect, and dBase.
7. How would you resolve the problem of accessing Lotus 1-2-3 from workstations having different display monitors, such as HGA, EGA, and VGA?
8. Develop a Novell menu selection that enables users to direct printouts to either their local workstation printer or to a network printer using PRINTQ_2.
9. You have just installed WordPerfect. When you attempt to run it from a local workstation you get an out-of-memory message. Is this message a file server error or workstation error? What is likely to be the cause of the message? What would you do to solve the problem?

11

Utility Applications

INTRODUCTION TO UTILITIES

There are times the operating system will display an error message. Error messages are listed in the Novell manual *System Messages*. Some of the error messages recommend that a utility be run to correct the error. Such utilities are discussed in this chapter. In addition to utilities that deal with error conditions, there are utilities that enhance NetWare.

In general, NetWare is an operating system that provides a decentralized processing platform, shared network printing, and a shared network disk, all of which can be supported with utilities. They will be adequate in many situations. However, Novell sells technical information to encourage third-party developers to provide additional network utilities. Novell's openness has resulted in literally hundreds of new utilities that improve network management and enhance NetWare. This chapter discusses both Novell's utilities and third-party utilities, which support printing, remote workstation access, electronic mail, software licensing, troubleshooting user problems, remote dial-in, disk backup, diagnostics, and file server housekeeping.

PRINTING UTILITIES

Distributed printing is not available with NetWare 286. Instead, one file server can be configured for a maximum of five printers. These printers must be attached to the file server, and are subject to parallel and serial cable limitations. A user is limited to his or her local printer or to the network printer to create output. It is likely that some network users will be too far away from the network printer to be able to use it conveniently. To extend printer sharing, utilities are installed on the file server. Printer utilities permit any user on the LAN to print to a local printer.

Fresh Technology Group offers Printer Assist, a utility to add local printers to the network. This allows any user to access a printer that is connected to the network. Printer Assist reroutes jobs sent to the standard NetWare queues on the file server to the workstation printer. It also provides for logging the number of pages and lines printed, as well as the user and server/queue.

Printer Assist can be installed, either dedicated or nondedicated, with NetWare 286 and 386. Dedicated Printer Assist requires a dedicated workstation. Nondedicated Printer Assist allows a workstation to run the program in the background while other applications are running.

Installing Nondedicated Printer Assist

The following instructions apply to a file server with NetWare and with a workstation logged in as the supervisor.

1. **Use the Printer Assist INSTALL routine to copy the Printer Assist diskette to the UTIL directory.** If another directory is used, make sure the directory is mapped as a search drive.

2. **Define the print queues.** Shared local printing requires that you first create the desired queues with the NetWare PCONSOLE utility. The steps are:

   a. Run PCONSOLE and select the *Print Queue Information* option. Add a queue by pressing the INSERT key after the list of existing queues appears. PRINTQ_0 and perhaps PRINTQ_1 should already be there.

   b. Enter the name of the queue to be added. Associate the name of the queue with the local printer to be shared. For example, call a queue LASER for a laser printer. NetWare allows an unlimited number of queues to be added. Generally one printer services one queue. Actually, two printers (of the same type) can service one queue. The queue will route the output to the first available printer.

3. **Designate a user or group as a print server.** A user or a group on a workstation with a printer to be shared must be recognized by Net-Ware as a nondedicated print server. The PAQADD.COM program allows the supervisor to grant print server rights to a user or group of users in the following manner:

PAQADD PRINTQ_NAME GROUP_NAME or USER_NAME

Use PCONSOLE to create the PRINTQ_NAME. Use SYSCON to create GROUP_NAME and USER_NAME.

PAQADD.COM permanently enables the user with the local printer being shared the right to be a print server for that queue.

Setting Up the Workstation as a Print Server

On the workstation with the shared printer, the user or group member (as assigned by the PAQADD command) logs into the network.

1. **Setting up the workstation as a print server.** To load the resident print server software from the DOS prompt, type "PA" followed by the configuration switches to customize each print server worksta-tion. The Printer Assist manual explains the configuration switches. The switches determine the printer port to be used, the queue name, usage statistics, and the rate at which characters are sent from the queue to the printer. There are additional switches, but the following are enough for most configurations:

PA P=1 Q1=HP1

PA	The nondedicated print server program
P=1	Indicates the printer servicing jobs is attached to parallel port 1
Q1=HP1	Indicates Printer Assist is to reroute print jobs to the named queue HP1 (Hewlett-Packard Laser Printer 1) on the default file server

PA S=1 Q1=FS1/HP2 M=1000 L=HP2.LOG

S=1	Indicates the printer servicing jobs is attached to serial port 1
Q1=FS1/HP2	Indicates that Printer Assist is to reroute print jobs from file server FS1 on queue HP2 (Hewlett-Pack-ard Laser Printer 2).

M=1000   1,000 characters per second will be sent to the printer

L=HP2.LOG1 Enables recording of usage statistics for the print queue into the file HP2.LOG

In summary, print utilities are a must for networks with geographically dispersed workstations. Print utilities are not complicated to install. They do not require additional hardware, and, in the case of Printer Assist, they can use as little as 4 KB of the workstation's memory. Print server users are unaffected by having their printers used by other workstations.

REMOTE WORKSTATION ACCESS UTILITIES

Fresh Technology Group offers two utilities to support remote workstations. One is LAN Assist Plus, which allows authorized users to view, monitor, control, and assist any workstation on the network. With LAN Assist Plus, a network manager can help a user without leaving his or her office. Or a lab instructor can monitor the progress of students as they work through an assignment at their workstations.

Users have the ability to view another workstation screen as if sitting in front of that workstation. LAN Assist Plus also provides complete access to the screen and keyboard of other network workstations, even across bridged servers. Once LAN Assist Plus is installed, users load a 3 KB memory-resident file at their workstation.

LAN Assist Plus is copied to the UTIL directory, or to another directory for which there is an appropriate search path. It is then configured with LACONFIG.EXE. Some of the configuration options are:

- Allow keys to be entered remotely?
- Allow remote reboot?
- Display watching user name?
- Allow watched user to terminate look?
- Allow anyone to assist any computer?
- Allow multiple users to assist one computer?

A second utility from Fresh Technology Group is MAP Assist, which offers DOS-level, peer-to-peer disk access running under NetWare. Map Assist allows authorized users to "map" the physical drives of other workstations as their own logical drives. Users can also back up local drives, run applications, or copy and edit files residing on another workstation's local drives. Each workstation that shares a local disk loads a 6 KB memory-resident file. The local drive can be a floppy, hard, or CD ROM drive.

Installing MAP Assist requires the supervisor to copy the files into the UTIL directory, or into another directory with an appropriate search path. The host workstation that has the drive to share will load MAR.COM with a list of parameters; for example: MAR C:\APP RW=GROUP. This command creates a path to the APP directory and grants GROUP read and write access. The workstations wishing to access the host must load MA.COM. The host workstation can restrict access to one local workstation at a time or allow access to more than one at a time.

ELECTRONIC MAIL UTILITIES

Electronic mail allows users to send messages, letters, or drawings to individuals or mailing lists. The users reside on a single network, across networks, or on another mail system. Users can also attach spreadsheet, report, and DOS files. Mail users share the network hard disk and use it like a post office to send and receive mail. All of these features are available with an electronic mail system, such as CC:Mail, explained below to illustrate the benefits and ease of using a network mail system.

The network supervisor acts as mail administrator or designates a user to perform this role. The administrator installs the post office and maintains the database and program files. The administrator creates and manages the mail directory, public mailing lists, and bulletin boards. CC:Mail contains the following programs, which are important to a robust and secure mail system:

- A management statistics program to monitor the integrity of the database files
- A program that allows the administrator to reorganize the database files, minimizing the need to expand disk space as the mail system grows
- A program to allow users to dial into the post office
- A gateway to allow your post office to send and receive message traffic from CC:Mail users at other post offices
- An import/export program to move messages between CC:Mail and other applications
- A notify program that automatically alerts users of new mail

Installing CC:Mail requires creating three directories and granting the appropriate rights. First is the ADMIN directory, to which only the administrator has access. The programs in this directory permit the administrator to manage the mail directory, mailing lists, and bulletin boards. The CCMAIL directory has the mail program MAIL.EXE. The CCDATA directory contains the mail files or database.

CC:Mail is a menu-driven application. At any point in the program, the user highlights and selects the appropriate option. The mailing list is selected the same way. The following command is used to execute CC:Mail:

F:\CCMAIL\MAIL mailname pw M:\CCDATA

Mailname is the user's CC:Mail name, and pw is an optional password.

When the user first enters the mail menu, the highlighted selection will be either *Read Inbox Messages*, if there are any, or *Prepare New Message*, when no new mail is waiting to be read. A status box at the top of the screen informs the user of the number of new mail messages, how many total messages, and if bulletin board messages exist. When the *Read Inbox Messages* option is selected, headers of the mail messages are displayed with the latest message at the top of the list. Use the arrow key to highlight the message and the ENTER key to select the message to be read. After the message is read, use the ENTER key to display an "Action" menu. From the Action menu you can delete, attach items, move to folder, copy to folder, forward, reply, print, and archive. Each of these is selected by highlighting the choice and using the ENTER key.

Sending a message is a matter of selecting *Prepare New Message* from the main menu. Another screen with an "Address" menu is displayed. The options are to address to person, address to mailing list, address to bulletin board, copy to person, copy to mailing list, blind copy to person, and request receipt. The option *Address to Person* displays the mail directory. Highlight each person you wish to send mail to. The ESC key ends the selection. Second, type the subject. Third, type the mail message. The F10 function key ends the message step. Finally, a "Send" menu is displayed with the options to send message, attach copy of a DOS file, attach new items, display message, edit subject, and address message. Selecting *Send Message* will send the message.

Mail systems, such as CC:Mail, make a strong argument for installing LANs. Telephone tag is reduced, documents move faster, and communication is improved.

SOFTWARE LICENSING UTILITIES

Frequently, network versions of software are installed on a file server with no way to enforce the number of actual copies used at any one time. NetWare does not provide any utilities to restrict access to applications. Prudent network managers buy licenses for the *anticipated number* of users of an application at a particular time. For example, there is a network of thirty workstations. A site license of WordPerfect is purchased for twenty users. How is the twenty-first user prevented from using WordPerfect? The answer is to install licensing software. Not only is the legality of the license protected, but the software will also record the use of applications, as well as access rejections.

SiteLock is a licensing application that controls access to applications. It also records activity associated with the applications. Like Printer Assist, SiteLock is not difficult to install. It is a series of utilities that are executed from a batch file or menu, such as Novell's menu. To install and use SiteLock, follow the steps below. (Note: The supervisor must install the SiteLock utilities.)

1. **Create the SiteLock directory and add the group EVERYONE as a trustee.** Copy the SiteLock files to the directory SYS:SYSTEM-\SITELOCK. Use SYSCON and select *Group Information*. Select the group EVERYONE. Press ENTER and select *Trustee Information* from the menu. Use the INSERT key to add a trustee assignment. Enter SYS:SYSTEM/SITELOCK. Since this directory does not exist, answer "Yes" to add it. Modify the directory rights to read, write, open, create, and search.

2. **Add/update application locks with SiteLock.** Enter SITELOCK at the DOS prompt. A screen is displayed listing any locks. To ADD a lock, type the letter "a." Another screen will be displayed. You are prompted to enter:

   - The set name, which is a SiteLock record used to store information about access to an application
   - A brief description of the set
   - The number of simultaneous users

   To use WordPerfect as an example, the set name could be WPSET and the WordPerfect lock limitation could be set to fifteen licenses.

   Begin by entering WPSET as the set name. Next, enter a description, such as "WordPerfect Network Version." Enter 15 in the space for indicating the number of users. This procedure is repeated for each application software program. To update the set, re-enter SITELOCK and select the number of the set. If WPSET is listed as number one, then enter 1. A screen will display the current settings. Move to the location to be changed, and enter the updated information. A CTRL-D will delete a set.

3. **Add DOS batch commands to lock and unlock sets.** SLOCK.EXE sets a lock, reducing the number of application copies that can still be accessed. SUNLOCK.EXE releases the lock when the user exits the application. These commands are used in a DOS batch file or in a NetWare menu as in the following example:

```
ECHO OFF
SLOCK WPSET
IF ERRORLEVEL=100 GOTO GO
IF ERRORLEVEL=0 GOTO RETRY
:GO
WP
GOTO END
:RETRY
    ECHO "All licenses in use for WordPerfect"
    ECHO "Try later."
PAUSE
GOTO EXIT
:END
SUNLOCK WPSET
:EXIT
```

This batch file executes SLOCK, which returns a DOS error condition. The DOS error condition is a number that indicates whether an application can be accessed. A DOS condition of 100 shows that the application can be used. Any other DOS condition (error level 0) indicates all application licenses are in use.

BACKUP SOFTWARE UTILITIES

NetWare has two utilities to back up a network drive. LARCHIVE backs up the network directories to a workstation. The workstation could have a hard drive, tape drive, or it could direct the backup to a floppy drive. NARCHIVE backs up the directories to a network hard drive. Both of these utilities work well and are documented in the NetWare manuals. Network administrators find that backing up to a tape cartridge system attached to a workstation is the most desirable method.

A tape cartridge system has the advantage of storing large network drives (hundreds of megabytes) on one tape cartridge. This allows the supervisor to run the backup without intervention. Backing up to a local floppy drive requires the supervisor to insert diskettes during the backup. A 150 MB system would require numerous disk swaps. A backup to another network disk drive assumes your system has the available space. The following criteria should be used when selecting a backup system:

Network Backup Selection Criteria

- The software should back up both the directories and the bindery information. This is critical when restoring the backup onto the file server. When directories and the bindery information are not restored properly, the information has to be reentered. This includes trustee rights and login scripts.

- The software must allow for batch or custom backups. The supervisor should be able to select the directories or conditions easily for backing up files.

- The software must allow the backup to span more than one volume or tape.

For more information on system backup and disaster recovery, refer to Chapter 12.

DIAGNOSTICS AND MAINTENANCE UTILITIES

Diagnostic utilities allow the network manager to monitor network traffic. Maintenance utilities rebuild corrupt files and update network binderies.

PERFORM

PERFORM.EXE is a NetWare utility that measures the data throughput of a particular workstation. PERFORM can be run on a single workstation or several workstations at one time. PERFORM.EXE is on the

FIGURE 11.1
Network Performance Test

```
                  Novell Network Performance Test V2.3

                  Read record/Write record    (R/W)     WRITE
                  Overlayed or Sequential     (O/S)     OVERLAYED
   Parameters     Record Size             (1-4096)      4096
                  Iterations to perform   (1-1000)      1
                  Stations in test                      1

                                                   Aggregate
                                                 KB/S |80.0
   Results        Type  Size  I/Os  Bytes  I/O  Time  |
                  W O   4096   0     4096        0:05  80:0 |Aver
                                                         |80.0

   Status         Select Options and Press <F1> to start test.

                                                <ESC> to exit
```

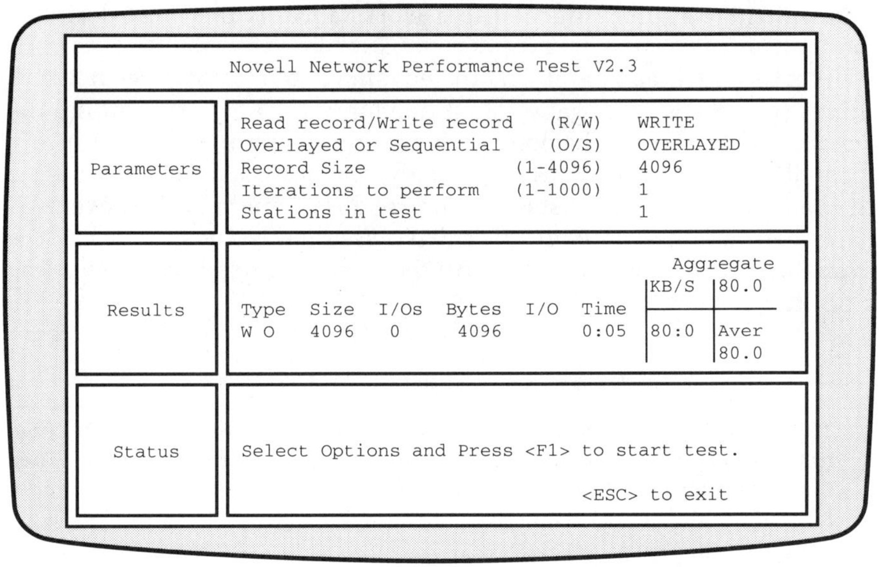

troubleshooting NetWare diskette. To run PERFORM, copy PER-FORM.EXE and PERF$RUN.OVL to a network drive. Change to that directory and enter PERFORM. The screen is displayed in Figure 11.1. You can change the parameters to determine how the network traffic changes as the parameters are changed.

NWCARE

NWCARE is another utility used to monitor a network. NWCARE is not included with NetWare, but can be purchased separately from Novell. NWCARE gathers and displays information related to the performance and efficiency of file servers, workstations, and the network topology.

NWCARE tests communication between any two nodes. One node can send a series of packets to another node. The results of sending packets are displayed in graphs. The graphs show errors in transmission and utilization of shell software. The screen in Figure 11.2 displays menu options that demonstrate the functionality of NWCARE. When NWCARE is run, it queries the network for all active nodes to

FIGURE 11.2
NetWare Care Current Nodes Diagram

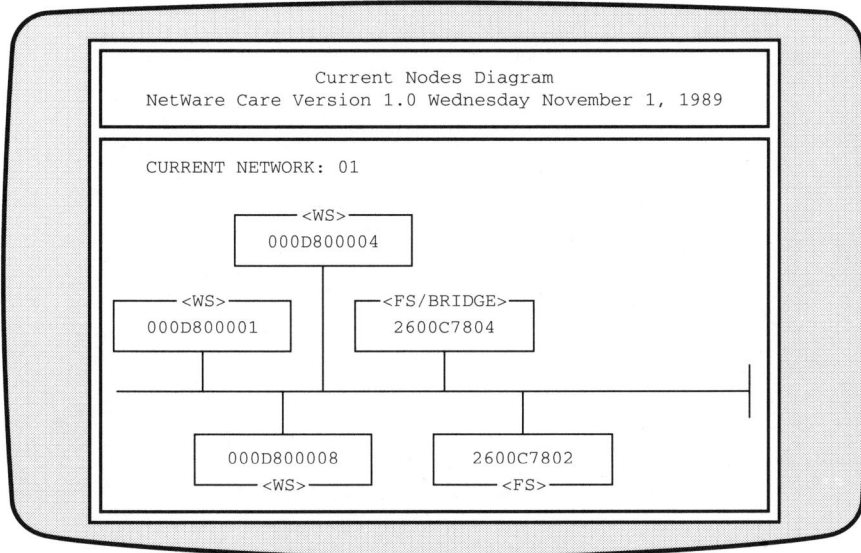

```
Current Nodes Diagram
NetWare Care Version 1.0 Wednesday November 1, 1989


CURRENT NETWORK: 01

            ─────<WS>─────
           │   000D800004   │

   ─────<WS>─────        ─────<FS/BRIDGE>─────
  │   000D800001   │    │      2600C7804      │


      ┌──────────────────┐    ┌──────────────────┐
      │    000D800008    │    │    2600C7802     │
      └──────<WS>────────┘    └──────<FS>────────┘
```

get their addresses. The first screen displays a representation of the active nodes.

Use the arrow keys to highlight a node. The ENTER key displays the next screen, which is the "Node Information" menu shown in Figure 11.3. These options can then be selected to determine how a workstation is performing on the network.

The F2 key displays the next screen, which is the "Network Options" menu, as shown in Figure 11.4.

PERFORM and NWCARE are NetWare utilities that monitor network performance. Restrict these utilities for use by the supervisor.

BINDFIX

BINDFIX is a NetWare utility for repairing the NetWare bindery files, NET$BIND.SYS and NET$BVAL.SYS. (These files contain all the information on network users and their passwords, groups, and trustee assignments.) Use BINDFIX when a user name cannot be deleted, a password cannot be changed, rights cannot be modified, the "unknown server" error occurs during spooling, or errors referring to the

FIGURE 11.3
NetWare Care Node Information Menu

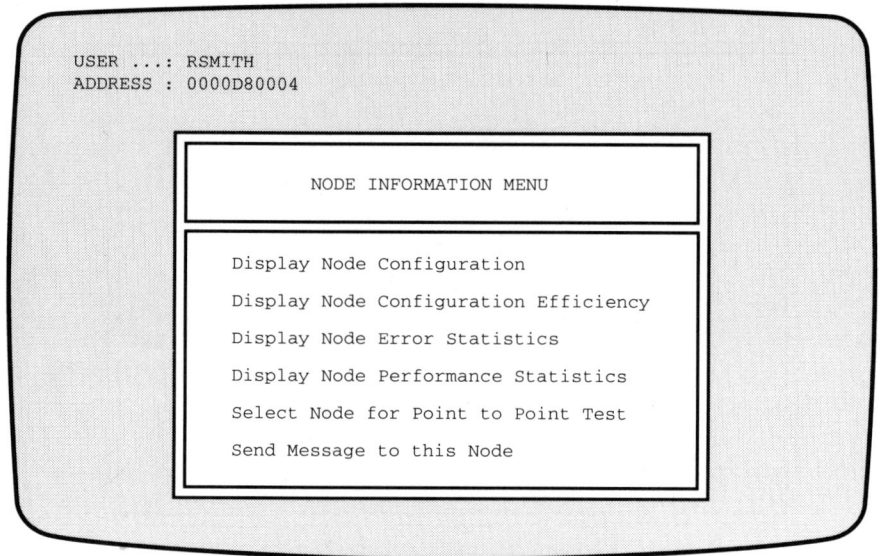

```
USER ...: RSMITH
ADDRESS : 0000D80004


                        NODE INFORMATION MENU


             Display Node Configuration

             Display Node Configuration Efficiency

             Display Node Error Statistics

             Display Node Performance Statistics

             Select Node for Point to Point Test

             Send Message to this Node
```

FIGURE 11.4
NetWare Care Network Options Menu

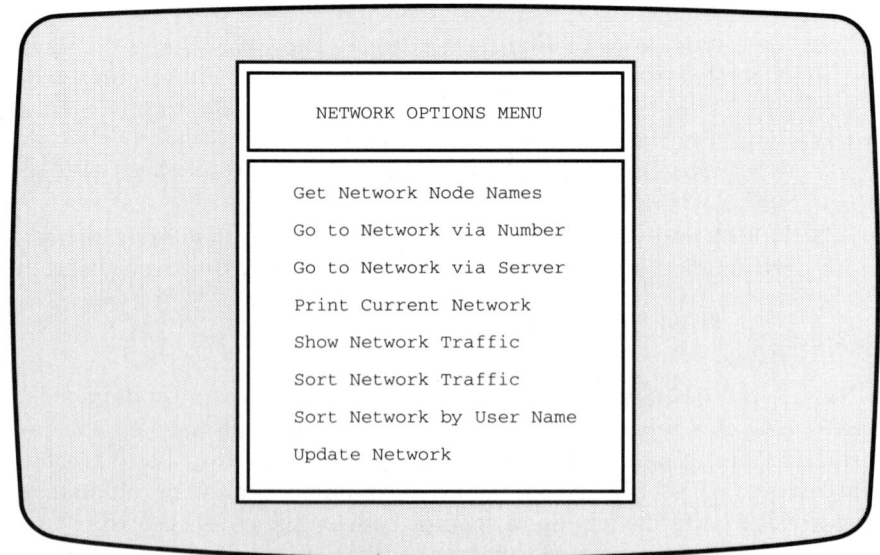

```
                        NETWORK OPTIONS MENU


             Get Network Node Names

             Go to Network via Number

             Go to Network via Server

             Print Current Network

             Show Network Traffic

             Sort Network Traffic

             Sort Network by User Name

             Update Network
```

FIGURE 11.5
BINDFIX Status Screen

```
Rebuilding Bindery. Please Wait

  Checking for invalid nodes.
  Checking object's property lists.
  Checking properties to see that they are in an
  object property list.
  Checking objects for back-link property.
  Checking set consistency and compacting sets.
  Building available lists and new hash tables.
  There are 100 Object Nodes and 100 Property Nodes
  free.
  Checking User Objects for standard properties.
  Checking group objects for standard properties.
  Checking links between users and groups for
  consistency.
  Delete mail directories of users that no longer exist?
  (Y/N):
```

bindery are displayed on the console. BINDFIX should also be run when users or groups are added and deleted, because the bindery is not purged of the deleted user and group information until BINDFIX is run. Mail directories linked to the bindery are also not removed when a user is deleted. Running BINDFIX once a month will ensure a properly maintained bindery.

BINDFIX is in the SYSTEM directory, and can be run by the supervisor by entering BINDFIX. The file server must be up and running. All users other than supervisor must be logged off. (See Figure 11.5.)

Before the bindery files are rebuilt, the existing bindery files are closed and backed up with the extension .OLD. This procedure protects the existing bindery information from being destroyed in case the rebuilding is not successful. BINDFIX will then scan the current bindery files, looking for inconsistencies. If the program finds an inconsistency, the prompt in Figure 11.6 is displayed.

A "Yes" to this prompt causes BINDFIX to search all disk volumes and remove the directory trustee rights for all users who have been deleted. When the bindery operation is complete, the message in Figure 11.7 is displayed.

FIGURE 11.6
BINDFIX Mail and Trustee Screen

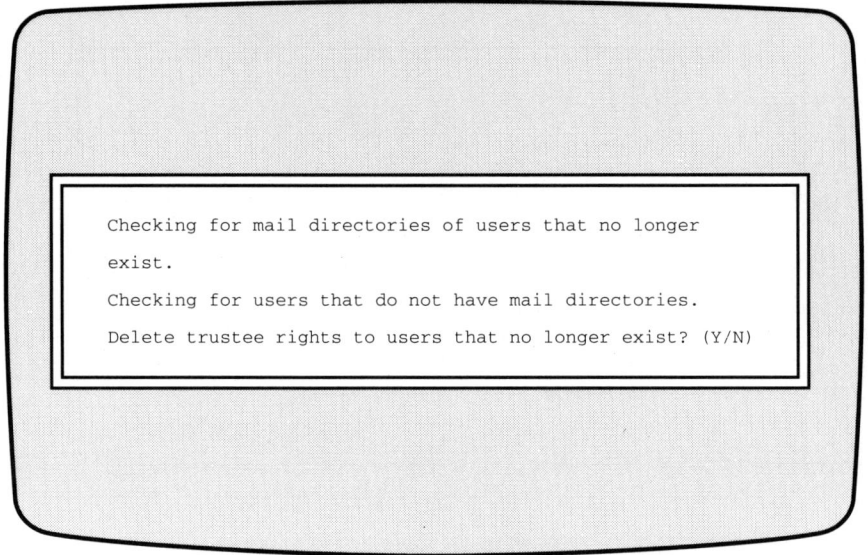

```
Checking for mail directories of users that no longer
exist.
Checking for users that do not have mail directories.
Delete trustee rights to users that no longer exist? (Y/N)
```

FIGURE 11.7
BINDFIX Volume Screen and Completion Status

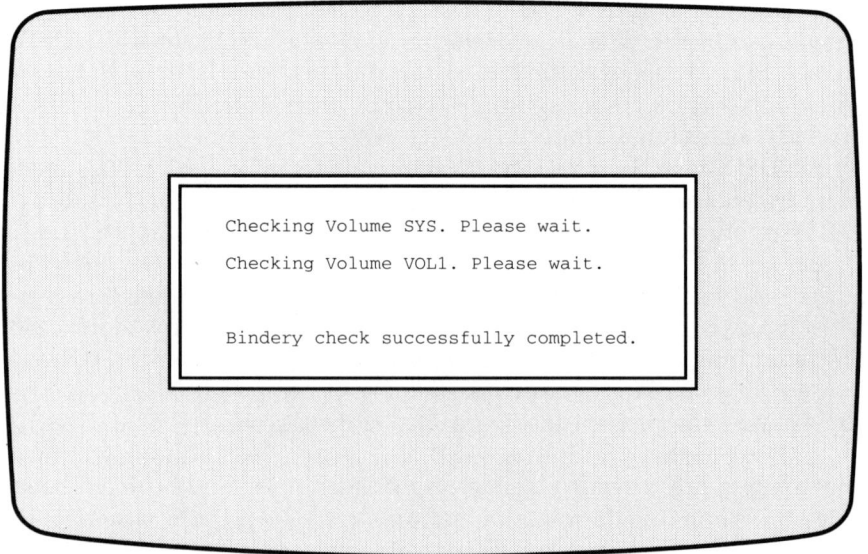

```
Checking Volume SYS. Please wait.
Checking Volume VOL1. Please wait.

Bindery check successfully completed.
```

FIGURE 11.8
FIGURE 11.8
BINDFIX Screen Showing Unsuccessful Completion

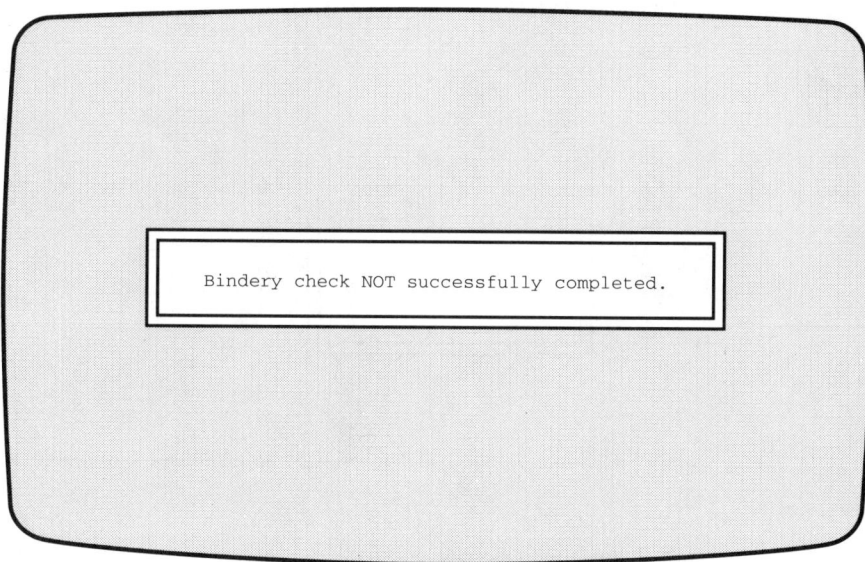

```
              Bindery check NOT successfully completed.
```

An unsuccessful BINDFIX will display the message in Figure 11.8.

After BINDFIX is run, you should down the file server. Type DOWN at the file server console. Next reboot the server. This causes the updated bindery files to be loaded into memory on the file server. Should a problem occur after running BINDFIX, the original bindery files can be restored by running BINDREST from the SYSTEM directory.

VREPAIR

VREPAIR recovers data from a disk on a file server after corrupt or incorrect data has been written. This situation occurs when the file server has been turned off or loses power before the DOWN command is issued.

VREPAIR is on the working copy of the UTILEXE-2 NetWare disk. To use it, first down the file server. Next, boot the file server with DOS. Put the UTILEXE-2 diskette in the A: drive and enter VREPAIR. A window similar to Figure 11.9 is displayed.

Select the drive you wish to repair. The next display prompts for a volume name. See Figure 11.10.

FIGURE 11.9
VREPAIR Screen Displaying Disks to Repair

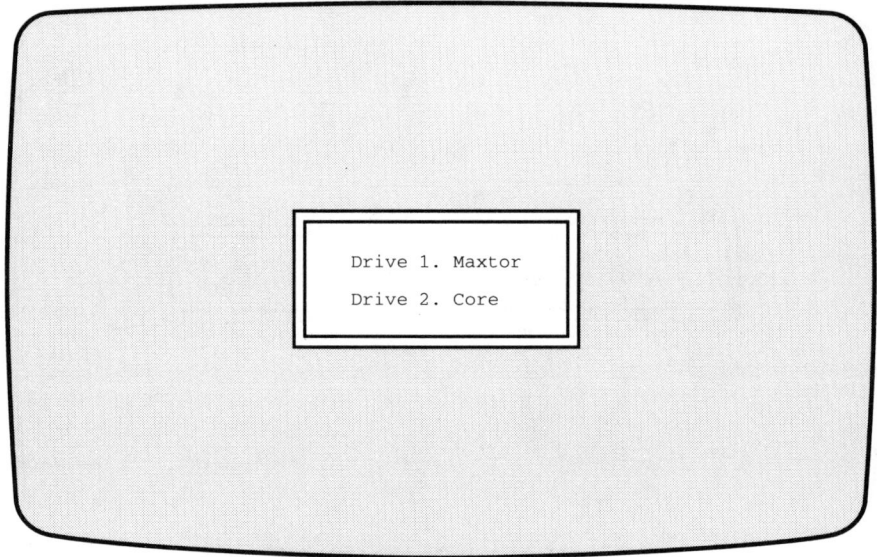

```
Drive 1. Maxtor

Drive 2. Core
```

FIGURE 11.10
VREPAIR Prompt for Volume

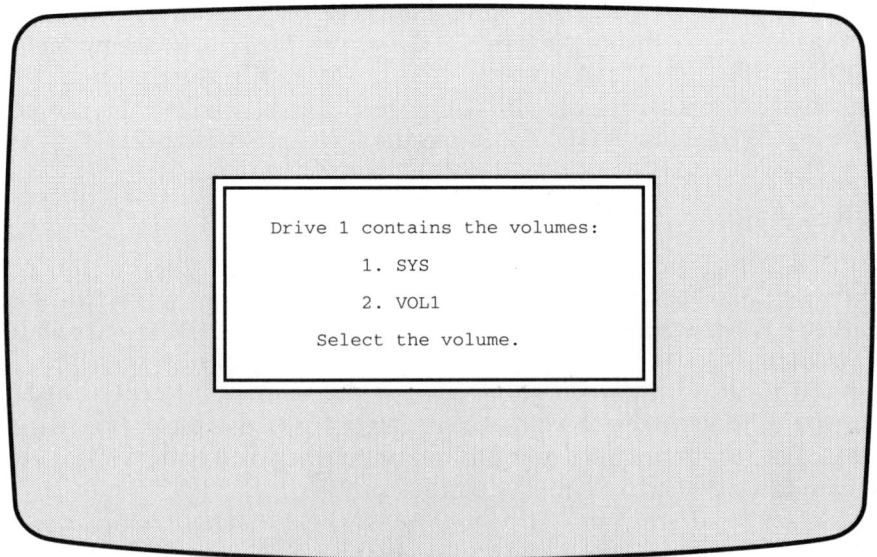

```
Drive 1 contains the volumes:

        1. SYS

        2. VOL1

Select the volume.
```

FIGURE 11.11
VREPAIR Prompt for Printed Output of Errors

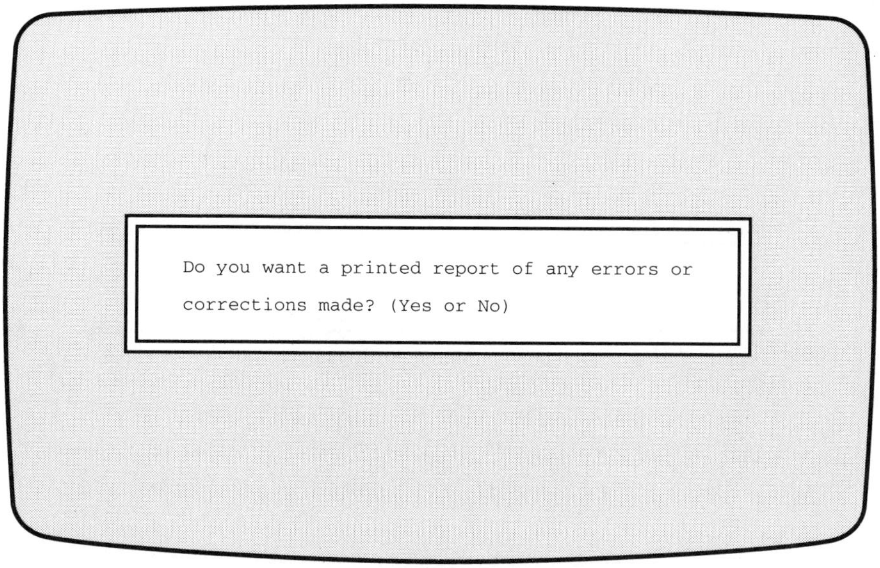

```
Do you want a printed report of any errors or

corrections made? (Yes or No)
```

At this point you have the option of printing the errors to the screen or to the printer. Enter "No" if there is no printer attached to the file server. See Figure 11.11.

Next, you are asked if you want to test for bad blocks. Enter "Yes" to test for bad blocks. See Figure 11.12.

If VREPAIR encounters an error, it provides information about the error and a suggested solution. VREPAIR will then check for bad data blocks, attempt to write them to another block, and update the bad block table.

After you type "Yes" to test for bad blocks, VREPAIR asks if you want to recover lost blocks as files. Enter "Yes" to this prompt (see Figure 11.13). When VREPAIR encounters used blocks not connected to a file, these blocks are saved to files in the root directory. After VREPAIR is completed, you have the option of examining these files and determining whether to save or delete them. Examining the files can help you to determine what data has been lost and whether the data needs to be rebuilt.

Figure 11.14 displays the selections made to this point in VREPAIR.

FIGURE 11.12
VREPAIR Prompt to Test for Bad Blocks

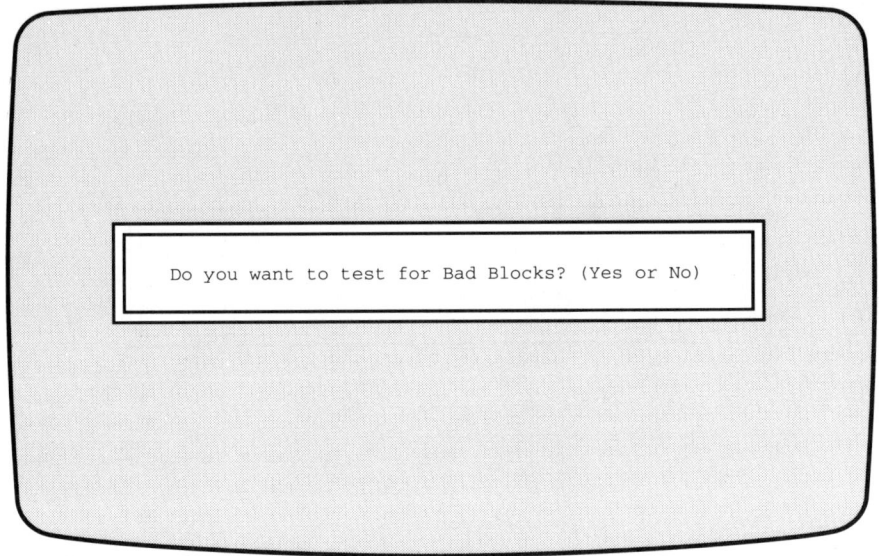

```
Do you want to test for Bad Blocks? (Yes or No)
```

FIGURE 11.13
VREPAIR Prompt to Recover Lost Blocks as Files

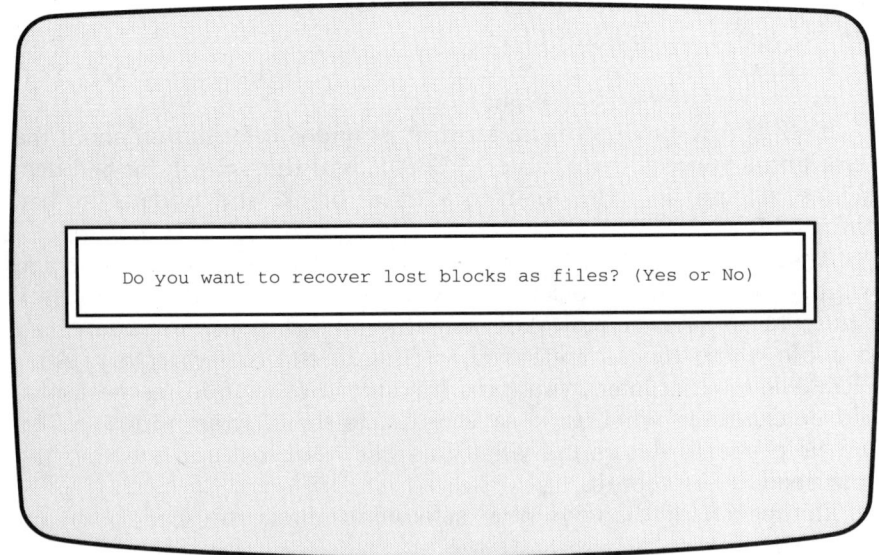

```
Do you want to recover lost blocks as files? (Yes or No)
```

FIGURE 11.14
VREPAIR Showing Selections

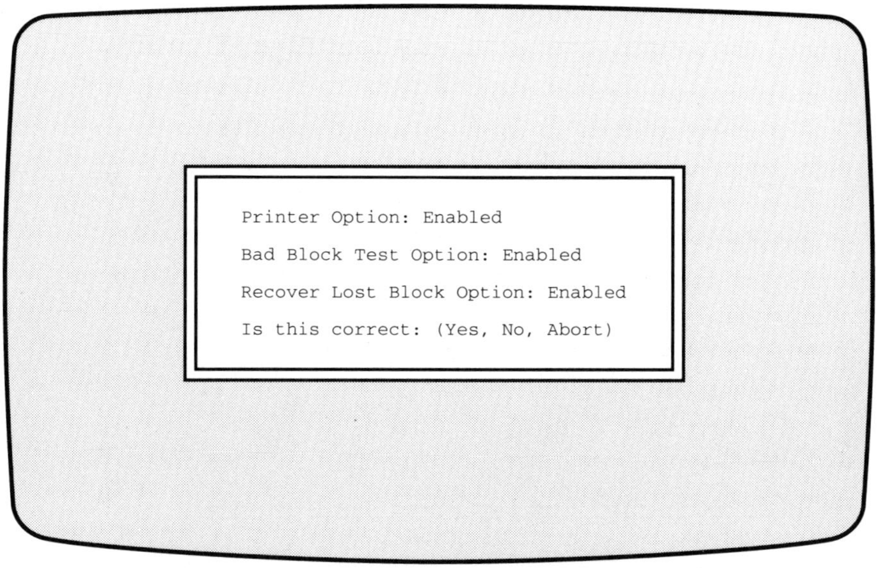

```
Printer Option: Enabled

Bad Block Test Option: Enabled

Recover Lost Block Option: Enabled

Is this correct: (Yes, No, Abort)
```

After you enter "Yes" to confirm, the screen in Figure 11.15 appears.

If VREPAIR discovers errors and makes the corresponding corrections, the next screen is displayed as in Figure 11.16. To save the corrections, enter "Yes."

If VREPAIR finds no errors, it displays the screen in Figure 11.17. Then it returns to the original screen as in Figure 11.9.

DCONFIG

DCONFIG is a utility to view or change the file server operating system or workstation shell. The following parameters can be changed:

- The network address assigned to a NIC
- The disk driver type and configuration on the file server
- The number of communication buffers assigned on the file server
- The shell configuration on a workstation
- The configuration options (IRQ, DMA, base memory address, and base I/O address) used by each NIC

FIGURE 11.15
VREPAIR Test Screen

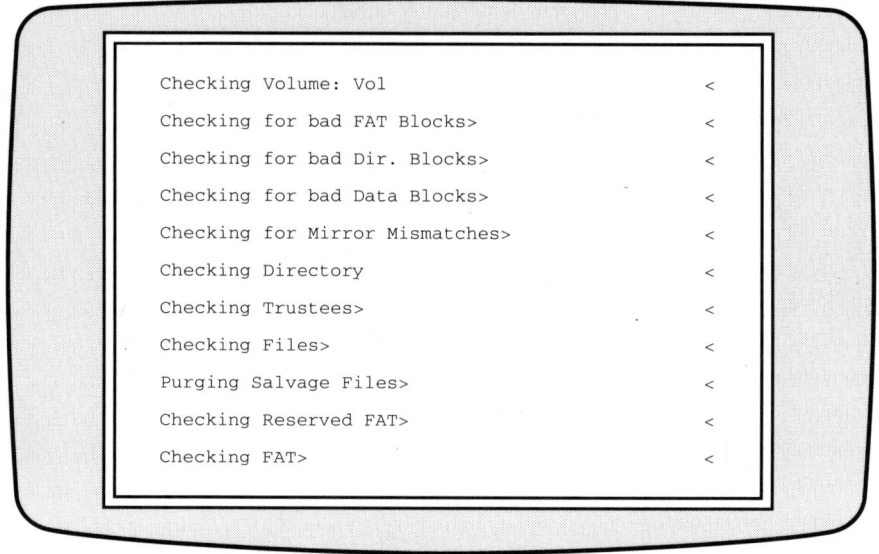

```
        Checking Volume: Vol                            <

        Checking for bad FAT Blocks>                     <

        Checking for bad Dir. Blocks>                    <

        Checking for bad Data Blocks>                    <

        Checking for Mirror Mismatches>                  <

        Checking Directory                               <

        Checking Trustees>                               <

        Checking Files>                                  <

        Purging Salvage Files>                           <

        Checking Reserved FAT>                           <

        Checking FAT>                                    <
```

FIGURE 11.16
VREPAIR Prompting to Make Changes Permanent

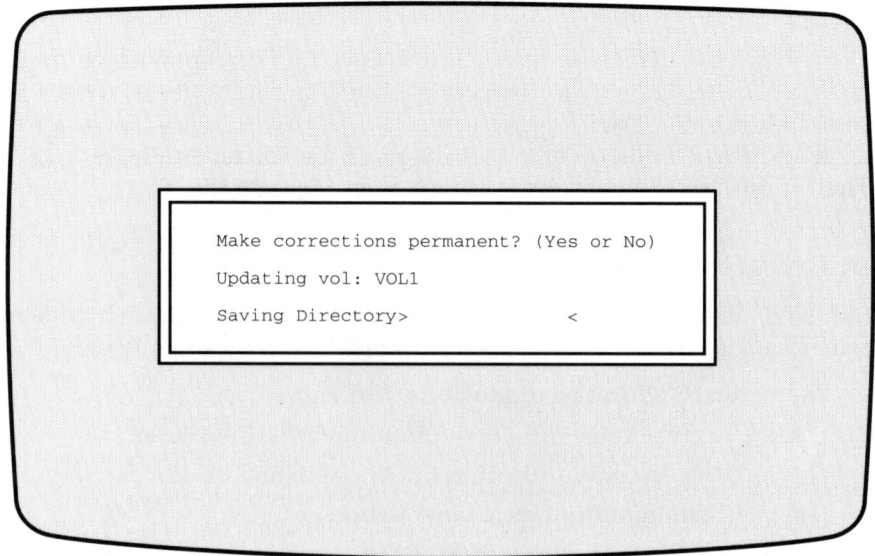

```
        Make corrections permanent? (Yes or No)

        Updating vol: VOL1

        Saving Directory>                <
```

FIGURE 11.17
VREPAIR Exit Screen

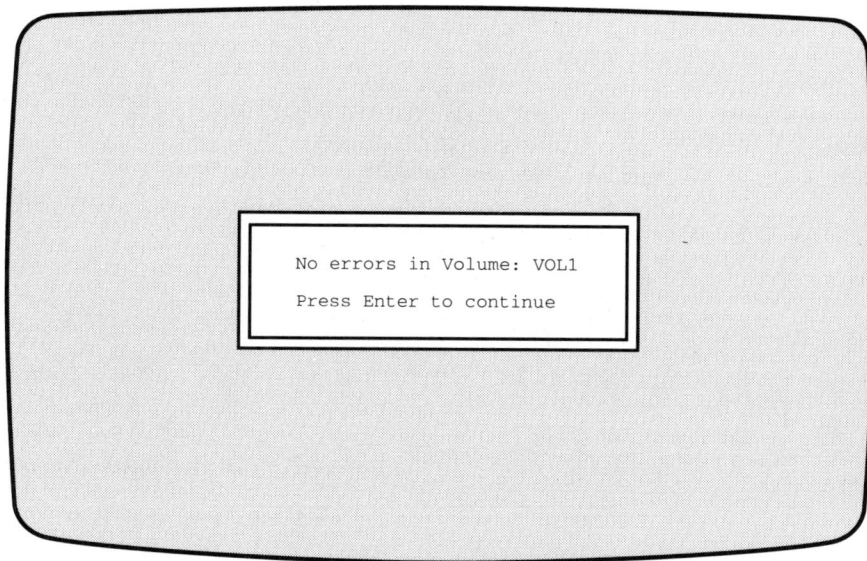

```
No errors in Volume: VOL1

Press Enter to continue
```

DCONFIG can be run when the file server is running. It can change parameters; it cannot add network drivers.

DCONFIG is on the AUXGEN disk. To execute DCONFIG on the network operating system when the file server is running:

1. Copy DCONFIG.EXE to the SYS:SYSTEM directory, then change to that directory.

2. Enter the command FLAG NET$OS.EXE RW to flag the operating system read/write.

3. Display the current operating system configuration by entering DCONFIG NET$OS.EXE. Figure 11.18 is an example of what DCONFIG will display. The information provided in the figure shows the file server is configured for eighty communication buffers. It has one NIC, designated as LAN A. The network address is set as 1. The NIC is an Interlan NI5210 set at IRQ 3, IO address 318h, and buffer address CC00:0. (Note that the asterisk indicates which setting is used.) The disk driver is for an IBM AT compatible disk controller.

FIGURE 11.18
DCONFIG Information on the Operating System File

Buffers: 80
LAN A Configuration:
    Network Address: 00000001
    Node address is determined automatically
        Hardware Type: Micom-Interlan NI5210 802.3 Driver
            0: IRQ = 2, IO Address = 300h, Buffer = D000:0
            1: IRQ = 2, IO Address = 300h, Buffer = C000:0
            2: IRQ = 3, IO Address = 310h, Buffer = C800:0
          * 3: IRQ = 3, IO Address = 318h, Buffer = CC00:0
            4: IRQ = 4, IO Address = 320h, Buffer = D000:0
            5: IRQ = 4, IO Address = 320h, Buffer = D400:0
            6: IRQ = 5, IO Address = 328h, Buffer = D800:0
            7: IRQ = 5, IO Address = 330h, Buffer = DC00:0
            8: Factory Defaults: IRQ = 2, IO Address = 360h, Buffer = C000:0
    Disk Driver: IBM AT hard disk controller or compatible Channel 0
        Configuration:
      * 0: AT controller I/O base = 1F0h, Interrupt = 14 Channel 1 unused.

The information provided in the figure shows the file server is configured for eighty communication buffers. It has one NIC, designated as LAN A. The network address is set as 1. The NIC is an Interlan NI5210 set at IRQ 3, IO address 318h, and buffer address CC00:0. (Note that the asterisk indicates which setting is used.) The disk driver is for an IBM AT compatible disk controller.

Here are two examples that show how you would use the DCONFIG utility to change the operating system file:

1. To change the network's address on LAN A to 20, enter:

    DCONFIG NET$OS.EXE A:20

2. To change the number of communication buffers to 100, enter:

    DCONFIG NET$OS.EXE BUFFERS:100

When you're finished with DCONFIG, flag NET$OS.EXE to shareable read only:

    FLAG NET$OS.EXE SRO

To put the configuration into effect, the file server must be downed and restarted. This will reload the modified NET$OS.EXE.

SUMMARY

This chapter has explained utilities used to enhance network activities and to diagnose network problems. Utilities that enhance the network include print-server software, such as Printer Assist, which makes a workstation's printer available to other network workstation users. Electronic mail is another example of software that enhances a network. Electronic mail enables users to share messages and files.

Network problems are diagnosed with software like PERFORM and NWCARE. These packages assess the data transmission rates and show problem or broken connections on the network. BINDFIX is another program that addresses network problems. It repairs data associated with user ID information. Finally, VREPAIR and DCONFIG were discussed. VREPAIR restores damaged files and operating system information. And DCONFIG permits the supervisor to reconfigure the operating system or workstation shells.

CHAPTER QUESTIONS

1. What is the difference between dedicated and nondedicated printer servers?

2. What are the advantages of installing electronic mail on a network?

3. Why is it important to monitor software licenses on a network?

4. You are in SYSCON and discover that it will not let you change a user's password. What utility do you run to remedy this problem? Explain how you would run the utility.

5. Your file server has gone down because of a power failure. When you boot it up, you discover it has file allocation table errors. What should you do to address this problem? What utility would you run?

6. Your network is slowing down because there are not enough routing buffers. What should you do?

7. What features should you look for when purchasing a tape back-up system?

8. Is it possible to have access to a workstation's local hard drive from a network? If so, how?

12

LAN Management: Taking Control

INTRODUCTION

While the LAN is in the installation and testing stage, take the opportunity to develop a plan for its administration. This plan will involve these steps:

- Establishing the duties of the network manager
- Selecting the network manager
- Training the network manager
- Establishing a backup person for the network
- Defining network standards
- Developing a plan to prevent and solve network problems
- Establishing security procedures for the network
- Developing a network disaster recovery plan
- Creating a plan for user training
- Identifying ways in which users can report problems
- Purchasing equipment to help resolve network problems
- Finding ways to expedite growth and modifications in the network

When developing a management plan for the network, keep in mind that the network exists for users; it is their tool. In an industrial setting, this means a LAN can become a cornerstone to facilitate the productivity of workers and management. Within educational settings, a network is vital for classroom, laboratory, and general academic endeavors.

Users will quickly become dependent on the LAN to complete their work. When something goes wrong, they will expect a quick solution. As their LAN expertise develops, they will have increasing expectations for LAN services, coupled with LAN growth. With an effective and responsive management plan, it will be possible to correct problems more quickly. Further, it will be easier to address the needs for increased services and growth.

DUTIES OF THE NETWORK MANAGER

The network manager provides the link between the organization and the technical aspects of the LAN. If the network manager's duties are defined clearly, it will be easier for this person to keep the LAN operating reliably.

A primary duty of the network manager is to administer the *technical side* of the LAN. This entails setting up and maintaining hardware on the LAN. As mentioned earlier, the hardware comprises the file server (or servers), workstations, printers, modems, repeaters, gateways, cable, cable connectors, and other equipment.

Once the hardware is installed, it's good practice to establish service contracts on network components, such as the file server, workstations, printers, and other critical equipment. Preventive maintenance schedules, especially for printers and plotters, will ensure uninterrupted network performance.

On the technical side, the network manager plans the transition from the test phase of the LAN to full-scale production. This involves fully testing the SFT operating system, establishing user directories, establishing access restrictions and file protection, invoking security measures, such as passwords, and installing and testing application software. An added part of the transition to full production is converting data files from other computer systems to the LAN for use by specific LAN applications.

Another technical feature is the selection of LAN utilities to enhance access and performance of the LAN. For instance, such utilities as print-server applications enable the network manager to establish remote printers at workstations other than the file server. Remote printing enables users to direct their printouts to any printer on the LAN, which reduces equipment requirements, and permits the network manager to put a printer at any location on the LAN. Utilities, such as Remote2 or Carbon Copy enable users to dial into the LAN through the telephone system. In this way, it is possible for the vice president of a company to access a LAN at a manufacturing site in Denver while working at his or her desk at corporate headquarters in New York.

There are also utilities that facilitate LAN maintenance activities, such as maintenance-menuing systems. These provide quick access to LARCHIVE, NARCHIVE, BINDFIX, and other common maintenance functions. There are also programs available that enable automatic deletion of residual log-on files, like batch files associated with the Novell menu system.

Here is a list of the technical responsibilities of the network manager, as viewed by the *NetWare System Manager* manual. This information is used in the System Manager Course, taught by Novell and Novell Authorized Education Centers:

1. Establishing and maintaining the network's users, directories and security
2. Loading and updating software applications as required
3. Updating the NetWare Operating System as required
4. Responding to the needs and questions of users relative to their access of the network and performance of their duties
5. Maintaining backups of all files
6. Training qualified persons to act as back-up managers when needed
7. Monitoring network performance periodically to determine system requirements for:
   - additional memory
   - cache blocks
   - directory entries
   - file handles
8. Remaining abreast of changes in user and systems software and hardware requirements as they apply to:
   - additional file servers
   - hard disks
   - workstations
   - mainframe and remote PC access
   - fault tolerance

9. Cleaning up the directory structure periodically to maintain system organization and eliminate unused and outdated files

10. Keeping system information up-to-date and orderly*

The network manager is responsible for both the technical and *business* aspects of the LAN, maintaining familiarity with the use and cost of the equipment, which can vary among vendors. Some less-expensive components can be used instead of costlier ones. Some brands of cable, for instance, may be as effective and reliable as other brands, but they may cost less.

The most important business responsibility of the manager is to maintain relationships with vendors. The broader the range of vendors, the more likely it is the network manager will be able to take advantage of support and price differences among them.

Writing requests for proposals (RFPs) is another key business responsibility. An RFP outlines all of the organization's hardware and software requirements that must be met by a vendor. The completed RFP is sent to vendors. Vendors who believe they can meet the requirements in the RFP will typically submit a formal written response, showing how they intend to fulfill the requirements.

If the RFP is written well, it can be invaluable in a number of ways. First, it forces the organization to analyze its LAN needs as comprehensively and clearly as possible. Second, it enables vendors to determine if they can offer a solution to the organization's needs. And third, it provides a recourse if the vendor makes promises that are not kept; or if the vendor supplies equipment and services that do not meet the original specifications in the RFP.

When writing an RFP, it is particularly important to specify all equipment requirements in as much detail as is feasible. This includes requirements for mean time between equipment failure, software compatibility specifications, warranty needs, and statements showing who is responsible for hardware and software support. See Figure 12.1.

Even more important than developing RFPs and maintaining relationships with vendors is the necessity for the network manager to understand the environment in which the LAN will be used. In business, LANs may be used in a variety of areas: accounting, order entry, manufacturing, inventory, internal communications, or any combination of these. In the school environment, LANs may be used for teaching classes, for administrative functions, or scientific research. If you understand the needs of the production environment, you will also understand how the LAN should be managed. For example, if a par-

*Copyright © by Novell, Inc. All rights reserved. Reproduced by permission.

FIGURE 12.1
Request for Proposal (RFP) Outline

What to include in an RFP

- A description of the organization
- A description of the organizational goals
  to be fulfilled via the LAN
- Equipment specifications
- Equipment reliability requirements
- Equipment locations (including information
  about buildings that will house the equipment)
- All communications needs (including details
  about existing communications equipment)
- Software specifications
- Specifications regarding application software
- Compatibility with specific Novell operation
  system environments
- Connectivity requirements with other LANs or
  with mainframes or minicomputers
- Software and hardware support requirements
- Warranty requirements

ticular LAN is used to generate payroll, there will be critical times during each pay period when the LAN must function at its optimum level.

Part of understanding the production environment is developing direct communication lines with other managers whose areas are affected by the LAN. To a large extent, they will need to have an impact on how the LAN is managed and what applications are used on the LAN.

Especially important responsibilities of the network manager are training and documentation. The network manager has a vested interest in training LAN users and in providing documentation for software applications. The training role is as important as the technical role. Users need to know how to use specific software applications. They also need to know how to route printouts to the appropriate printers. And they need to know the basics of logging on, logging off, and using menus.

As users learn about basic operations, many will quickly gain an interest in developing more-sophisticated applications skills. They will begin to see even more uses for the LAN, and will ask that more applications be installed. New applications mean more demand for training, which makes the training role a continually expanding area.

Installing documentation on the LAN is a good way to address some of the need for training. There is a host of computer-aided training packages for commonly used applications, such as Lotus 1-2-3, dBase, WordPerfect, WordStar, and PageMaker. Many of these packages offer training at beginning and advanced levels. The Novell user manuals can be installed on-line for convenient access.

SELECTION AND TRAINING OF THE NETWORK MANAGER

Demands on the network manager necessitate finding someone with technical training in computer science or a related area, as well as experience in supporting microcomputer applications. They also require an individual with experience in host communications, since many LANs are connected to host computers.

Knowledge of communications protocols and microcomputer internals is another important ingredient. The ability to test communications signals and the ability to upgrade microcomputers are two additionally useful skills. Strong writing and oral capabilities are also important.

Further, the network manager needs to be prepared to seek additional training and education to keep current in the field. New hardware architectures and enhancements to operating systems are a given in the networking business.

ESTABLISHING BACK-UP PERSONNEL

In addition to the network manager, there must be back-up persons who can provide support when needed.

Back-up individuals need to know how to keep the LAN functioning smoothly. They need information about how to manage print queues, how to operate software, how to back up and restore LAN data, and how to diagnose problems. It's also important to have at least one back-up individual who understands the directory structure, how to create new users, how to write menus and login scripts, how to grant trustee rights, and how to use system functions, such as SYSCON and PCONSOLE within the NetWare operating system.

DEFINING NETWORK STANDARDS

If there are no standard approaches to setting up a network, management of the network will quickly become chaotic. Standard approaches include ways of creating groups, writing login scripts, defining users, mapping search drives, and creating boot diskettes.

Without standardization, the network will quickly get out of hand. For example, in the absence of planning and coordination of efforts, the directory structure can quickly become complex. Standard applications programs may end up in any of several directories or subdirectories. Multiple versions of the same program may exist in different directories. As the complexity grows, it becomes more difficult to upgrade software, since one directory might hold several different sets of programs. The most recent version of programs may be difficult to separate from older versions; and mapping to the correct directory becomes problematic.

The following sections offer some concrete ways to standardize network setup procedures.

STANDARDIZING DIRECTORIES

A good place to start is in standardizing directories and subdirectories. Novell NetWare creates four key directories: PUBLIC, SYSTEM, LOGIN, and MAIL. The PUBLIC directory stores utilities and programs used by the Novell network. This directory should be reserved strictly for software provided through Novell. For example, the directory provides a good location for installation of the on-line Novell manual documentation provided in the FOLIO program.

The SYSTEM directory contains files and programs used by the NetWare operating system. Like the PUBLIC directory, this directory should also be reserved strictly for operating system files. The LOGIN directory is used for log-in by users. It can also display available file servers to users who have not yet logged into the network. The MAIL directory is used to store mail files for electronic communications. All four directories, PUBLIC, SYSTEM, LOGIN, and MAIL, should be reserved for Novell use only.

Other directories can be created by the network manager and authorized users as the need arises. First, develop a naming convention when establishing new directories or subdirectories. For example, applications such as word processors, spreadsheets, and database programs can be placed in an APP directory. Within the directory, there can be subdirectories for specific applications, such as WP for a word processor and DB for a database program. It's advantageous to keep the names of directories and subdirectories short by using descriptive abbreviations.

If you need to install more than one application package, such as two different word processing applications, create a subdirectory for each separate application. For instance, you may have purchased both

FIGURE 12.2
Applications Directory

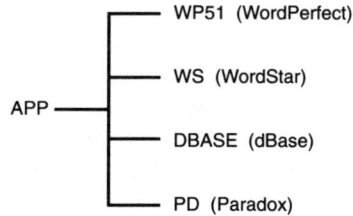

```
                                 ┌──── WP51  (WordPerfect)
                                 │
                                 ├──── WS  (WordStar)
                    APP ─────────┤
                                 ├──── DBASE  (dBase)
                                 │
                                 └──── PD  (Paradox)
```

WordStar and WordPerfect for installation. You may also have copies of dBase or Paradox to install. Create separate subdirectories under an applications directory for each package. Figure 12.2 is an example of what the directory and subdirectory structure might look like.

Within each subdirectory, you may want to create yet another subdirectory. As an example, applications such as WordPerfect are supplied with a learning diskette. The files on this diskette can be placed in a subdirectory under the WordPerfect subdirectory. Then, if it's later decided the learning material is no longer needed, it's a simple matter to delete the subdirectory. This is easier than trying to determine which programs are associated with the learning diskette in one large WordPerfect directory. In addition to the learning material, you may also wish to have a subdirectory for WordPerfect text documents, such as letters, macros, .SET files, and graphics. (See Figure 12.3.)

As you create directories and subdirectories, avoid creating an excessive number of levels. Normally, it's hard to manage more than

FIGURE 12.3
Applications Directory with Subdirectories

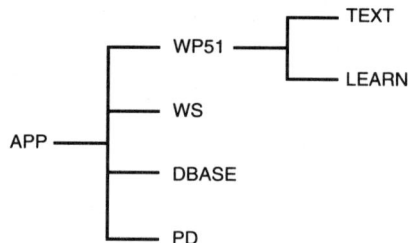

```
                                              ┌──── TEXT
                              ┌──── WP51 ──────┤
                              │                └──── LEARN
                              │
                              ├──── WS
                  APP ────────┤
                              ├──── DBASE
                              │
                              └──── PD
```

three or four levels of subdirectories. Once you know what software is to be installed, develop a chart or tree diagram to document the directory structure before you begin installation.

Besides APP, there are other viable names for the kinds of directories you are likely to create. Compilers may be installed under a COMPILER directory, and utilities might go under a directory called UTIL. A print server application is an example of software that might go into a subdirectory under the UTIL directory. A utility application that monitors the number of available licenses for given software is another example of an application to put in the UTIL directory. Monitoring applications, such as SiteLock, ensure that access to software does not exceed the number of copies for which the LAN is legally licensed. For instance, if there are ten licenses for WordPerfect, this type of utility will ensure that no more than ten users access WordPerfect at one time.

Many Novell LANs have a user directory or directories to enable users to store their personal files. This directory might be called USERS or USERID. Within the directory, there can be subdirectories for each user. (See Figure 12.4.)

If there are categories of users, such as marketing users, accounting users, data systems users, and management users, then it is useful to create subdirectories based on these areas in a company. Lower subdirectories can then be built for every user within each area of the company. (Refer to Figure 12.5.)

With the directory structure established in this fashion, the system login script or the login script of each user should have a map to the individual's user subdirectory. The marketing group for example,

FIGURE 12.4
Users Directories

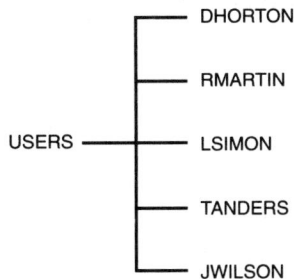

	DHORTON
USERS	RMARTIN
	LSIMON
	TANDERS
	JWILSON

FIGURE 12.5
Users Directories Within Departments

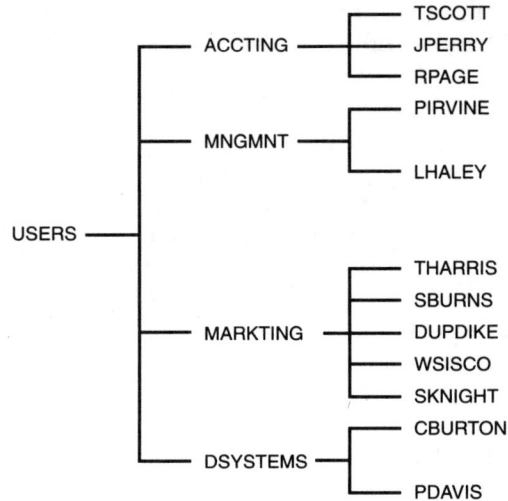

```
                                                  ┌─── TSCOTT
                           ┌─── ACCTING ──────────┼─── JPERRY
                           │                      └─── RPAGE
                           │                      ┌─── PIRVINE
                           ├─── MNGMNT ───────────┤
                           │                      └─── LHALEY
                           │                      ┌─── THARRIS
    USERS ─────────────────┤                      ├─── SBURNS
                           │                      │
                           ├─── MARKTING ─────────┼─── DUPDIKE
                           │                      ├─── WSISCO
                           │                      └─── SKNIGHT
                           │                      ┌─── CBURTON
                           └─── DSYSTEMS ─────────┤
                                                  └─── PDAVIS
```

might have a portion of the system login script, which includes a statement block like:

    IF MEMBER OF "MARKTING" BEGIN
      MAP H:=SYS:USERS/MARKTING/%LOGIN_NAME
      DRIVE H:
    END

Or the user's login script might have a statement block of:

    MAP H:=SYS:USERS/MARKTING/%LOGIN_NAME
    DRIVE H:

Making the statements above, the user is automatically switched to his or her home subdirectory. In these examples, the first level of the home directory will be USERS on the volume (disk drive) called SYS. The general group under USERS will be MARKTING, for those in the marketing department. And the log-in ID, such as THARRIS, will be derived from the system variable, %LOGIN_NAME. This variable, or identifier, always captures the user's log-in ID for the network and for login scripts or menus.

With a user directory established this way, you can create groups to reflect the directory structure. In the example, the user groups are ACCTING, MNGMNT, MARKTING, and DSYSTMS. These groupings enable the network manager to declare trustee rights by group membership or via the individual log-in ID.

NAMING THE FILE SERVER

Although your organization may start with only one file server, others may be added in the future. Additional file servers can be connected to an existing LAN or you may decide to install a wide-area network backbone to which several LANs will be attached. Plan for this possibility by establishing naming conventions for each file server.

Naming conventions for LANs may focus on any of the following characteristics of the organization:

- The group that will use the file server, such as sales staff or secretarial services
- The building where the file server resides, such as Building A or Physical Plant
- The specific department or division that uses the file server, such as the engineering division or accounting department
- The function of the file server, such as research/development or word processing

For example, if one file server is used for engineering, it might be called ENG. If there are two file servers for different engineering groups, they might be called ENGI and ENGII. Thus, an organization might have an ACCT file server for accounting, an ENGI server, an ENGII server, and a BUS server for the business office.

When naming a server, keep in mind the value of brevity. Short names are easier to type when establishing search drives and mappings.

LOG-IN ID NAMES

Log-in IDs work best when they reflect the user's name. They should also be designed so individuals can easily be reached by electronic mail. Nicknames, such as Dr_Byte or BigRed, are not particularly helpful in identifying the user. The simplest naming convention is to use the individual's first initial and last name. For example, Thomas

Scott's log-in would be TSCOTT. If there are two Thomas Scotts, you might include the middle initials: TJSCOTT and TMSCOTT.

An alternate log-in ID convention might consist of user initials. In our previous example, Thomas J. Scott and Thomas M. Scott would have the user IDs, TJS and TMS.

In some situations, there may be a workstation **pod** where a number of workstations are placed in a workroom or lab. These workstations are established for users who do not need to be identified by name. (A word-processing pod in a public library is an example of this kind of situation. Here, anyone from the community might come in to use word-processing facilities.) Log-in IDs would then reflect workstation names, rather than user names. If there are fifteen workstations, there might be user IDs WS1 to WS15. Individual boot disks could be made to use with each workstation.

GROUP NAMES

As mentioned in the section describing directories, group names can be developed and used within the directory structure. In this way, the directory structure becomes a mirror of the organizational structure. User subdirectories can branch according to the group to which a particular user belongs. This makes it easier to establish a user on the network, to troubleshoot problems, and to ensure establishment of the correct group rights.

In our earlier example, accounting department users TSCOTT, JPERRY, and RPAGE would have subdirectories under the subdirectory ACCTING and in the USERS directory on the file server ACCT as follows:

ACCT/SYS:USERS/ACCTING/TSCOTT

ACCT/SYS:USERS/ACCTING/JPERRY

ACCT/SYS:USERS/ACCTING/RPAGE

Notice we have used the naming conventions discussed to this point, observing the principles of brevity and descriptiveness.

Having groups and directories set up in this fashion expedites maintenance on directories and maintenance in establishment of group rights. Users in the ACCTING group can easily be given read, write, open, create, share, modify, and other rights to sensitive accounting data they manage. All that is necessary is to create the ACCTING group, place the appropriate users in this group, and grant the necessary trustee rights. When a new accounting user is hired, he or she can be added to the group.

Likewise, individuals in other selected groups can be prevented from modifying the data and even prevented from viewing it. Users in a management group might be granted rights to read the accounting or payroll data, but not to write or modify the database. Sales representatives might be prevented from having any access to the data through withholding trustee rights to this group.

SYSTEM LOGIN SCRIPTS

When a person logs onto the Novell network, the network first runs the system login script, then the user's individual login script. With prior thought and planning, the log-in sequence can be established to achieve two interrelated goals: low maintenance and clarity of performance.

Low maintenance calls for designing the login scripts so it's easy to make modifications. This is done by accomplishing most of the log-in set-up work in the system login script, instead of in each user's login script. Minimize the commands in the user's login script. When you need to make changes to the log-in procedures, you will need to make changes only to the system login script. This is much easier than making repetitive changes to each user's login script, particularly when you might have to do this twenty, forty, or more times.

Clarity of performance entails writing the login scripts so they are internally documented and so commands follow a logical sequence. This improves the ability to maintain the scripts after they've been written. Figure 12.6 contains an example of a system login script.

Notice that the login script in Figure 12.6 is divided into several different sections, each separated by a beginning REM statement. (REM statements are used for comments.) The first section contains DOS and Novell controls that are standardized for all users. The BREAK OFF prevents users from exiting before the system login script is finished. The MAP DISPLAY OFF command suppresses display of the search drive mappings. And the DOS SET PROMPT="PG" sets the prompt sequence so it shows the directory path and the (>) prompt.

The next commented section establishes search drives. Search drive 1, or drive Z:, is mapped to the PUBLIC directory. Search drive 2, which becomes drive Y:, is mapped to the directory containing the version of DOS the logged-on user has on his or her machine. Note that the first two search drives should always be allocated in this way. The PUBLIC directory contains commands each user will need to access. The DOS directory is important for DOS commands, such as FORMAT and PRINT.

FIGURE 12.6
System Login Script

```
REM ** ESTABLISH DOS AND NOVELL CONTROLS **
BREAK OFF
MAP DISPLAY OFF
DOS SET PROMPT="$P$G"

REM ** ESTABLISH SEARCH DRIVES **
MAP S1:=ACCT/SYS:PUBLIC
MAP S2:=ACCT/SYS:PUBLIC/BIN/%MACHINE/%OS/%OS_VERSION
COMPSPEC S2:COMMAND.COM
MAP S3:=ACCT/SYS:APP/MENUS

REM ** DISPLAY GENERAL MESSAGE TO USERS **
FDISPLAY ACCT/SYS:UTIL/MESSAGES/ALL.MSG

REM ** SET UP CUSTOMIZATIONS FOR GROUPS ***
IF MEMBER OF "ACCTING" BEGIN
  MAP H:=ACCT/SYS:USERS/ACCTING/%LOGIN_NAME
  ENDCAP
  FDISPLAY ACCT/SYS:UTIL/MESSAGES/MNG.MSG
END

REM ** SET USERS TO DEFAULT DRIVE H:
DRIVE H:
```

The statement, COMSPEC S2:COMMAND.COM, tells the system to reload the COMMAND.COM file from the DOS directory that matches the version of DOS the user has on his or her PC workstation. It is extremely important that the COMMAND.COM file in this path is the same as the COMMAND.COM file that resides on the user's workstation. If the two don't match, the user will see an "INVALID COMMAND.COM" message on his or her screen and will have to reboot the workstation. Many application programs require COMMAND.COM to be reloaded when the user exits the program. WordPerfect and Lotus 1-2-3 are two examples. When you exit one of these programs, it reloads the COMMAND.COM file from the file server into the memory of the workstation. Since there are many versions of DOS, there are also many COMMAND.COM versions. The version they load must be identical to the version loaded at the time the program was started.

The different versions of DOS are loaded into a subdirectory under the PUBLIC directory. In our example system login script, the subdirectory path is:

ACCT/SYS:PUBLIC/BIN/%MACHINE/%OS/%OS_ VERSION

The notations %MACHINE, %OS, and %OS_VERSION are Novell identifiers. The identifier %MACHINE contains the workstation type, such as IBM_PC. The %OS identifier holds the operating system name, such as MSDOS. Finally, the %OS_VERSION identifier contains the specific version of the operating system, such as V3.10. If the workstation is using MSDOS 3.1, the map established to DOS for that user will be:

Y:=ACCT/SYS:PUBLIC/BIN/IBM_PC/MSDOS/V3.10

If another user logs in using MSDOS 3.3, he or she will be mapped to:

Y:=ACCT/SYS:PUBLIC/BIN/IBM_PC/MSDOS/V3.30

Of course, for all of this to work properly, it's necessary to have each version of DOS used by the LAN workstations loaded onto the file server.

Refer back to Figure 12.6 and notice there are only two search drives established other than those to the PUBLIC directory and DOS subdirectory. One is a search drive to the menu subdirectory, the other is to the utilities directory. This provides access to network utilities that might need to be used. It also provides access to menus so they can be run at the command level, if necessary.

It is best to establish a minimum number of search drives. Network security is enhanced with fewer search drives, and the entire system is handled more efficiently. If you need a mapping to run an application or to access data, create it via a MAP INSERT statement in the menu system. Delete the mapping with a MAP REM once the application session has been completed. Keeping the number of search drives low yields more control over who can access which applications on the file server. The example menus in Chapter 10 and the example in Figure 12.9 in this chapter illustrate the MAP INSERT and MAP REM statements.

It's also good practice to establish a procedure for use of drives on a file server. Normally, drives A: through E: are reserved for workstation floppy and fixed drives, including hardcards. Drive F: is the network default drive. Drives G: to N: are used for user-specific drive mappings, such as home directories. Also included in the G: to N: mapping are individualized software programs not designed for shared access on the network.

Drives O: through V: are used to create search drives and temporary mappings as created in menus. Drive W: is reserved for network utilities. Drive X: is mapped to the menu directory or subdirectory. Drives Y: and Z: are mapped to DOS and to the PUBLIC directory. Figure 12.7 contains a summary of drive-mapping standards.

FIGURE 12.7
Explanation of Search Drives

DRIVE	FUNCTION
A: to E:	Used for workstation floppy and fixed disk drives
F:	Used as the network default drive
G: to N:	Used to customize individual user home drives and non-shared software applications
O: to V:	Used for login script search drives and customized menu search drives
W:	Used for network-wide utility applications
X:	Used for user and system menus
Y:	Used for the workstation operating system version
Z:	Used for the PUBLIC directory

Refer back to the example system login script in Figure 12.6. After establishing search drives, the login script provides an opportunity to include a system-wide message to all users. This is accomplished through the statement: FDISPLAY ACCT/SYS:PUBLIC/MESSAGES/ ALL.MSG. The text of the message is contained in the file ALL.MSG. Here is an opportunity to share information about the system with all users. The information might pertain to new software available, new employees, or anticipated "down" time for network maintenance. If there is no system-wide information to share, this statement can be commented out with a REM statement. Once a new message is prepared, the REM portion of the statement can be deleted so the message is displayed.

Another portion of the example system login script is an area for establishing customized procedures that pertain to specific groups on the file server. One set of statements is for the accounting (ACCTING) group, another is for the management (MNGMENT) group. The statements used for the accounting group include:

IF MEMBER OF "ACCTING" BEGIN

    MAP H:=ACCT/SYS:USERS/ACCTING/%LOGIN_NAME

    CAPTURE P=0 NB NT TI=1 F=1

END

The block within the IF statement sets the user's home drive to H: and creates a map to the user's subdirectory. The identifier, %LOGIN_ NAME, holds the specific user ID. The CAPTURE statement customizes printouts so they'll be spooled to Printer 0. In this instance, Printer 0 might be a shared laser printer connected to the file server. The set of statements for the management group is similar to those for the accounting group:

```
IF MEMBER OF "MNGMENT" BEGIN
    MAP H:=ACCT/SYS:USERS/MNGMENT/%LOGIN_NAME
    ENDCAP
    FDISPLAY ACCT/SYS:PUBLIC/MESSAGES/MNG.MSG
END
```

Here, the user's home drive is again set as drive H:. The ENDCAP statement is used to customize printing for this group. It assumes each management user has a printer at his or her workstation. Finally, the statement FDISPLAY ACCT/SYS:PUBLIC/MESSAGES/MNG.MSG says to display a special message for management users only. This message might remind managers to have employee timecards in by a certain time.

The final statement in the example system login script sets the default drive to H:. Once the logged-on user is mapped to his or her home directory, this statement sets the default drive to that home directory.

USER LOGIN SCRIPTS

User login scripts provide an opportunity to further customize network activities to individual users. This may entail calling special menus, specifying individualized printing parameters, or running a particular program.

As mentioned earlier, you can reduce system maintenance by performing as much customization as possible in the system login script. Place only those customizations that cannot be generalized in the system login script into the user login script. The Figure 12.8 provides an example of a user login script.

Notice that the example user login script still contains internal documentation regarding what's being done. The script begins by calling user Scott's specialized menu. No map to the menu is necessary, because the menu's subdirectory was mapped into a search drive in the system login script. The #LOGOUT statement ensures that the user is not thrown into the command level mode if he or she presses

FIGURE 12.8
User Login Script

```
REM ** RUN THOMAS SCOTT'S MENU **
#MENU TSCOTT

REM ** LOG OUT IF USER PRESSES ESC TO EXIT **
#LOGOUT

REM ** SET DEFAULT DRIVE BACK TO F: **
DRIVE F:
```

the ESC key to exit the menu system. The last statement changes the session to the network home drive, which is drive F:.

MENUS

To keep a low-maintenance networking environment, standardize the menuing systems and menuing conventions. No matter how many file servers can be accessed via a LAN, plan to standardize on one menuing system whenever possible. The menuing system can be Novell's or one available through other sources, such as Saber Software or public domain software sources. Stay with one consistent menuing system for all users. In this way, you have to know only one menuing system well to make modifications for the addition of new software or network utilities.

Similarly, develop a consistent approach to menu design. The advantage of consistency is that once specific menu sections are created, they can be used again for other menus. If you develop a section of code to run a word processing application you can use the same code

FIGURE 12.9
NetWare WordStar Menu

```
Example NetWare WordStar Menu

%WordStar Menu
WordStar
        echo off
        cls
        capture p=0 nb nt ti=10
        map insert s4:=sys:app/ws >nul:
        ws
        map rem s4: >nul:
```

in any new menu. This enables you to spend time developing or installing new applications, rather than redeveloping menus. Figure 12.9 illustrates a menu written within Novell's menuing system.

BOOT DISKETTES

Many workstations without fixed drives will require special boot diskettes to connect to the network. Plan to keep the contents of boot diskettes as trim as possible. Besides the system files and COMMAND.COM file, the boot diskettes should contain:

- The IPX.COM and NETx.COM files
- Any needed device drivers, like ANSI.SYS
- A CONFIG.SYS file
- An AUTOEXEC.BAT file

The IPX.COM and NET3.COM files are needed for the network shell. The CONFIG.SYS file is needed to ensure that enough open files and buffers are provided for all software on the network. The ANSI.SYS or other device drivers are needed to meet the requirements of software that uses these device drivers. And the AUTOEXEC.BAT file is used to create a batch stream of commands for logging onto the network. The following is an example of what would be included in an AUTOEXEC.BAT file:

```
echo off
cls
ipx
net3
f:
login
```

In this example, the command stream turns off the echo display to the screen, clears the screen, runs the IPX.COM and NET3.COM network shell, switches to drive F:, and commences to log in the user. The AUTOEXEC.BAT file can be modified even further to supply the user's log-in ID and password.

Generally, boot diskettes are not intended to be altered or to store any data files. Existing files on a boot diskette can be protected by making them read-only files. The DOS Attrib command can be used to make files read-only. This prevents these files from being altered or deleted. If data files are accidentally written on a boot diskette, copy them to another data diskette and delete them from the boot diskette.

SECURITY PROCEDURES

Building appropriate security measures should be an integral step in establishing a network. Security involves the following:

- Making individual user information secure
- Limiting access to program and data files
- Limiting access to directories and subdirectories
- Training users to keep their information secure

A basic way to ensure network security is to require all users to have passwords. Whenever a new user is established, a password more than five characters long should be required. Users should be required to change their passwords on a regular basis, such as once every month or two. Users should also be required to have unique passwords. All of these security measures can be established through the

"Account Restrictions" menu, which is executed within SYSCON. You may also want to set restrictions on who can log in, according to the workstation location and/or time of day, combined with the day of the week. These options can be set for any individual user.

Assignment of flags, trustee rights, and directory rights is another way to implement security. NetWare enables you to alter or flag file attributes to control the way in which individual files are accessed. The flags that influence security the most include:

- Read Only
- Read/Write
- Execute Only
- Shareable
- Nonshareable
- Hidden

If you wish to prevent others from writing over or altering a file, flag it as read-only (FLAG filename RO). If a file has the extension, .EXE or .COM, you can mark it as execute-only (FLAG filename EO). This means that others can run the program file but cannot copy it onto their own diskette. If you have applications where there is only one license to run the application, you can mark the application files as nonshareable (FLAG filename N) to ensure that only one user can use the application. Then give only the authorized user trustee rights to that application directory. Last, if you want to hide specific files, flag them as hidden (HIDEFILE filename). No one can display these files while performing a directory command.

The flags read/write and shareable reduce the security on files. The read/write flag (FLAG filename RW) enables users to copy, delete, or alter a file. The shareable flag (FLAG filename S) enables multiple users to access or execute a file simultaneously. When files are copied onto the file server, the system automatically flags them as read/write and nonshareable. Change these flags so they meet the appropriate security needs.

Both trustee rights and directory rights consist of the same list of options:

- Open any files
- Read from any files that have been opened
- Write to any open files
- Create and open new files
- Delete any files

- Parental authority to create, rename, and delete subdirectories, as well as modify trustee and directory rights
- Search the directory and display the file names
- Modify file attributes of any file in a directory or subdirectory

When trustee rights are established in a directory, the default rights are read, open, and search. These rights are appropriate for software application directories. They allow users to execute programs, but not to copy program files or delete files. In networking environments where it is inappropriate for users to view file names, the S can be removed from the directory.

Normally, users should not have parental rights, since the directory structure of the file server should be administered by the network manager. Modify rights should also be given sparingly, because this option enables users to modify access to files that often are not intended for general access.

When the user's home directory is established, it is common to give the user RWOCD SM trustee rights. Once rights are established, they carry through to every subdirectory below the point where they are established. For instance, a parent directory might be titled APP, and there might be two subdirectories called WORK and WP. The WP subdirectory might be divided into two additional subdirectories, WP1 and WP2, with the WP1 directory containing a LEARN subdirectory. If trustee rights RWOCD SM are established for the APP directory, these rights will also be in effect for all of the subdirectories. If it's necessary to alter the rights for one directory, such as the WP1 directory, this must be done on an individual basis. For example, the rights ROS might be assigned only to the WP1 directory. Note that the ROS rights will be in effect for any subdirectories in the WP1 directory. (See Figure 12.10.)

Masked directory rights take precedence over trustee rights. If there is no W right assigned to a directory in the Maximum Rights Mask, then no one will have write authority to that subdirectory, regardless of whether the W right is granted through trustee rights.

FIGURE 12.10
Directory Structure with Rights

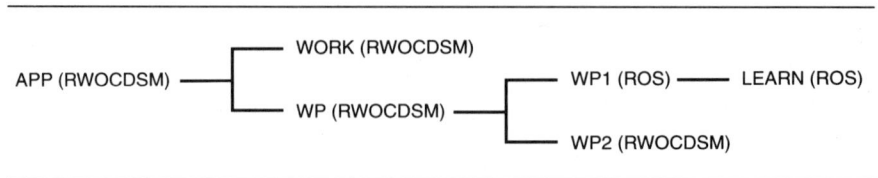

APP (RWOCDSM) —— WORK (RWOCDSM)
WP (RWOCDSM) —— WP1 (ROS) —— LEARN (ROS)
WP2 (RWOCDSM)

It is common procedure to leave the Maximum Rights Mask at RWOCDPSM for each directory and subdirectory. However, there might be instances where the network manager wants to ensure global security, such as protection against altering the directory structure or file attributes. This is easily accomplished by removing P and M rights in given directories.

Unlike trustee rights, masked directory rights are applicable only to individual directories or subdirectories. If the rights are changed for one directory, the changes do not automatically apply to subdirectories within that directory.

Another way to ensure security is to use the FILER utility to specify ownership of a directory or subdirectory. This is helpful when users have software applications for which they have licenses only on their specific workstation. Designating one user as the owner of the directory or subdirectory with appropriate trustee rights ensures that no one else can execute those programs.

A last security measure the network manager can emphasize involves training network users. Users need to be trained to keep their passwords secure. They should be discouraged from sharing passwords with associates, and they need to be encouraged to avoid writing passwords on slips of paper stored in a desk or posted on a wall.

SYSTEM BACK-UP AND DISASTER RECOVERY

Critical to any successful administration of a network is the formulation of a plan for disaster recovery. This plan makes it possible to restore important files and system information if a problem or emergency develops. Possible problems include fire, water and flood damage, unstable power damage, and equipment failure. Of these, equipment failure, such as the failure of memory or a fixed disk, is the most likely to occur. Unstable power is another frequent enemy of a network.

In disaster recovery one needs regular system back-ups. Although you can back up a file server with diskettes, you can do it better with a tape back-up system. Many tape back-up systems are available, the most reliable being those that are Novell-compatible and Novell-certified.

Most back-up systems use ⅛″ or ¼″ cassette tapes; they come in a variety of ranges. Some will back up to 60 MB of data. Others come in 150 MB and 300 MB maximum capacity ranges. For larger LAN systems, it's possible to purchase tape subsystems, which back up to 2.2 GB of data. These larger tape subsystems use 8-mm tape cartridges.

The larger capacity tape subsystems use helical scan recording techniques, which permit higher levels of data density on the recording medium.

Most tape subsystems perform error checking to verify the data on the tape as it is written. Typically this is done by quickly reading the data just after it is written, and comparing what is on tape with the data on the file server. Tape subsystems also come with tape verification utilities, which enable the tape to be checked for parity errors after the data is fully on the tape.

Tape subsystems generally comprise a tape drive and software used to manage the tape back-up and restore activities. The tape drive is physically connected to a workstation on the LAN, not to the file server. Depending on the manufacturer, the software may be accessed from the file server or from a physical drive on the workstation. It is also possible to connect more than one tape drive in tandem, for large-capacity LANs. The tape drives come in internal and external models. Internal drives, like disk drives, are installed in the workstation cabinet. External tape drives come in a stand-alone case, along with a circuit board, which is installed in the workstation.

Tape subsystem software often comes with the ability to back up systems file by file or in binary (or image) mode. As a rule, the best option is to back up the system file by file. This gives you the option of restoring only one file, one subdirectory, one directory, or any combination of files and directories, as well as the entire system.

A binary restore requires restoring all of the files at one time. Also, it is necessary to have the same fixed-disk configuration for the restore as was present for the binary save. Thus, if the original file server had a 40-MB fixed disk, it must be replaced with another computer that has the same 40-MB fixed disk.

When backing up the file server onto tape, the network manager needs to establish a regular schedule for back-ups. For instance, if users have the authority to create or change data files stored on the file server, back-ups should be performed daily with no user on the system. If only application software is stored on the file server, then back-ups are necessary any time new software or new users are added.

A system for making and rotating the tapes needs to be developed and recorded into a notebook. For instance, if back-ups are performed on a daily basis, the network manager is likely to have one or more tapes for each day of the week. Thus, there will be a Monday tape, a Tuesday tape and so on. In this way, if something goes wrong with Thursday's backup tape and a restore becomes necessary, there is always Wednesday's tape available, even though it may not be as current as Thursday's tape. Wednesday's tape can still be used for the restore, and only one day's worth of work is lost instead of two, three, four, or more.

For a daily back-up procedure, some network managers prefer to have two weeks' worth of tapes. This means a single tape is not recycled for two weeks. It provides more assurance, in case there is a need to view data historically, such as data as it existed in a file one or two weeks ago.

If data on the file server is critical to the organization, off-site storage of selected tapes is necessary. For example, once a week a tape might be taken to a safe deposit box in a bank. Then there will be a way to restore the file server in the event of fire or some other disaster.

An important drawback of some tape back-up subsystems is their inability to save trustee-rights data. When this is the case, it is necessary to perform the NARCHIVE SYSTEM procedure to save trustee rights and other user information. A handy way to accomplish this is to save the NARCHIVE data in a subdirectory under the SYSTEM directory or under the directory that contains the tape subsystem software. When this is performed prior to the tape back-up, the data is saved to tape for easy storage. This is easier than creating a separate diskette via LARCHIVE for trustee rights information in addition to the tape.

Besides tape back-up, there are other ways to provide for disaster recovery. One is to maintain a back-up file server. The back-up file server might run on a stand-alone basis or be connected to the network, in which case, it must have a server name that is different from the main server and a separate NetWare license. The back-up file server can be combined with tape back-up to ensure that a system is back on line as soon as possible. If the main server has a fatal hardware error, such as in the main CPU board, the back-up server can be restored, and users will be back on-line in a short time.

For even quicker restoration, the back-up file server can be attached to the LAN with its own licensed software. Programs designed to "shadow" data can be run so changes that occur on the main server are also copied onto the back-up server at regular intervals. The back-up server is then made accessible to users only when the main server can no longer function.

Another form of back-up is to enable disk mirroring through the Novell software. If two disk drives are present in the file server, data on the main server drive can be mirrored to another drive. Should the main drive fail, the second drive takes its place. This option works well in the event of a disk drive failure, but does not provide for immediate operations if the CPU board or another critical part fails.

As back-up alternatives are considered, it is important to adhere to software licensing requirements for both the Novell operating system and the application software on the file server. You must develop back-up procedures that honor all licensing constraints.

REPORTING LAN PROBLEMS

LAN problems may range from printer malfunctions to events that cause fatal error messages displayed at the file server console. Most problems have simple solutions, such as replacing a bad boot disk or helping a user to format a diskette. Other problems are more severe, such as file-server disk errors.

The key to solving problems quickly is to train users to resolve simple problems, and to report the more serious ones. Some users will work around even serious problems without informing the network manager. Others will report every small problem as it occurs. Training can help create a body of informed users who develop basic skills in addressing small problems. Likewise, users can be trained to record any serious error messages, along with LAN activities associated with the messages. This information can then be passed along to the network manager for appropriate action.

A simple way to ensure network error messages are reported is to ask each user to send a copy of the error message to the network manager via electronic mail. If the error message is judged to be extremely important, or the error interferes with the user's work, the best alternative is to call the network manager immediately.

Recording error messages in a centrally located notebook is another possibility. The notebook might have separate columns for the following:

- Error message
- Date and time of the message
- Circumstances under which the message occurred
- Person reporting the message

USER TRAINING

The key to effective use of a Novell network lies in training the users. Novell networks contain a host of options that make them very powerful user tools. The more users know about the network, the more productive they become.

Once users become sophisticated in how to use the network, the network manager can be relieved of solving small problems, such as how to delete a print job. This provides the network manager the opportunity to spend more time on preventive maintenance, installing and testing new software, and planning for future growth of the network.

There are several ways to offer training. One is to hold classes periodically in a lab or environment where users can access workstations to practice what they're learning. Classes taught in this manner are most effective if they are small, from five to twelve students. This enables both direct interaction with the instructor and the opportunity to try out what is learned on the network. Creating practice accounts for this type of training is also helpful.

One way to make training sessions even more effective is to supply handouts, each giving a summary of what is covered and a list of relevant user commands or actions. The results of the training are not likely to be long-lasting unless those who have attended are required to practice what they have learned in the days just after the training. This kind of practice is best if the trainee is isolated from interruptions during the practice.

Another way to offer training is through computer-aided instruction (CAI). A brief tutorial comes with many Novell systems. The tutorial can be placed on the user's menu or in a practice account. Also, customized tutorials can be made for specific work or school situations by purchasing software that enables creation of individualized tutorials.

A third option is to create a training video tape, which can be used in conjunction with hands-on practice. By using a video tape or CAI, or both, training can occur nearly any time without a scheduled class. And the training can be offered on an individualized basis.

Common topics to include in network training are:

- How to boot the workstation
- How to log on to the network
- How to use related DOS commands
- How to access and exit specific application software
- How to print on the network
- How to delete or manipulate printouts
- How to use print queues
- How to backup data in a home directory
- How to log out from the network

- What to do when problems occur
- How to perform basic maintenance on printers, such as loading paper
- How to take care of a workstation

EQUIPMENT FOR RESOLVING PROBLEMS

Cable trouble-shooting devices can be extremely useful in diagnosing many LAN problems. For example, an electrical short might develop in the LAN cable or in a connector to a workstation; or a length of cable might be added to the LAN, making the total length of a segment too long; or different brands of cable may cause incompatibilities; or a terminator may be defective. These situations may cause the LAN to behave in unpredictable ways or to fail entirely.

One device used to diagnose cable problems is called a Time Domain Reflectometer (TDR). This device detects breaks and shorts in the cable. It also measures the cable length. (Every LAN has a maximum effective length.) TDRs typically produce a printout of the results showing the cable length, impedance, pulse width, line noise, and other diagnostic information.

Cable-scanning devices (see Figure 12.11) are usually less expensive than a TDR, and yield information about breaks, shorts, and cable length. Many of these do not have a printout of information; instead they display the results on a small one- or two-line display. These results are often displayed briefly, such as "short at 100 feet." Most of these scanning devices work with different types of cable. Some cable scanning devices can be connected to an oscilloscope for more-detailed information. Connections to printers are also possible. Some generate an analysis of LAN traffic, as well as the need for additional bridges or repeaters.

When the LAN is down or not functioning properly, these cable diagnostic tools can prove essential to resuming service as soon as possible. They can also save money by reducing system down time.

LAN GROWTH AND MODIFICATIONS

Implementation of a LAN is an evolving process. As users become proficient with what they have, they'll soon find new applications they want to have on the LAN. Other stand-alone microcomputer users are likely to want a connection to the LAN. Requests for new printers

FIGURE 12.11
Cable Scanner *(Courtesy of Microtest)*

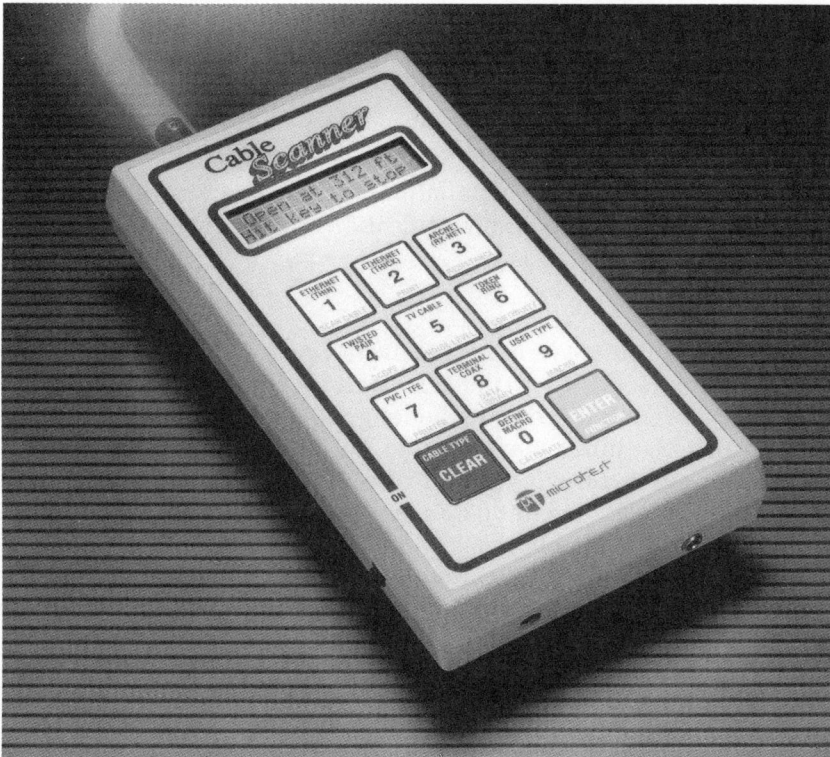

and more LAN capabilities will emerge. Simultaneously, users are likely to want customization of menus or applications. Some users will want to upgrade their workstations. Growth is a given in the workstation/LAN environment.

Network managers can prove their worth by accommodating this growth. They can represent both management and users in finding ways to expand the LAN services and to control costs.

The key to successful growth involves realistic needs analyses, accompanied by timely implementation plans. Each needs analysis should deal with these matters:

- What facilities are currently available
- The capacity left on current LANs
- What facilities are needed to increase user productivity

- A cost/benefit rationale for increasing facilities
- An analysis of extra personnel required to make LAN additions function

Implementation of additions to the LAN should include:

- Appropriate drawings of building layouts
- Well-defined responsibilities of vendors and of organizational resource persons, such as the network manager
- A realistic timeline for installation of cable, workstations, printers, application software, and modifications to user menus
- A plan for training users
- A plan for bringing users on-line

An important ingredient in this overall process is time to make the whole process work. No matter how well each step is planned, factors intervene to make the process take longer than expected. For example, portions of a building may need to be modified unexpectedly; the vendor may send the wrong kind of cable; several workstations may not work on arrival; or application software may take longer to install than anticipated.

If the new installation is brought up before everything is working and tested, problems are likely to occur. And users will initially lose confidence in the installation.

SUMMARY

This chapter has stressed LAN management. It begins with the importance of selection and training of the network manager. Particular emphasis is placed on the responsibilities of network managers. These responsibilities include managing the technical, business, and training aspects of the LAN. Training people who can support the LAN in the network manager's absence is another important topic of the chapter.

The chapter also discusses security and back-up issues. These include procedures for protecting information in directories and files, along with the need to establish regular LAN backup procedures as well as a disaster recovery plan.

Last, user training and planning for LAN growth were discussed. Both are interrelated, since well-informed users tend to feed the growth cycle of a LAN environment. Growth brings about the need to plan new LAN additions as a means for ensuring further success of these implementations.

CHAPTER QUESTIONS

1. Summarize the typical duties of the network manager.

2. What is an RFP for a LAN? What elements should go into the writing of an RFP?

3. Develop a list of standards that would apply to establishing directories on a file server you manage.

4. Show how to map a user's home directory in a login script.

5. Outline standards that apply to establishing user IDs and file-server names.

6. What is the function of the COMSPEC command?

7. Explain how drives are typically allocated for network functions.

8. What steps should be taken to ensure security on a network?

9. Explain each type of file attribute.

10. Explain each kind of trustee right.

11. You are the network manager of a LAN that has two file servers. One file server has important accounting and payroll information that is updated daily. The other has sales statistics and other information that is updated every Monday and Thursday. Develop a back-up plan for both file servers.

12. You have purchased a tape back-up system for your LAN, and you perform back-ups on a regular schedule. One day the disk drive on a file server will no longer function and you replace it. You install a new disk drive and restore the server files with your tape back-up system. When users log on, they discover they can no longer access the files and programs once available to them. You log on as supervisor and verify that the files and programs have been restored to the server. What would you do to diagnose this problem? What is the likely source of this situation? What steps should you take to fix it? How could you have prevented the problem?

13

Enterprise Networking: LANs and Beyond

INTRODUCTION TO ENTERPRISE NETWORKING (WIDE AREA NETWORKS)

Local Area Networks are effective for distributing computing, applications, and disk space to a small geographic area of an organization. The full benefits of networking are achieved, however, when the total enterprise is networked. In most situations the enterprise is "geographically dispersed," which means it encompasses offices and buildings outside of what could be connected with LAN technology. Enterprises also have mini and mainframe computers, which must be included in the enterprise's network. Users also would like to dial into a network. Therefore, an organization must provide the following networking solutions before achieving total enterprise networking:

* Networked remote and local LANs
* LANs networked to mini and mainframe hosts
* Remote workstations networked to LANs

NETWORKING LANS TOGETHER

An important objective is to connect LANs so that workgroups are not aware of using more than one LAN or that a LAN is in another city.

273

One way to connect LANs is by bridging. A **bridge** consists of hardware and software configured to allow packets to move among LANs. Thus, a bridge connects different LANs, permitting communication among devices on the separate LANs. For example, a bridge might connect a NetWare ethernet LAN to an AT&T Starlan network. A NetWare bridge connects NetWare LANs having different topologies, such as ARCNET and ethernet. There are two kinds of NetWare bridges: **internal** and **external bridges**. An internal bridge is a NIC in the file server. An external bridge is a workstation configured with Novell's bridging software.

INTERNAL AND EXTERNAL NETWORK BRIDGES

Internal bridges can provide one or more of the following: increase the performance of a large LAN; allow different kinds of media to be used; and extend the cable distance. Installing a bridge in a large, heavily used network can increase performance, because the bridge isolates the network traffic. Packets that are local to one LAN are kept local. They do not cross the bridge. Only packets destined for a remote node on another LAN cross the bridge.

An internal bridge is particularly useful for an ethernet topology. It increases the speed of communications and permits different topologies with different cabling to be joined.

Another feature of the internal bridge is that it extends cable distance by adding the cable distance of one LAN to that of another LAN. Figure 13.1 illustrates an internal bridge connecting an ethernet segment and an ARCNET segment.

The internal bridge hardware consists of NICs installed in a file server. For example, one file server might contain an ethernet NIC and an ARCNET NIC.

An external bridge serves the same function as an internal bridge in NetWare. However, the external bridge resides on a node (workstation) other than the file server. The node can be dedicated to work only as a bridge, or it can be nondedicated. Nondedicated external bridges can double as a workstation.

REMOTE BRIDGES

NetWare Remote Bridge software enables users to transparently connect to distant or remote local area networks. For example, a network in Denver might connect to one in Chicago.

FIGURE 13.1
Internal Bridge Connecting an ARCNET and Ethernet

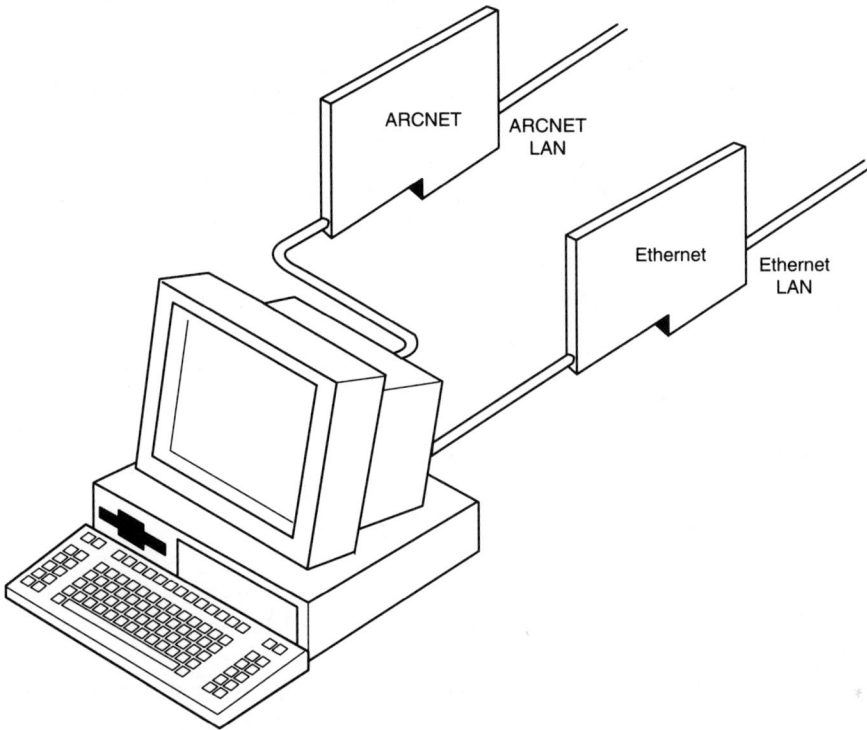

Remote bridges are external bridges connected to communications equipment, such as a modem. NetWare supports four remote bridging products. The appropriate bridge solution depends on the application to be supported and the cost of the bridge. These bridge solutions are:

- asynchronous
- X.25
- high speed 64 Kbps
- T1

Asynchronous Remote Bridges

An **asynchronous** bridge uses modems and RS-232 serial connections. Asynchronous communication is a low-cost way to transmit data. In asynchronous communication, the data is placed in a block and surrounded by framing bits. There are one or more framing bits placed in front of the data and at the end of the data. These bits indicate where the data starts and where it ends.

On each LAN, an asynchronous modem is connected to the bridge, and a communication line is connected to the modem. Data is transmitted at speeds of up to 2,400 baud on voice communication lines. Speeds of 19.2 Kbps can be achieved on dedicated data lines.

The components needed for an asynchronous bridge include:

- NetWare asynchronous software
- one or more Novell WNIM+ adapters or COM1/COM2 ports with cabling
- an asynchronous modem

X.25 Bridges

NetWare also offers an **X.25** solution for bridging remote LANs. X.25 is a protocol used by many Public Data Networks, such as Telenet and Tymnet. Both of these networks provide connections through local telephone lines. Subscribers are charged a fee for their use of the network. Public Data Networks span international borders, with the X.25 protocol especially popular in Europe. X.25 networks are accessed through voice and dedicated leased communication lines.

Figure 13.2 represents an X.25 network.

X.25 bridges can operate at speeds of up to 56 Kbps. Any number of workstations can access a remote LAN. NetWare security and fault tolerance are supported across the bridges. The bridge can run dedicated or nondedicated (which combines a bridge and workstation into one computer). A nondedicated bridge with DOS and the NetWare shell requires 320 KB of memory. A Novell X.25 adapter is inserted into the bridge to provide an RS-232 port. A **synchronous** modem with speeds of up to 56 Kbps can be attached to the adapter.

Synchronous communication is faster than asynchronous communication. Synchronous communication uses a clock to time when data blocks are sent. Thus, there is a constant time interval between each block. The time interval makes it possible to distinguish between each block that is transmitted. The framing data bits used in asynchronous communication are not needed.

FIGURE 13.2
A LAN Configured to Use an X.25 Network Protocol

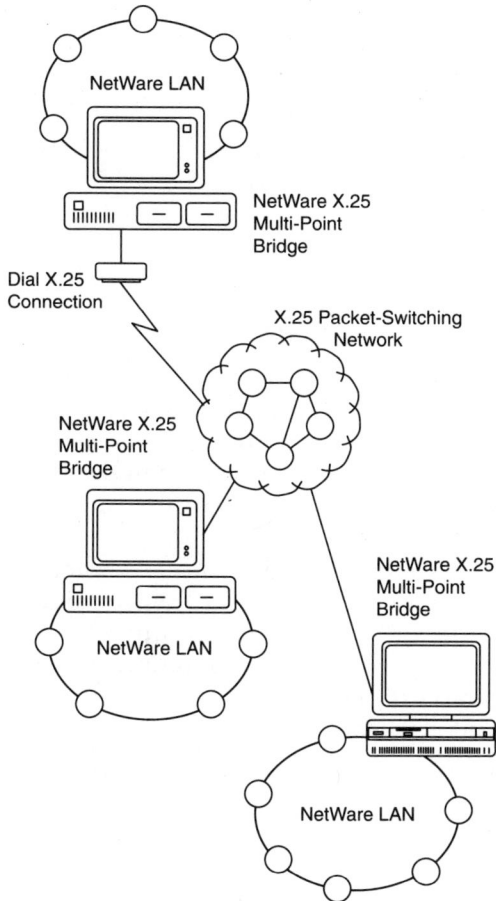

The requirements for an X.25 bridge are:

- X.25 software
- X.25 adapter board in a bridge workstation
- Full duplex synchronous modems for sending and receiving

High-Speed Bridges

The fastest LAN-to-LAN connections use NetWare Link/64 or NetWare Link/T1. Both provide real-time remote LAN access. An enterprise

FIGURE 13.3
LANs Networked with High Speed Data Links

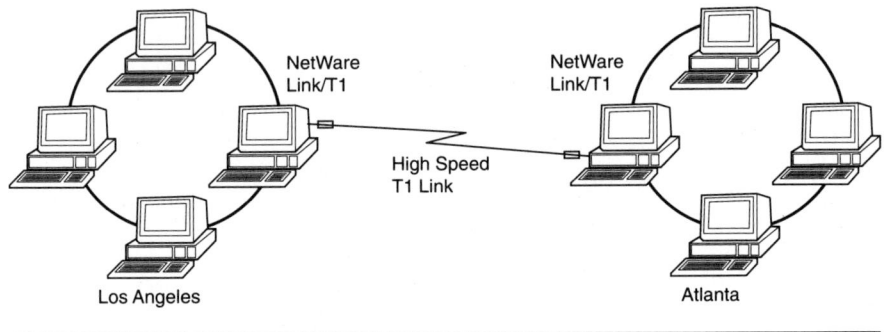

may have several LANs with databases located in several cities. With NetWare Link/64 or NetWare Link/T1, the user can query all the databases at once. These two communication products offer great flexibility in designing applications requiring significant transmission throughput.

NetWare Link/64 offers a maximum data transmission rate of 64 Kbps. NetWare Link/T1 supports data transmission rates from 9,600 Kbps to 1.544 Mbps. These products support electronic mail, file transfer, and host access (mainframe and minicomputers). Figure 13.3 represents remote LANs connected with high-speed data links. The following are needed to configure a Link/64 or Link/T1 bridge:

- NetWare Link/64 or NetWare Link/T1 software
- One or more synchronous adapters with cabling
- Customer Service Unit (CSU), Data Service Unit (DSU) or combination CSU/DSU at the sending and receiving LANs
- 80286 or 80386 dedicated workstation

The software should be installed on an 80286 or 80386 microcomputer on each LAN to be bridged. The bridge must be dedicated. The synchronous adapters provide the physical connections from the workstation to the CSU/DSU, a device that converts signals to send over the high-speed line. (See Figure 13.3.)

NETWORKING LANS WITH HOST GATEWAYS

Enterprises have used mini and mainframe computers for many years to provide multi-user applications. These computers are also required for large accounting and manufacturing applications, and on-line transaction processing. Also, there are substantial investments in mini and mainframe systems. This prevents short-term conversion to LANs. Enterprise connectivity, therefore, requires connecting LANs to mini and mainframe host computers. There are two host computing environments: IBM and asynchronous.

IBM Gateways

Connecting LANs to an IBM host requires a **gateway.** Gateways are translators between networks that use different protocols. For example, a gateway permits a workstation using IPX/SPX to communicate with another device using the SNA protocol. Just as a human might translate French into English, the gateway translates SNA protocol to IPX/SPX and vice versa. **SNA** is the Systems Network Architecture protocol used by IBM mainframes to communicate with terminals and other IBM computers.

Connecting a NetWare LAN to an IBM host requires converting NetWare packets to SNA packets. IBM host computers require a connected workstation or LAN to emulate an IBM-type terminal. There are 3270- and 5250-type IBM terminal emulators.

NetWare's SNA gateway allows up to ninety-seven workstations using SPX or NetBIOS to communicate with an IBM SNA host computer. The SNA gateway requires the following:

- NetWare SNA Gateway software
- Adapter installed in the gateway server
- NetWare 3270 LAN workstation software

The SNA Gateway is installed in any NetWare LAN workstation. The workstation can be dedicated or nondedicated, but the gateway cannot be installed on the file server. The gateway on the LAN manages mainframe communications for all LAN users.

An SNA Gateway also allows different topologies access to an IBM host. The Gateway supports ethernet, ARCNET, or Token-Ring topologies.

A token-ring LAN uses a token-ring adapter to physically connect to the host computer or controller. A token-ring workstation can be used also as the SNA gateway. Novell recommends an 80286 dedicated Token-Ring workstation be used for the gateway. The token-ring connection allows up to 128 simultaneous host terminal and printer sessions.

Remote SNA connection is provided with synchronous (SDLC) connections. SDLC (synchronous data-link control) is a communications protocol. Connecting a LAN via a synchronous connection allows up to sixteen host terminal/printer sessions with speeds of up to 19.2 Kbps. A synchronous adapter is required for the workstation to connect to a synchronous modem.

A coax adapter with the SNA Gateway software provides local access to five host terminal/printer sessions. The coax adapter provides

FIGURE 13.4
A LAN Networked with an SNA Gateway

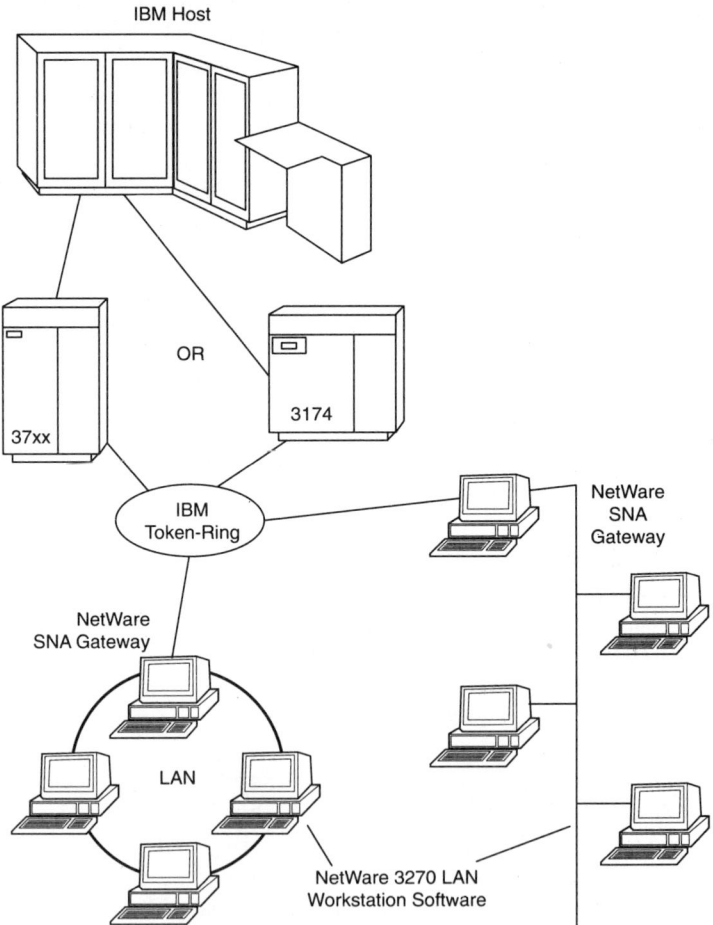

IBM Host

OR

37xx

3174

IBM
Token-Ring

NetWare
SNA Gateway

NetWare
SNA
Gateway

LAN

NetWare 3270 LAN
Workstation Software

Token-Ring Host Connectivity Option

the physical connection for using coaxial cable from the LAN SNA Gateway server to the host. (See Figure 13.4.)

NetWare 5250 Gateway products are another solution that allows LANs to be connected to host IBM minicomputers, such as the System 34, 36, or 38 and AS/400. The NetWare 5250 Gateway allows NetWare workstations to emulate IBM 5250 and other IBM terminals. The following is a list of requirements for 5250 host connections:

- NetWare 5250 Gateway software
- Adapter installed in the gateway server
- NetWare 5250 LAN workstation software
- Synchronous modems

The NetWare Gateway software is installed in a workstation, not in the file server. This configuration permits nine concurrent host/printer sessions at the gateway, with up to five of those sessions available to any workstation. Synchronous modems are used to connect to the minicomputer host from the NetWare Gateway. A synchronous adapter is installed in the NetWare Gateway to provide the physical connection. The gateway is capable of data transmission of 19.2 Kbps.

Each LAN workstation has NetWare 5250 Workstation software installed. This software lets the workstation emulate a variety of IBM 5250 compatible terminals and printers. The 5250 emulation permits up to five concurrent host sessions and one DOS session. Figure 13.5 illustrates a LAN-to-IBM minicomputer network configuration.

FIGURE 13.5
A LAN Networked to an IBM Host Computer

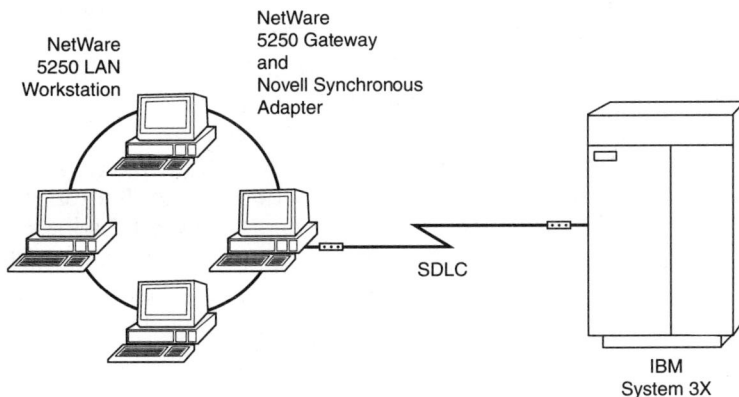

Asynchronous Gateways

Many non-IBM computers use asynchronous communication protocols. For instance, asynchronous communication is used by Digital Equipment, SUN, and Hewlett-Packard. To realize enterprise connectivity, asynchronous computers must be connected to NetWare LANs. The two NetWare approaches to connecting to an asynchronous host are NetWare Asynchronous Communications Server (NACS) and NetWare X.25 Gateway.

NACS software allows any workstation on a LAN to communicate with any asynchronous device. Up to sixteen workstations using a single-server workstation can connect to a remote host. They dial out from a LAN workstation to a remote host and dial into a LAN workstation from a remote workstation. Any number of NACS can be installed on a LAN. A NACS configuration includes the following:

- NACS software
- One or more Novell WNIM+ adapters installed in the server workstation
- Asynchronous modems, if the workstations are not directly connected to the host
- Terminal emulation software

NACS software is installed in any dedicated workstation designated as the NACS server. The WNIM+ adapter provides four asynchronous ports. A cable is then attached from the port to an asynchronous modem or asynchronous device. The asynchronous device can be the host computer or communications processor. Finally, each workstation loads terminal emulation software. Novell offers ASCOM IV as a terminal emulation package. ASCOM IV provides emulators for such common terminals as VT100, VT220, IBM 3101, Tektronix, Televideo, and WYSE. XMODEM, Kermit, ASCII, and other file transfer protocols are also supported with ASCOM IV. NACS provides asynchronous communication over voice-grade telephone lines. Figure 13.6 illustrates an asynchronous network.

Some computer vendors also offer X.25 communication products. These vendors include Digital Equipment, Hewlett-Packard, Prime, and Tandem. The NetWare X.25 Gateway increases the enterprise connectivity by providing a high-speed link. It uses X.25 protocol to connect to host computers using the same protocol. The X.25 Gateway requirements are the following:

- NetWare X.25 Gateway software
- Novell X.25 Adapter

FIGURE 13.6
A LAN Networked to an Asynchronous Host with NACS

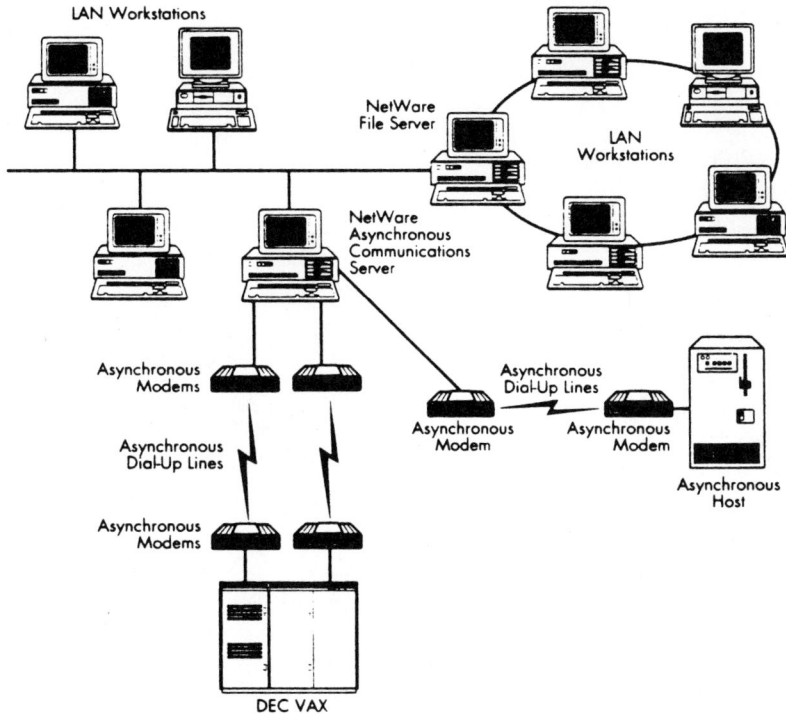

- Synchronous modems
- Terminal emulation software

The X.25 Gateway software is installed in a workstation that will function as the gateway server; an 80286 workstation should be used. The server can support up to eight terminal emulation sessions. The adapter provides the physical port for connecting to a synchronous modem for remote access. No modem is required for direct connection to an X.25 network. Each user loads the appropriate terminal emulation software into his or her workstation to emulate a terminal. Figure 13.7 illustrates a NetWare X.25 network solution.

TCP Gateway

TCP, or Transmission Control Protocol, is software that bundles data into packets and also unbundles it. TCP was developed by the Depart-

FIGURE 13.7

A LAN Networked to an Asynchronous Host Using an X.25 Asychronous Gateway

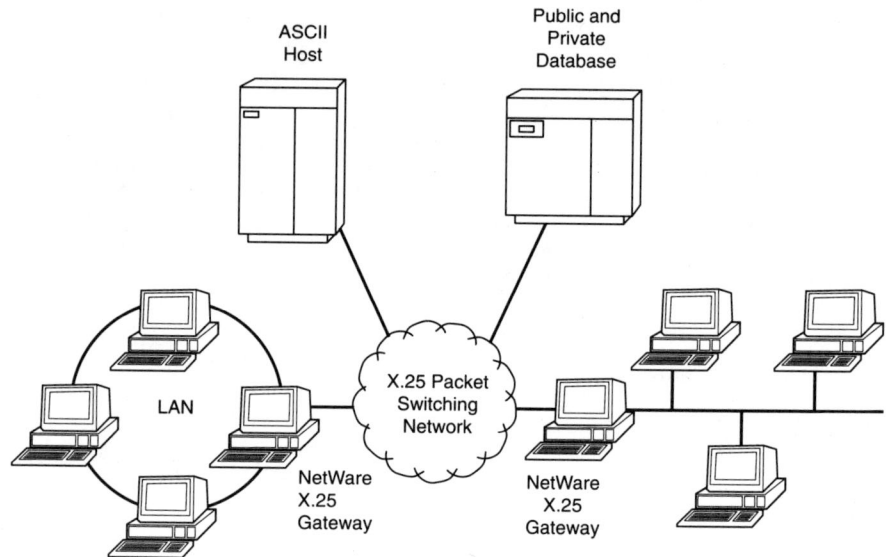

ment of Defense to provide reliable communications under demanding conditions. It is implemented on LANs, minicomputers, and mainframes, and is used extensively on education networks.

A **TCP** gateway allows a NetWare LAN to communicate with a network that uses TCP. TCP offers FTP, or File Transfer Protocol, for sending and receiving files. FTP allows either the sending or receiving computer to act as the host.

A TCP product, called WIN/TCP for DOS, offered by the Wollongong Group, uses the services of NetWare's IPX protocol. TCP becomes a layer of software that allows a NetWare LAN to communicate with TCP host computers and NetWare nodes. TCP is used primarily with ethernet networks using **TCP/IP** software. The **IP**, or Internet Protocol, was also developed by the Department of Defense to enable different computer systems to communicate using a common communications protocol. IP software keeps track of the address of nodes to guarantee a packet reaches the right node.

Another approach to connecting a NetWare LAN to a TCP/IP network requires configuring the workstation shell and file-server operating system. For the workstation, configure IPX.COM. For the file server, configure NET$OS.EXE. The configuration process requires obtaining a utility program, such as ECONFIG.EXE.

REMOTE DIAL-IN ACCESS TO LANS

Perhaps the best alternative for heavy remote access is Novell's NetWare Access Server, which permits up to fifteen remote users to dial into a LAN. The NetWare Access Server is a dedicated 80386 workstation, functioning as sixteen individual virtual workstations. One virtual workstation controls the other fifteen virtual workstations. These workstations are actually 640-KB segments of the 80386's memory and WNIM+ adapters. A remote workstation can be an IBM compatible computer, a Macintosh, or ASCII terminal.

A remote workstation dials into the NetWare Access Server, using an asynchronous modem and remote control software, such as NetWare AnyWare. Processing is done on the LAN at the Access Server, so processing is as fast as if the remote user were actually on the LAN. Only screen updates and keystrokes are transmitted between the remote workstation and the Access Server. Figure 13.8 depicts a LAN using an access server for remote dial-in access.

For enterprises requiring a single remote user, there is a single remote access solution. Single remote workstation access is available, using remote-control software and a LAN workstation. There are several remote-control software applications, such as Carbon Copy, that permit a remote workstation to dial into a LAN using asynchronous communications. The remote-control software is installed on the remote workstation and the LAN workstation. This single remote user solution functions like the NetWare Access Server, except only one user can dial into the LAN at a time.

SUMMARY

NetWare offers a variety of alternatives providing enterprise-wide connectivity. Performance requirements, existing equipment, and cost constraints narrow these alternatives. To connect a NetWare LAN to an IBM host computer, it is necessary to use either 3270 or 5250 terminal emulation and the appropriate gateway hardware and software. Connecting a NetWare LAN to non-IBM hosts requires a NetWare Asynchronous Communications Server. This solution also requires a LAN workstation to emulate a terminal. The last connectivity product

FIGURE 13.8
Remote Access Server for Dial-In Access to a LAN

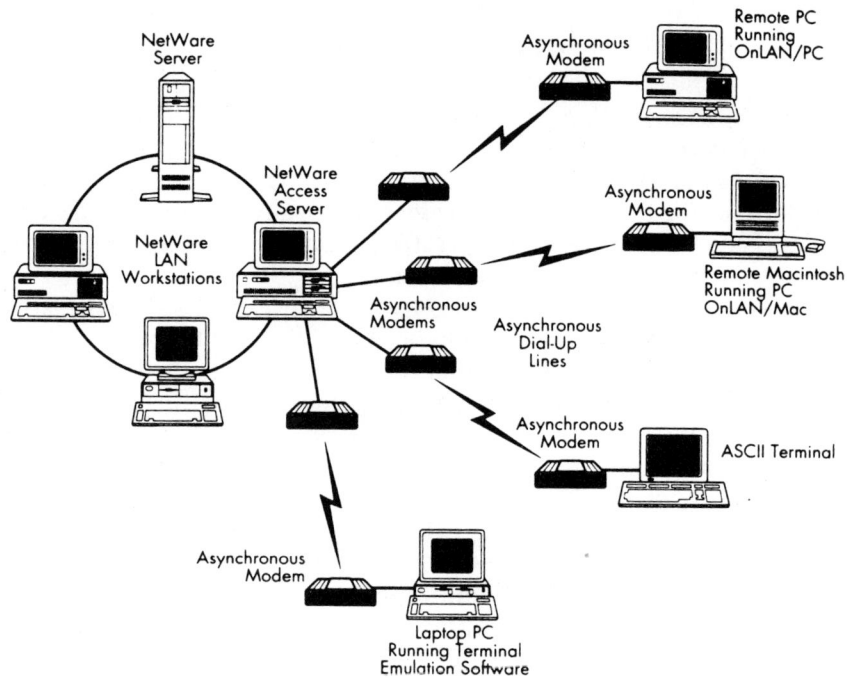

discussed was recommended for remote users dialing into the LAN. These networking alternatives provide solutions for obtaining enterprise-wide connectivity.

CHAPTER QUESTIONS

1. What is a bridge? What is a gateway?
2. Explain the differences between internal and external bridges.
3. What are the advantages of using a bridge on a Novell network?
4. Why would you use a gateway on a Novell network?

5. What is a remote bridge?

6. Compare asynchronous communications to synchronous communications.

7. What links are required for high-speed bridges?

8. Describe the type of gateway used to connect an IBM host computer to a NetWare LAN.

9. How would you connect a DEC computer to a NetWare LAN?

10. You have two NetWare LANs. One is ethernet and one is ARCNET. Both are in the same building, but on different floors. Also, you have a DEC mainframe computer and you want to connect to the BITNET educational network. How would you design a solution to connect both LANs, the DEC mainframe, and the BITNET network?

Glossary

Active Hub A device used on ARCNET LANs. This device will amplify and split signals. It enables the cabling distance to be lengthened.

Asynchronous This communication method places data in a discrete block. The block is surrounded by framing bits. Thus, there are framing bits at the beginning and end of the block. These bits show where the block begins and where it ends.

Backbone A large cable segment that joins two or more LANs in the same building or across several buildings.

Bandwidth This refers to the capacity of a cable to carry data on different channels or frequencies. Baseband cable has only one channel, whereas broadband cable has several channels for data transmission.

Baseband A network cable that has only one channel for carrying data signals.

Bindery This is NetWare's database of information about users, groups, and printers that have been defined by the supervisor. Each record of information is called an object.

Bits Per Second The transmission speed of data on a network. Depending on the type of cabling and the LAN topology, transmission speeds range from 1 Mbps to 100 Mbps.

BNC A **bayonet-locking connector** used with coax cable. This is a T-shaped connector with one end connected to a NIC and the other two ends connected to the LAN cable. (BNC is the abbreviation of Bayonet-Neill-Concelman.)

Bridge A device that connects different LANs so a node on one LAN can communicate with a node on another LAN. Bridges connect LANs with different topologies and protocols.

Broadband A network cable with several channels for carrying data signals at the same time.

Bus Topology The physical layout of a LAN where all nodes are connected to a single cable. The ends of the cable are fitted with terminating devices.

Cache Memory Part of a computer's random access memory used to temporarily store data. A Novell file server divides memory into 4-KB blocks of cache memory. The most recently accessed programs and data files are stored in cache to make them instantly available to the next requestor.

Centralized Communications A system of control used by mainframe and minicomputers that assigns a priority on communications with the CPU. For example, some terminals, have more access (higher priority) to computer functions than other terminals. Mainframe and minicomputers also are centralized, in that software is run on the computer, not on the terminal or workstation.

Coaxial Cable A cable consisting of a single piece of metal surrounded by insulation, which is surrounded by a braided or foil outer conductor. This type of cable has a plastic outer covering.

Communication Buffer Also called a **routing buffer,** this is a storage area in a Novell file server's memory. One-half kilobytes in size, each buffer stores data until the file server can process it.

Decentralized Communications   A system of control on a LAN where all devices have equal priority when communicating with the LAN. Also, software is distributed so it is run on the workstation and not on the file server.

Dedicated Server   A file server that only has the NetWare operating system on it.

Device Driver   A software program that enables the NetWare and DOS operating systems to work with NICs, disk controllers, and other hardware.

Disk Channel   A line or route reserved for data transmission between the disk controller and the CPU.

Disk Controller   A circuit board contained in a computer that is connected to one or more floppy and hard disk drives. This circuit board oversees the read and write activity on the disk drive.

Electrical Topology   The electrical aspects of LAN cabling. These involve electrical interference, cable bandwidth, and the way data packets are transmitted.

Emulator   Software that enables one device or program to imitate another. The NETBIOS.COM software from Novell causes NetWare to imitate the NETBIOS protocol used by IBM networks.

Environment Variable   A variable used by DOS to enable it, or a program to find specific files. For example, the MicroSoft C compiler program uses a set of library files in a subdirectory. An environment variable can be set to show DOS how to find these library files.

External Bridge   A microcomputer configured to act as a NetWare bridge, joining NetWare LANs with different topologies.

FAT   The **File Allocation Table** contains pointer information showing where a file is located on a disk.

Fiber-Optic Cable   A cable consisting of glass or plastic fibers. The fibers are contained in a cladding, which is surrounded by a protective outer covering.

File Server A computer that enables other computers to share resources. The file server contains a network operating system, such as NetWare. It also stores programs and files that can be accessed by other computers.

Gateway A device acting as a translator between networks that use different protocols. The gateway permits a workstation using one protocol, such as SNA, to communicate with a workstation using a different protocol, such as IPX/SPX.

Group A listing of users on a NetWare file server, all of whom can be assigned the same directory rights.

Indexed File A large file marked for individualized handling to speed access to the file's contents. A separate file allocation table, called a Turbo FAT, is kept in memory for each indexed file. The Turbo FAT enables the records in the file to be accessed quickly. Files 1 MB or larger are marked for indexing.

Internal Bridge A NIC in a NetWare file server which connects one NetWare LAN topology to another NetWare LAN topology.

Internetwork Two or more physical networks connected to one another. They may be connected through bridges, gateways, or routers.

Internetwork Packet Exchange (IPX) One of two data transmission protocols used by NetWare. The other protocol is Sequenced Packet Exchange. IPX permits the transmission of message packets or requests between the file server and workstations.

Interrupt A communications channel used by a device, such as a disk drive, to get the attention of a computer's microprocessor.

IP **Internet Protocol** developed by the Department of Defense to ensure data is routed to the correct node.

Links Sections of cable that go from workstation to workstation on a network.

Local Drive Floppy and hard drives on a workstation are local drives.

Local Printer A printer connected to a workstation, which is not used as a shared network printer.

Logical Drive This is a NetWare drive, which exists through software. Logical drives can be manipulated (mapped) to any directory or subdirectory on a file server. One physical hard drive can be mapped to have logical drives F-Z.

Map This involves associating a logical NetWare drive letter with a directory. For example, the logical drive L: could be mapped to SYS:APP/WP. When you switch to drive L:, NetWare will place you in this directory. The MAP command and the SESSION menu enable you to create a mapping.

Multi-user This term refers to more than one user accessing a device or software. For example, a software package is a multi-user package if it will allow more than one user to access it at one time.

NETBIOS A communication protocol used by IBM's PC LAN system. Some applications are written for a NETBIOS environment. Novell provides a program (NETBIOS.COM) that simulates this protocol.

NetWare Loadable Module (NLM) A program that runs as though it is part of the NetWare 386 operating system. However, the NLM is written separately from the operating system. An NLM can be written by Novell, a third-party vendor, or a user. It is loaded along with the operating system. NLMs are a feature of NetWare 386 and replace VAPs used in NetWare 286.

Network Drive A drive on a file server that contains information workstations can access.

Network Printer A printer shared by network users. The printer can be attached to the file server or to a print server.

NIC The **network interface card** is a circuit board installed in the file server and in each workstation. It works with the Novell operating system to send and receive data on the network.

Node A workstation, file server, print server, bridge, or other device that has an address on a network.

Nondedicated Server   A file server that can run operating systems in addition to the Novell operating system. For example, Advanced NetWare 286 permits DOS and NetWare to run at the same time. With this option, the file server can also be a workstation.

Open Data-Link Interface   A feature of NetWare 386 that handles commonly used protocols, such as IPX/SPX, TCP/IP, and AppleTalk.

Operating System   The software on a computer that controls execution of input/output processes, program execution, and the handling of files. DOS and NetWare are examples of operating systems.

Packet   A discrete unit of data bits transmitted over a network. The unit includes addressing information, error control information, and data.

Partition   A portion of a hard disk allocated to an operating system, such as NetWare or DOS.

Passive Hub   A device used on an ARCNET LAN to split the transmission signal. It does not amplify the signal like an active hub.

Physical Drive   An actual drive (device) on a file server or on a workstation. This is a piece of equipment.

Physical Topology   The physical cabling layout of a LAN, such as bus, ring, or star.

Pod   A group of workstations located in a workroom or laboratory that are available for shared use.

Point-to-Point   A form of data communications in the bus and ring topologies where data is transferred from one node to the next.

Print Queue   A way to manage printing tasks. A NetWare print queue directs printouts to specified printers. And the queue determines which print jobs will print first.

Print Server   A device or software application that enables users to share printers attached to the network. A dedicated print server performs printing tasks only. A nondedicated print server enables the print management device to perform other functions, such as doubling as a workstation.

Protocol   A set of rules that establishes how computers communicate with one another.

Remote Bridge   A bridge joining two LANs that are miles apart, such as a LAN in New York and a LAN in Omaha.

Ring Topology   This topology connects all nodes in a logical ring-like pattern.

Sequenced Packet Exchange   One of two data transmission protocols used by NetWare. The other protocol is Internetwork Packet Exchange.

Shell   Software used on a workstation to enable it to communicate with NetWare. The workstation shell directs command requests to DOS or NetWare. The shell is loaded into a workstation's memory. It stays in memory while a user is logged into NetWare. The shell files are IPX.COM and NETx.COM.

SNA   **Systems Network Architecture** protocol used by IBM mainframe computers for connecting to terminals and printers.

Star Topology   In this topology, each node is connected by a single cable link to a central point, called a hub.

Synchronous   This is a method of communication using a time interval to distinguish between transmitted blocks of data. A clock ensures that the time interval is the same between each block that is transmitted.

System Fault Tolerance   A set of procedures in software or hardware that enable a system to recover after a power or computer failure. The procedures prevent or minimize lost and corrupt data. They also minimize down time.

TCP   **Transmission Control Protocol** developed by the Department of Defense, which performs extensive error checking to ensure the integrity of transmitted data.

TCP/IP   A combination of the TCP and IP protocols used to achieve common communications between many different LANs, mini, and mainframe computers. This protocol is used on national defense and education networks.

Terminate-and-Stay-Resident   A program that remains in the workstation's memory even when that program is not currently in use.

Token   The type of data packet used to carry information on LANs using the ring topology.

Topology   The way nodes on a LAN are connected. The three LAN topologies are bus, token ring, and star.

Transaction Tracking   A feature in SFT NetWare that prevents incomplete transactions from being written to a file. This is important if updates to one or more files are interrupted by a system or power failure. If the transactions are incomplete, they are automatically backed out.

Trunk Segment   A length of cable connecting several nodes. The trunk spans all of the cable from the terminator at one end of the cable to the terminator at the other end.

Trustee Rights   A feature of NetWare that enables access rights to be assigned to any file server directory or subdirectory. The access rights are given to users and groups. The rights govern whether a user can read files, open files, search for files, create files, or perform other activities in a directory.

Turbo-FAT   The **Turbo File Allocation Table** is a one-table index that NetWare constructs for large data files over 1 MB. Pointers to data in the file are kept in the Turbo FAT instead of the regular FAT. The Turbo-FAT permits fast access to data.

Twisted Pair   This type of cabling consists of two insulated wires twisted around each other. They may be accompanied by similar pairs. The pairs are surrounded by an outer protective covering. There is shielded and unshielded twisted-pair cable. Shielded cable has a foil electrical shield between the twisted pairs and the outer covering. Unshielded cable does not have the foil.

Uninterruptible Power Source   This device keeps computer equipment running after a power failure, providing back-up power from batteries for a short period of time.

VAP   A **value-added process** to the NetWare operating system provided by an independent vendor. For example, there is a VAP that enables Macintosh computers to be connected to a Novell LAN. VAPs are used on NetWare 286.

Wide Area Network   Wide area networks use telecommunications facilities to link computer users separated by large geographical distances.

Workstation   A microcomputer connected to a host mainframe computer, minicomputer, or LAN. A workstation has its own CPU and can be one of many brands of computers, such as a Macintosh, IBM, or Zenith.

X.25   A communication protocol used on Public Data Networks, such as Telenet.

Bibliography

Bowker, Richard., *Racal InterLan on Interoperability.* Boxborough: Racal InterLan, 1988.

Corrigan, Patrick H., and Aisling Guy. *Building Local Area Networks With Novell's NetWare.* Redwood City: M&T Books, 1989.

Fritz, James S., Charles F. Kaldenbach, and Louis M. Progar. *Local Area Networks Selection Guidelines.* Englewood Cliffs: Prentice-Hall, 1985.

Jordan, Larry E., and Bruce Churchill, *Communications and Networking for the IBM PC and Compatibles.* 3rd ed. New York: Brady, 1990.

Liebing, Edward., *NetWare User's Guide.* Redwood City: M&T Books, 1989.

McCann, John T., *NetWare Supervisor's Guide.* Redwood City: M&T Books, 1989.

Schwaderer, W. David., *Programmer's Guide to NetBIOS.* Indianapolis: Howard W. Sams, 1988.

Stacy, A., *The MAP Book: An Introduction to Industrial Networking.* Santa Clara, Industrial Networking Inc., 1987.

Stallings, William., *Business Data Communications*. New York: Macmillan Publishing, 1990.

Stallings, William., *Handbook of Computer-Communications Standards: Volume 1, The Open Systems Interconnection Model and OSI-related Standards, Second Edition*. Indianapolis: SAM, Macmillan, 1987.

Stallings, William., *Handbook of Computer Communications Standards Volume 2 Local Network Standards*. Indianapolis: Howard W. Sams, 1988.

Tanenbaum, Andrew., *Computer Networks*. Englewood Cliffs: Prentice Hall, 1988.

Tangney, Brendan, and Donal O'Mahony., *Local Area Networks and their applications*. London: Prentice-Hall, 1988.

Index